£20

KT-146-548

Au.

Tit

Access

WITHDRAWN FROM
THE LIBRARY

UNIVERSITY OF

KA 0022801 X

SEMIOTICS OF ART

SEMIOTICS OF ART

Prague School Contributions

Edited by
Ladislav Matejka and Irwin R. Titunik

The MIT Press
Cambridge, Massachusetts, and London, England

Copyright © 1976 by
The Massachusetts Institute of Technology

All rights reserved. No part of this book may be reproduced in any form
or by any means, electronic or mechanical, including photocopying, re-
cording, or by any information storage and retrieval system, without
permission in writing from the publisher.

This book was set in IBM Composer Univers by Margaret Hayman,
and printed and bound by The Murray Printing Company in the United
States of America.

Second printing, 1977

Library of Congress Cataloging in Publication Data
Main entry under title:

Semiotics of art.

    CONTENTS: Mukařovský, J. Art as semiotic fact.—Bogatyrev, P.
Costume as a sign.—Bogatyrev, P. Folk song from a functional point
of view. [etc.]
    1. Semiotics—Addresses, essays, lectures. 2. Arts—Addresses,
essays, lectures. 3. Pražský linguistický kroužek. I. Matejka,
Ladislav, 1919- . II. Titunik, I. R.
P99.S39   301.2'1   75-32405
ISBN 0-262-13117-X

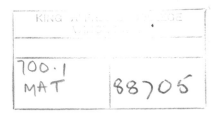

Contents

PREFACE

Ever since man first became aware of the phenomenon of communication, he has recognized the fundamental role of the sign in human life. Throughout the ages his inquisitive mind has sought answer to the questions: What constitutes a sign? What are the laws that govern signs? The history of man's inquiry into the nature of sign is an integral and continuous part of the history of philosophy in general; contributions to the theory of sign are evident, for instance, in the doctrines of Plato, the Stoics, the medieval Scholastics, the seventeenth-century mentalists and empiricists. The crystallization in the twentieth century of a new interest in the principles of sign systems represented a conscious revival of those older traditions of human thought. Indeed, as if explicitly acknowledging that fact, the American pragmatist, Charles Sanders Peirce, chose as the appellation for his theory of sign John Locke's term "semiotic," derived from the Greek word *semeion*. The same classical derivational base served for the coinage of "sémiologie," which the Geneva linguist, Ferdinand de Saussure, Peirce's contemporary and the cofounder of modern semiotic thought, employed to designate the general science of sign.

Both Peirce's *semiotic* and Saussure's *semiology,* whether imported directly from America and Geneva or indirectly via Russia and Vienna, came to Prague, Czechoslovakia, during the early 1930s and found fertile ground in the extraordinary humanistic trend, then developing there, that has come to be known under the various titles of the *Prague Linguistic Circle,* the *Prague School,* or *Prague Structuralism.* For the Prague theoreticians the model of sign yielded the most revealing results in studies of art, studies of verbal art, in particular. Numerous instances of the impact of these studies on the recent phenomenal upsurge of semiotic theory and analysis in the United States, Western Europe, and the Soviet Union amply testify to the fact that the investigations of the Prague School retain to the present day a high degree of validity and a power to enlighten and inspire.

The anthology here presented is predicated upon this belief in the continuing and generative relevance of certain Prague School contributions. Our selection of articles was guided paramountly by the ambition to demonstrate the profundity and diversity of the Prague scholars' analytical application of the model of sign to the problem of art. At the same time, we have also endeavored to bring into focus the historical development of Prague Structuralism, particularly in regard to its relationship with the school of Russian Formalism, which flourished in the Soviet Union during the 1920s and of which Prague Structuralism may be regarded, to a significant degree, as both a continuation and a reassessment.

The first section of the anthology, its theoretical introduction, is represented by the programmatic paper of Jan Mukařovský, "Art as Semiotic Fact" (1934). In it Mukařovský, inspired by the semiotic framework of Prague School phonology, arrives at the conclusion that the objective study of art must regard the work of art as a sign involving (1) a perceivable form created by an artist (i.e., *signans*), (2) an internalized signification (i.e., *signatum*), and, moreover, (3) a relationship of an oblique kind, metaphoric or other, with the social context to which the binary character of sign refers (i.e., *designatum*). Thus the work of art is viewed as an intermediary between the creator and the community capable of meaningful interpretation of the artifact. Mukařovský warns that failure to recognize the semiotic nature of art, with its indissoluble structure of signans and signatum, subjects a work of art to potential distortion or loss of meaning.

If its semiotic properties are disregarded, a work of art may appear as a mere design of formal constituents or, at the other extreme, a kind of psychological or even physiological case study or a piece of evidence about ideological, economic, or social conditions. The work of art, Mukařovský insists, precisely owing to its semiotic character, stands in a special relationship with its social context, and only after interpretations of that oblique relationship can the work's "documentary value" be properly assessed. It is only the semiotic point of view, Mukařovský asserts, that "allows theorists to recognize the autonomous existence and essential dynamism of artistic structure and to understand evolution of art as an immanent process but one in constant dialectical relationship with the evolution of other domains of culture."

The second section of the anthology consists of a selection of folkloristic studies by Petr Bogatyrev that played an essential role in the gradual crystallization of Prague School semiotics. The domain of folklore served particularly well for illuminating multifunctional structures and hierarchical transformations induced by contextual changes and, implicitly, by diachrony. In his article, "Costume as a Sign" (1936), Bogatyrev concentrates on the folk costume (national dress) to illustrate its numerous and varied functions. "In all cases," Bogatyrev points out, "costume is both material object and sign." Accordingly, some functions pertain to the folk costume as an object, whereas other functions are performed by the folk costume as a sign referring to other domains. Bogatyrev persuasively argues that the functional approach, by taking semiotic values into consideration, opens new vistas for folklore studies in particular. He is convinced that analyses based on purely formal criteria have proved to be unsatisfactory. In this connection he singles out as an example of failure the rigorously formalistic analyses which, in their approach to folktale, disregarded the profound difference between fairy tales and historical tales. In Bogatyrev's view, the functional approach, oriented semiotically, would correct that deficiency and could contribute to the analysis of narrative in general, provided that oral narrative be strictly differentiated from narrative in the medium of written literature.

The functional, semiotically oriented approach is more specifically elaborated in Bogatyrev's study, "Folk Song from a Functional Point of View" (1936). The functional method applied to the multifunctional structure of folk song helps clarify, as Bogatyrev illustrates, obscure points in the development of folk songs, including their diffusion, modification, and particularly, functional transformation. The numerous functions of folk song, in Bogatyrev's view, are constantly changing. Accordingly, the structure of functions is viewed as a dynamic hierarchy subject to rearrangement and reevaluation in terms of dominating or dominated functions. The changes reflect contextual and, implicitly, temporal changeability. As compared with folk costume, which can be at the same time an object and a sign, the folk song is only a sign. From this point of view, concludes Bogatyrev, the folk song is appreciably more akin to such sign systems as oral tales, legends, proverbs, and oral genres in general.

While the folk costume in itself is simultaneously a material object and a sign, or more exactly, the bearer of a structure of signs, when it is used on the stage it becomes in Bogatyrev's formulation "a sign of a sign." Bogatyrev's study, "Semiotics in the Folk Theater" (1938), is specifically devoted to the problem of a sign of a sign, as illustrated by the concrete examples of folk theater. Theater is treated by Bogatyrev as a medium which transforms everything into a semiotic structure so that even real objects become for the spectator a sign of a sign or a sign for a real object. Accordingly, the language used by the actor on the stage becomes a very complex system of signs. It retains all the properties of poetic language, but, in addition, it becomes a constituent of dramatic action. This duplexity permeates all aspects of stage performance and can serve, from Bogatyrev's point of view, as a particularly rewarding area of semiotic investigations.

The transformational aspect of the stage was specifically discussed by Bogatyrev in the study entitled "Forms and Functions of Folk Theater" (1940) [a chapter from his book on Czech and Slovak folk theater] ; in our anthology, this chapter of Bogatyrev's book concludes the folkloristic section. In Bogatyrev's view, "one of the most important and fundamental features of the theater is transformation: the actor changes his appearance, dress, voice, and even the features of his personality into the appearance, costume, voice, and personality of the character whom he represents in the play." Bogatyrev, however, points out that we find the basic theatrical element of transformation also in the practice of various rituals and folk ceremonies that have a dominant magical or religious function. The intrinsic relationship between rituals and art should be studied, as Bogatyrev suggests, with due distinction between folklore and nonfolklore being made. Only then will the folk theater, precisely in its differentiation from nonfolklore theater, prove most revealing. Bogatyrev's predilection for concreteness and specificity does not prevent his semiotic observations about folklore from having profound significance for the study of the semiotics of art in general, whether folklore art or nonfolklore art. It was particularly Bogatyrev's analysis of folk theater that provoked active response among theorists of theater and dramatic genre as is implicitly illustrated by the following section of this anthology devoted to theatrical and cinematic art.

The third section begins with a study of sign systems in the theater that argues the fundamental necessity of grasping the rules underlying such systems in their particular spatial and temporal settings. This thesis is convincingly demonstrated in Karel Brušák's paper, "Signs in the Chinese Theater" (1939), devoted to a discussion of the tightly knit sign system that has survived for centuries and still is operative today in the classical Chinese theater. He distinguishes two basic types of signs: visual signs, associated with dramatic space, and acoustic signs, associated with dialogue and music. In the Chinese theater, "the elaborated system of signs enabled the Chinese actor to give a comprehensive portrayal of the most varied actions without having to re-create reality on the stage." Brušák points out that the conventionalized action-signs never aim at imitation of reality and are, in fact, deliberately constructed so as to be as far removed from realism as possible. In many respects, the classical system of Chinese theater furnishes rich material not only for the semiotics of dramatic art but also for the theory of sign in general. It is apparent that adequate understanding of the system is the basic prerequisite for an understanding of the values generated by that system. On the other hand, an inadequate grasp of the system would necessarily result in the distortion of the values. Thus, Brušák's study unveils important principles not only for understanding Chinese theater but also for understanding different cultures in general.

The multifarious implications of the fact that on the stage everything stands for something else are comprehensively discussed by Jindřich Honzl in his study, "Dynamics of the Sign in the Theater" (1940). In Honzl's view, the specific character of the theatrical sign, implemented by acting, has to be considered in every attempt to define the theater as an art distinct from other arts. Action, taken as the essence of dramatic art, is figuratively compared by Honzl to a single current which unifies word, actor, costume, scenery, and music by passing from one to another or simultaneously flowing through several components at one time. He does not claim, however, that there are permanent laws or invariable rules for the unification of dramatic devices via the flow of dramatic action. Rather he sees the dramatic action as a permanently changeable phenomenon. In his opinion it is this permanent changeability that makes dramatic art so distinctively itself but, at the same time, so elusive of definition.

In contradistinction to Honzl's emphasis on action as the dominating feature in dramatic art, Jiří Veltruský in his study, "Dramatic Text as a Component of Theater" (1941), emphasizes that the semiotics of theater is brought about by the confrontation of two sign systems which are invariably present: language and acting. In his view the linguistic sign system, which enters via the dramatic text, always combines and conflicts with the acting, which fundamentally belongs to an entirely different sign system. Since the semiotics of language and the semiotics of acting are diametrically opposed in their basic characteristics, there is, in Veltruský's opinion, a dialectical tension between the dramatic text and the action. The interrelationship of the two poles of this antinomy is viewed as a variable one in which the two sign systems operate not only so as to check but also so as to enrich each other. Thus, the variability of sign is explained in its dialectical unity with its opposite, the stability of sign.

In another article, "The Hierarchy of Dramatic Devices" (1943), Jindřich Honzl returns to his earlier observations by elaborating his view on the relationship between the verbal aspects and the performance of dramatic art. The words of a drama, as Honzl sees it, may constitute the principal component through which action and, indeed, all other aspects of dramatic structure are expressed. Such is the case of ancient Greek tragedy that, Honzl argues, always remained what it was by origin—a poem. It is precisely the "flexibility of the dramatic sign," as Honzl conceives it, that made possible the bond in Greek tragedy between dramatic text and stage presentation. Not to recognize the significance of the principles involved, that is to say, to separate the language of drama from the stage performance as disparate structures, means, in Honzl's opinion, to fail to grasp the essential unity of dramatic art as such.

Quite a different tack is taken again by Jiří Veltruský, who argues that the drama as a genre belonging to literature should be investigated apart from the theater, which represents, in his view, an entirely different art. In "Basic Features of Dramatic Dialogue," selected from his comprehensive study *Drama as Literature* (1942), Veltruský points out that the usage of language in dialogue clearly distinguishes drama from the literary genres dominated by monologue. Since dialogue involves more than one speaker, it necessarily unfolds not only in time but also in space, that is to say, in a specific "here and now." This peculiarity of dialogue, which distinguishes it from monologue, is complemented, according to Veltruský, by the fact that, unlike monologue, dialogue is always integrated in the extralinguistic situation. Moreover, in dialogue several contexts interpenetrate and alternate. In dramatic dialogue, which is the primary target of Veltruský's observation, the situation is still more complicated than in an ordinary conversation because the writer uses dramatic dialogue as an instrument of art.

In "Construction of Semantic Contexts" (1942), which was also selected from *Drama as Literature,* Veltruský elaborates three fundamental principles of contextual semantics: (a) the unity of sense of the entire context, (b) the accumulation of meanings, and (c) the oscillation between the semantic statics and dynamics. The specificity of dramatic dialogue is skillfully used by Veltruský as a base for his attempt to tackle the principles of contextual semantics from a new point of view.

The fourth section of our anthology is concluded by Roman Jakobson's article, "Is the Cinema in Decline?" (1933). Written at a time when the transition from the silent film to the sound film provoked theoretical controversy, Jakobson's study contains a number of observations that still remain highly relevant. Jakobson advances the notion that an entirely new semiotic system of art can always develop and enlarge the number of existing arts. With reference to cinema, the questions dealt with are whether film art is autonomous, what the nature of the material it transforms is, and where its specific hero is to be found. Jakobson asserts that signs are the material of every art, including that of the cinema. The director Kulešov's dictum, "The shot must operate as a sign, a kind of letter," proves that the semiotic essence of cinematic elements is clear to film makers. "For this reason essays on cinema always speak in a metaphorical way about the language of the film and even introduce the notion of film-sentences, with subject and predicate, and of film subordinate clauses, or look for verbal and nominal elements in film."

The section of the anthology devoted to verbal art opens with Jan Mukařovský's "Poetic Reference" (1936), which deals specifically with the referential usage of sign in the domain of verbal art. He defines poetic reference as any verbal reference appearing in a text which has a dominant aesthetic function. In such a text, the verbal context itself plays the role of the primary target of reference so that reference to reality becomes oblique, being subordinated within the hierarchy of referential functions. In Mukařovský's view, it is precisely this decline in the direct relationship to extralinguistic context which makes reference a poetic process. The internal arrangement of the complete poetic work appears at the focus of attention. However, such a focusing on the sign structure of the work of verbal art does not mean that the poetic reference is completely disengaged from any connection with reality. In fact, the obliqueness of the reference to the extralinguistic context becomes essential for the role of art in the community. It makes the verbal art an autonomous semiotic process that appears in a subtle but essential relationship with other social values.

The autonomy of the aesthetic function of art, implied by its semiotic nature, is also emphasized by Roman Jakobson in his paper, "What Is Poetry?," which was first published in 1933. With reference to the groundwork of modern phenomenology, Jakobson points out that the phenomenological inquiries demonstrated the prime importance of the distinction between a sign, with its signifying and signified properties, and the designated object and, implicitly, between the meaning of a word and the content toward which the meaning is directed. In accordance with such a distinction, Jakobson views the semiotic system of art as "an integral part of the social structure, a component which interacts with all the others and is itself mutable, since both the domain of art and its relationship to other constituents of social structure are in constant dialectical flux." At the same time, he makes it emphatically clear that what is at stake is not the separation of art but the autonomy of aesthetic form. Throughout Jakobson's comments on "What Is Poetry?," there is a distinctly detectable echo of theses he formulated in 1928 in cooperation with the outstanding Russian literary theorist and writer Jurij Tynjanov, where the scholastic and taxonomic predilection of certain trends in early Russian Formalism or of its later offshoots was decisively rejected in favor of a relational, hierarchical, and, thus, structural approach to art.[1]

The evolution of a literary system in complex coordination with other social systems is discussed in Jakobson's "Signum et Signatum," which was selected from his comprehensive study (1936) about Czech poetry in the Hussite period. Here Jakobson confronts the problem of how to deal with the literature of fifteenth-century Bohemia, literature written during a time of religious revolution when iconoclasm was rife, and art, if tolerated at all, was required to serve as ideological propaganda. Jakobson admits that he himself was mistaken in trying to project the results of his intrinsic analysis of fourteenth-century poetry into the poetry of the Hussite period without taking into consideration the specificity of aesthetics during the Hussite religious revolution. "To fully grasp the newness of Hussite poetry," he asserts, "we must place it in a broader context: the development and

differentiation of Czech poetic forms is contingent upon the proliferation
of the functions of the Czech poetic language; the history of poetry and
the history of language are closely intertwined." At the same time, he emphasizes the necessity of treating poetic structure through the conception
of sign and, via the sign, of proceeding to the social context "where a given
system of signs, language, and especially poetry comes to fruition."

The correlation of the literary system with other social systems does not,
in Jakobson's view, contradict the notion that poetry is a self-contained
entity, defined by its own system of signs and determined by the dominating
feature of poeticity. Although poetry, he argues, is to certain extent autonomous, it is also a constituent of a more comprehensive system of culture
and of the overall system of social values: "Each of these autonomous yet
integral parts is regulated by immanent laws of self-propulsion, while at the
same time depending upon the other parts of the system to which it belongs; if one component changes, its relationship to the other components
changes, thereby changing the components themselves."

Roman Jakobson, already during his Prague years, endeavored to dis-
close what he considered the basic and truly universal characteristics of
verbal art in the dichotomy of metaphor and metonymy, viewed as eternal
sources of figurative usage of language in general and of verbal art in particular. In his postscript to the Czech translation of Boris Pasternak's lyric
autobiography *The Safe Conduct* (1935), Jakobson presents Pasternak as a
poet of metonymy and, thus, as a poet gravitating toward prose in contradistinction to his contemporary Vladimir Majakovskij, a poet with a predilection for metaphor, disinclined to do any writing in prose. Jakobson
approaches metonymy and metaphor as the general principles underlying
verbal signs, the two poles of a binary opposition: metonymy is based on
contiguity and is, therefore, syntagmatic in nature, whereas metaphor is
based on similarity and represents a paradigmatic operation. It is the gravitation toward one of the two poles, rather than exclusive adherence, that,
in Jakobson's view, characterizes individual poets. By the nature of their
predilection poets may represent distinct literary traditions, even when
they belong to the same generation, as is the case of Pasternak, Majakovskij,
and Xlebnikov. Thus, there is a co-occurrence of individual predilections
and of distinct literary traditions at each synchronic stage of literary evolution. Consequently Jakobson insists that to regard the writers of one

particular period "as individual links in a single chain of literary evolution and to determine the sequence of these links" is to take a one-sided view. It is apparent that Jakobson's search for universal invariants is coupled in his study with an acute sense of the variability of phenomena relevant to evolution—whether the evolution is displayed as a chain of links or co-occurrence at each stage.

In spite of differences between Pasternak and his contemporaries, Jakobson sees as their common feature the tendency to make the sign independent of the object. This tendency, in his interpretation, is the guiding principle of the whole of modern art that arose as the antithesis to Naturalism. With obvious reference to Pasternak's party-line critics, Jakobson declares: "the attempts to link this specifically artistic phenomenon with a limited social sector and an ideology corresponding to it are typically mechanistic aberrations: if we infer from the nonobjective character of art that the artist's conception of the world is nonrealistic, we artifically obliterate an important antinomy."

The tasks of literary history in contradistinction to literary criticism were broadly outlined in Felix Vodička's comprehensive study *Literary History* (1942). One of its chapters appears in our anthology under the title "Response to Verbal Art." It deals with the reception of verbal art from the point of view of a historian who is aware of the fact that the criteria for evaluation as well as the literary values themselves continuously change over the course of history. To record these changes is, in Vodička's view, precisely the literary historian's proper task. He must concern himself with the literary norms of each given literary period and must endeavor to reestablish its hierarchy of literary values. Among his tasks, furthermore, should be the study of the actualizations of a literary work within the framework of various periods, and, finally, the study of the impact exercised by the work of art on extraliterary spheres. Tendentious literature, in which the extraliterary effect constitutes an essential part of the authorial design, Vodička believes is best investigated by other sciences more suitable to judge the scope of the extraliterary effect. It follows that for Vodička the most fundamental task of a literary historian is to distinguish a work of verbal art from nonart.

Both Lubomír Doležel and Jiří Levý, our next two contributors, belong to the younger generation of the literary theorists who have been trying to revive the tradition of Prague School structuralism after the hostile anti-structuralist period of the 1950s. Both Doležel and Levý have in common a clear predilection for algebraic analysis, classificatory procedures, and rigorously formalized descriptions. In his concise study "A Scheme of Narrative Time" (1973), Doležel shows that even the most complicated patterns of time in the narrative work are derived from physical time by transforming physical aspects of time into semiotic ones in two steps, one having to do with selection, the other being formative. His abstract scheme of classification is skillfully applied to Milan Kundera's *Joke,* one of the better modern Czech novels. The results confirm the view that the modern novel appears in the process of increasing liberation from the norms of physical time, although physical time remains, of course, the underlying concept. Doležel's study represents one branch of the Prague School tradition that has been strongly attracted by the formal features of verbal art. It may be claimed that this branch of the Prague School has remained closer to Russian formalism or rather to that trend in Russian formalism connected with the names of Viktor Šklovskij and Vladimir Propp. Thus, Doležel's development illustrates the fact that the Russian heritage has remained a strong undercurrent in the Prague School tradition, notwithstanding the fact that certain members of the Prague Linguistic Circle approached it highly critically.

The specific features that characterize verbal art in contradistinction to the nonartistic usage of language are, of course, a perennial problem for translators of verbal art. It is precisely that aspect of translation which represents the most crucial topic for Jiří Levý in his study "The Translation of Verbal Art," selected from his book *Genesis of Verbal Art and Its Translation* (1963). The literary work is explained by Levý as a subjective transformation of objective reality, which necessitates differentiating objective reality from literary reality and existential facts from artistic facts. In his view the seminal problem of the translation process is the relationship of three basic components: (a) the objective text, (b) the actualization by by the reader of the original, and (c) the actualization by the reader of the translation. Consequently, the translator has to face (a) linguistic problems in contrasting the grammar of two languages, (b) problems of style and poetics in contrasting two systems of aesthetic norms, and (c) problems of two traditions of literary criticism concerned with the ultimate values of the work interpreted synchronically. Thus the translator has to combine the erudition of a linguist, a literary theorist, and a literary judge.

The first of the two articles that comprise the fifth and final section, devoted to the theoretical problems of the visual arts, is Mukařovský's penetrating paper "The Essence of the Visual Arts" (1944), in which the concept of sign, viewed as an intermediary of some suprapersonal meaning, is applied anew as an explanatory model. Although a work of art could be defined merely in terms of its material properties as a material object, it fulfills its autonomous, unsubordinate aesthetic function only when the material properties are understood as transformed by the creative act into a sign structure capable of conveying meanings intended by the artist. Or, as Mukařovský puts it, "the material by which particular arts differ from one another and by which, of course, the visual arts as a whole differ from the others is not a merely passive basis of artistic activity but is an almost active factor that directs the activity and constantly intervenes—whether positively or negatively—in it."

Jiří Veltruský, in his recent contribution, "Some Aspects of the Pictorial Sign" (1973), also emphasizes the fact that painting radically differs from other semiotic systems in general and from language in particular. Thus, a picture is a specific type of sign. Veltruský views this specificity as definable according to several criteria among which the most relevant are (1) the material, (2) the manner in which the *signifiant* (expressed) is connected with the *signifié* (meant), (3) the mutual relationship of the referential, expressive, and connative functions of the pictorial sign, and (4) the construction of its total sense. Veltruský points out that the material properties of the pictorial sign determine the specific way in which the picture conveys meaning. The pictorial sign is capable of conveying meaning independently of any referential function just through the psychophysical effects of the material itself. In fact, the material properties of the artifact always produce psychophysical effects that necessarily have semiotic implications, no matter whether, or to what extent, the sign has an aesthetic function. The semiotic basis of pictorial art is explained by Veltruský in terms of three essential categories: (1) subject matter, (2) the differential value that each component acquires within the picture as a whole, (3) the role of pictorial norms.

In connection with the psychophysical effects of the material, Veltrusky emphasizes that that particular feature characterizes not only the pictorial sign but also sculpture, architecture, theater, dance, and even music. At the same time, however, he makes clear that the problem of meaning derived from the psychophysiological stimulation requires additional investigation.

Finally, as a supplement to the anthology proper, the reader is provided an overview of Prague structuralism in the postscriptural essay "Prague School Semiotics."

Notes

1. "Problemy izučenija literatury i jazyka," *Novyj Lef,* 12 (1928), pp. 36-37 = "Problems in the Study of Literature and Language," *Readings in Russian Poetics: Formalist and Structuralist Views,* ed. by L. Matejka and K. Pomorska, M.I.T. Press: Cambridge, 1971, pp. 79-81.

Part I

1. Art as Semiotic Fact

Jan Mukařovský

It becomes increasingly evident that the basic constitution of the individual consciousness, even at its innermost levels, derives from content belonging to the collective consciousness. As a consequence, crucial importance accrues to problems of sign and meaning, seeing that any mental content that exceeds the bounds of the individual consciousness acquires the character of a sign by the very fact of its communicability. The science of signs (called semiology by Saussure, sematology by Bühler, semiotic by Peirce) needs to be elaborated to its fullest extent. As contemporary linguistics (see the investigations of the Prague School, that is, the Prague Linguistic Circle) expands the field of semantics by treating all the elements of the system of language, even including sounds, from the semiotic point of view, the results of linguistics need to be applied to other domains of sign usage and to be differentiated according to their special characteristics. There are a number of sciences particularly concerned with the problem of signs (as well as with the problems of structure and value, which problems, incidentally, are closely related to those of signs—a work of art, for instance, is at one and the same time sign, strucrure, and value). In fact, all sciences known as humanities (*sciences morales, Geisteswissenschaft*) deal with phenomena that have the more or less pronounced character of signs due to their double existence both in the world of sense perception and in the collective consciousness.

A work of art is not identifiable, as psychological aesthetics would like to think it is, with the state of mind and spirit of its creator or with any of the possible states of mind and spirit induced in its perceivers. Clearly, every state of the subjective consciousness involves something individual and momentary that makes it impossible to grasp and communicate in its entirety, whereas the work of art is meant expressly to serve as an intermediary between its creator and the community. Moreover, there is always some "thing," some "artifact," that represents the work of art in the outside world and may be perceived by one and all. However, it is not possible to reduce the work of art to that "artifact," since it may happen

"L'art comme fait sémiologique." *Actes du huitième Congrès international de philosophie à Prague 1934* (Prague: 1936), pp. 1065-1072. Translated by I. R. Titunik.

that the artifact, shifted in time or space, will completely alter its appearance and inner structure. Such changes are readily detectable if, for instance, we compare several different, successive translations of the same poetic work. The artifact, thus, functions merely as an external signifier (*"signifiant"* in Saussure's terminology) for which in the collective consciousness there is a corresponding signification (often labeled "aesthetic object") given by what is common to subjective states of mind aroused in individuals of any particular community by the artifact.

In addition to this central core of the collective consciousness, there are in every act of perceiving a work of art psychological elements that are very nearly equivalent to what Fechner covers by the term the "associative factor" of aesthetic perception. These subjective elements can themselves be objectified, but only insofar as their general quality or quantity is determined by the central core located in the collective consciousness. So, for instance, the subjective states of mind and spirit aroused in any viewer of an Impressionist painting will be of an entirely different kind than those evoked by a Cubist painting. As for quantitative differences, clearly the number of subjective notions and feelings aroused will be considerably greater with respect to a poetic work of the Surrealist type than one of the Classicist type: the surrealist poem makes it incumbent upon the reader to imagine virtually the entire contexture of theme, whereas the classicist poem all but precludes the free-play of subjective associations due to its exactness of expression. It is only in this way that, indirectly at least—via the intermediary of the core belonging to the collective consciousness, the subjective constituents of the perceiver's mental state acquire an objective semiotic character similar to that possessed by a word's "secondary meanings."

Concluding these brief general remarks, we must also mention that by denying the identification of a work of art with any subjective mental state we also, at the same time, reject any hedonist theory of aesthetics. The feeling of pleasure aroused by the work of art can at best achieve indirect objectification as a potential "accessory signification"; to assert that it necessarily forms part of the perception of any work of art would be a mistake. Though the evolution of art exhibits periods that do strive to arouse pleasure, still it also exhibits periods that regard pleasure with indifference or even aim at its contrary.

According to its current definition, a sign is a reality perceivable by
sense perception that has a relationship with another reality which the first
reality is meant to evoke. Thus, we are obliged to pose the question as to
what the second reality, for which the work of art stands, might be. True,
we could merely assert that the work of art is an *autonomous* sign characterized solely by the fact of its serving as an intermediary among members
of any one community. However, to do so would mean to put aside unre-
solved the question of the contact of a work of art with the reality it refers
to. If signs not relating to any distinct reality are possible, still a sign always does refer to something by simple consequence of the fact that a sign
must be understood the same way by both sender and receiver. Only, for
autonomous signs, that "something" is not determined distinctly. What,
then, is the indistinct reality to which the work of art refers? It is the total
context of all phenomena that may be called *social,* for example, philosophy,
politics, religion, economics, and so on. It is for that reason that art, more
than any other social phenomenon, has the power to characterize and represent the "age." It is also the reason why for so long a time the history of
art has been confused with the history of culture in the broad sense of the
word and, vice versa, why general history has seen fit to borrow the
peripeteiae of art history for the mutual delimitation of its own periods.

True, connection with the total context of social phenomena may be
tenuous as regards certain works of art, such as, for instance, is the case of
the "poètes maudits" whose works are alien to the contemporary system
of values. However, it is precisely for that reason that they remain outside
literature and are not accepted by the community until such time as, in the
course of the evolution of the social context, they become capable of expressing it. One other explanatory remark must be added here to preclude
all possible misunderstanding: in saying that the work of art refers to the
context of social phenomena, we by no means assert thereby that the work
necessarily coincides with that context in the sense that, without further
ado, it can be taken as direct evidence or passive reflection. As is true of
any *sign,* the work of art can have an indirect relationship with the thing
signified (for example, a metaphoric or other kind of oblique relationship)
without ceasing on that account to refer to it. It follows from the semiotic nature of art that a work of art must never be utilized as an historical
or sociological document without preliminary interpretation of its

documentary value, that is to say, without preliminary interpretation of the quality of its relationship with the particular context of social phenomena involved.

To summarize the main points of our argument thus far, we may say that the objective study of the phenomenon "art" must regard the work of art as a sign composed of (1) a perceivable signifier, created by the artist, (2) a "signification" /= aesthetic object/ registered in the collective consciousness and (3) a relationship with that which is signified, a relationship which refers to the total context of social phenomena. In the second of these constituents lies the structure proper of the work.

We have not, however, exhausted the problems of the semiotic of art. Besides its function as automomous sign, the work of art has another function, that of informational sign. Thus, a poetic work, for instance, functions not only as a work of art but also, simultaneously, as an "utterance" expressing a state of mind, an idea, an emotion, etc. In certain of the arts this informational function is very evident (poetry, painting, sculpture), while in others it is veiled (dance) or even invisible (music, architecture). We shall leave aside here the formidable problem of the latent presence or total absence of the informational element in music and architecture (though we are inclined to recognize a diffuse informational element even in these domains; thus, for example, the relatedness of melody in music to verbal intonation, the informational power of which is evident) in favor of concentrating on those arts where the functioning of the work as informational sign is beyond doubt. These are the representational arts or "subject" arts (subject = theme, content) in which the subject would seem, at first glance, to function as the work's communicative signification. In actuality, every component of a work of art, not excluding even the most "formal" ones, possesses an informational value of its own independent of the "subject." Thus, the lines and colors of a picture signify "something" even in the absence of any subject (see, the "absolute" painting of Kandinsky or the works of certain surealist painters). It is in this virtual semiotic character of their formal constituents that the informational power (which we have called diffuse) of subjectless arts consists. If we were to be precise, we would have to say that it is once again the entire structure which functions as the signification of a work of art, the informational signification included. The subject of a work simply plays the role of an axis of crystallization with respect to that signification which, otherwise, would remain vague. The work of art, then, has a two-fold semiotic function, autonomous and informational, the latter being reserved especially for the representational arts. Hence, the dialectical antinomy between the autonomous and informational functions of sign can be seen operating to greater or lesser effect in the evolution of these arts. The history of prose fiction supplies particularly typical examples.

Complications of an even more intricate type arise, however, once we pose the question of the relationship of art to thing signified from the informational point of view. This relationship is different from the one that connects art, in its capacity as autonomous sign, with the total context of social phenomena, since art as informational sign refers to some distinct reality, for example, a particular event, a certain person, and so forth. In this respect art resembles signs that are purely informational. Only—and the qualification points to the essential difference—the informational relationship between the work of art and the thing signified does not have existential value, even when such is asserted. In regard to the subject of a work of art, no question as to its documentary authenticity can be postulated as long as the work is held to be a product of art. This does not mean that *modifications* of the relationship to thing signified are without importance for a work of art; they function as factors of its structure. For the structure of any given work it is very important to know whether it treats its subject as a "real" (perhaps even documentary) one or a "fictitious" one or whether it oscillates between these two poles. Indeed, works may be found which are based on a parallelism and counterbalance of a two-fold relationship to a distinct reality, in one instance without existential value and in the other purely informational. Such is the case, for example, of portrait painting or sculpture that is at one and the same time information about the person depicted and a work of art devoid of existential value. In literature, the same duality characterizes the historical novel and the fictionalized biography. Modifications of the relationship to reality do, therefore, play an important role in the structure of any art working with a subject, but the theoretical investigation of these arts must never lose sight of the true essence of the subject which is to be a unity of meaning and not a passive copy of reality even in the case of a "realistic" or "naturalistic" work.

We should like to remark, in concluding, that unless the semiotic character of art is adequately elucidated, the study of its structure will remain necessarily incomplete. Lacking a semiotic orientation, the theorist of art will always be inclined to regard the work of art as a purely formal structure or, on the other hand, as a direct reflection of the psychological or even physiological states of its creator or direct reflection of the distinct reality conveyed by the work or direct reflection of the ideological, economic, social or cultural situation of the milieu in question. This train of thought will lead the theorist either to treat the evolution of art as a series of formal transformations or to deny evolution completely (as in the case of certain currents in aesthetic psychology) or, finally, to conceive of it as passive commentary on an evolution exterior to art. Only the semiotic point of view allows theorists to recognize the autonomous existence and essential dynamism of artistic structure and to understand evolution of art as an immanent process but one in constant dialectical relationship with the evolution of other domains of culture.

Our sketch of the semiotic study of art was meant: (1) to provide partial illustration of a certain aspect of the dichotomy between the natural sciences and the humanities; (2) to bring out the importance of semiotic considerations for aesthetics and for the history of art.

Having now completed our presentation, perhaps we may be allowed to summarize its principal ideas in a set of theses:

A. The problem of sign, together with the problems of structure and value, is an essential problem for the humanities, all of which deal with phenomena that have the more or less pronounced character of signs. For that reason the results obtained by research in linguistic semantics must be applied to the phenomena of the humanities—especially to those whose semiotic character is most clear-cut—in order to be differentiated according to this specific characteristic.

B. The work of art bears the character of a sign. It can be identified neither with the individual state of consciousness of its creator nor with any such states in its perceiver nor with the work as artifact. The work of art exists as an "aesthetic object" located in the consciousness of an entire community. The perceivable artifact is merely, by relation with this immaterial aesthetic object, its outward signifier; individual states of consciousness induced by the artifact represent the aesthetic object only in terms of what they all have in common.

C. Every work of art is an autonomous sign composed of: (1) an artifact functioning as perceivable signifier; (2) an "aesthetic object" which is registered in the collective consciousness and which functions as "significa-tion"; (3) a relationship to a thing signified (this relationship refers not to any distinct existence—since we are talking about an autonomous sign—but to the total context of social phenomena, science, philosophy, religion, politics, economics, and so on, of any given milieu).

D. The representational arts, the arts with a "subject" (= theme, content), have, in addition, a second semiotic function, which is the informational function. Naturally, the perceivable symbol remains the same in this case as in the preceding one; the signification is here, too, given by the aesthetic object in its entirety, but it possesses among the components of that object a privileged carrier that functions as an axis of crystallization for the diffuse informational power of the other components: the subject of the work. The relationship to thing signified refers, as in any informational sign, to a distinct existence (an event, a person, a thing, and so forth). Through this quality, the work of art thus resembles purely informational signs. Only—and this is the essential difference—the relationship between the work of art and thing signified does not have existential value. In regard to the subject of a work of art, it is impossible to postulate the question as to its documentary authenticity insofar as the work is held to be a product of art. This does not mean that modifications of the relationship to thing signified (that is, different degrees along the scale "reality—fiction") are unimportant for a work of art; they function as factors in its structure.

E. The two semiotic functions, autonomous and informational, coexisting in the representational arts, constitute together one of the essential dialec-tical antinomies of the evolution of these arts; their duality makes its effect, over the course of evolution, in constant oscillations of the relationship to reality.

Part II

2. Costume as a Sign

(The Functional and Structural Concept of Costume in Ethnography)

Petr Bogatyrev

Urban and rural styles of dress, used as national costumes, have many functions: practical and aesthetic functions, and often, in association with the aesthetic function, erotic and magic functions, as well. Costume also functions as an indicator of the age of its wearer and as a distinguishing marker between married and unmarried people. Such a sociosexual function is closely related to the moral function (in Slovakia, for example, a special costume designates an unwed mother, called *závitka*). Moreover, there are festive and professional functions, as well as functions indicating social status, class, region, nationality, religion, and so forth. In all cases, costume is both material object and sign.

Therefore, let us first focus on the difference between material object and sign.[1] The world around us displays two kinds of material objects. One kind is without any ideological significance, for example, natural objects, implements of production, things of everyday use. We can use them, become familiar with their structure, learn how they are made or what role they play in production. In this case, we do not suppose that a stone or a hammer, for instance, is a sign which denotes something else: another object or another event. However, if we take a stone, paint it white, and then place it between two fields, something different happens. Such a stone will accrue a specific meaning. Now it will no longer be merely itself, namely a stone as an item of nature, but will acquire the special significance of indicating something other than itself. It will become a marker, that is, a sign with a particular and variously usable meaning. A sign for what purpose? A sign to mark the border between two plots of ground. Similarly, when we see the crossed hammer and sickle prominently displayed, they represent for us not merely tools, a picture of tools, but a symbol of the U.S.S.R. What exactly has happened? A phenomenon of material reality has become a phenomenon of ideological reality: a thing has changed into a sign (which is also of a material nature, of course). Signs, too, are

"Kroj jako znak," *Slovo a slovesnost,* 2 (1936), pp. 43-47. Translated by Yvonne Lockwood.

particular, tangible things. As we have seen, any item of nature, technology, or everyday use can become a sign whenever it acquires meaning beyond the bounds of its individual existence as a thing in and of itself.[2] Some objects can be used equally as material things and signs; for instance, costume with its several functions is a material thing and a sign at the same time. This close connection of thing and sign in one object is not the property of costume alone. We have a fine example in the famous legend about Theseus. Theseus was supposed to have agreed that, if he lived, his ship would return with white sails, if he died, it would return with black sails. In both cases, the sails remain material objects: they must satisfy all the requirements of sails with respect to quality, firmness, durability of material, suitability of shape, and so on. But besides being sails as such, they also became a sign indicating whether Theseus was dead or alive. Thus, from this legend, we see that sails had a different function as a sign than as a material thing. Yet, while functioning as a sign, they continued to fulfill their practical role as a material thing. Likewise, costume always has a practical function; hence, it is not only a sign but also a practical thing at the same time. Cases where costume is only a sign are quite rare. Even the Chinese actor's paper costume, which functions predominantly to signify that the actor is playing the role of a Chinese, is, after all, not only a sign but also something that covers the actor's body.

If we examine each individual function of costume, we again see that they all pertain to costume in some respects as a practical thing, in other respects as a sign. Among all the functions of costume already mentioned, only the practical and, in part, the aesthetic function pertain to costume strictly as something in itself.[3] Many other functions pertain both to the clothing itself and to other domains that the costume represents. For example, the role of holiday apparel has very much to do with the clothing itself—that is, it is supposed to be made of costly material, supposed to look "dressy," while, at the same time, certain details—including even the expensive cloth—are not just matters of clothing but also serve to signify that this day is a holiday and not an ordinary day. The case of the function indicating class is similar. The fact that expensive fabric is used for the clothing worn by the rich has a bearing on the matter of the clothing itself but at the same time also denotes the social class of the wearer. However, I repeat, in this case, dress also changes as a thing. Let us imagine that we obtain the dresses of a rich peasant woman and of a poor peasant woman from some village, for instance from Vajnor in the Bratislava area where formerly rich peasant women embroidered their sleeves with gold and the poor only with silk, and that we send these dresses to a secondhand dealer in town. Even if the dealer should not know that both costumes were symbols of class distinction between peasants, he still would appraise the sleeves differently, judging them as material objects. In certain special cases, however, the social distinctiveness of a costume may appear as a sign only. A military uniform, for example, has on it certain details that indicate the rights of the wearer and his rank in the army. When a private sees a uniformed officer, he knows that he is obliged to obey his command; in this case, the quality of the material or the aesthetic value of the uniform is irrelevant. If we take a rich soldier's uniform, made of better material than the officer's uniform, and send it to a secondhand dealer who does not know about military distinctions, he may attach higher value to the uniform of the rich soldier. Or, if there is no difference in the quality of material, the dealer might assess the uniforms as equal, despite the fact that in the army these uniforms differ substantially as signs. In order to comprehend the social functions of costumes and uniforms, we must learn to understand these objects as signs in the same way that we learn to understand different words of a language. For example, in some areas darker colors indicate nationality: Germans in Slovakia wear darker colors than the Slovaks; in other areas darker colors signalize a difference in religion between Protestants and Catholics, whereas elsewhere they indicate age differences. Just as soldiers learn to distinguish the various insignia of a military uniform, so villagers learn from childhood to recognize what darker colors in clothing mean.

Some of the functions of folk costume derive solely from its property as a sign. When an unwed mother has to wear certain items of costume, the neighborhood takes note that she is wearing those items and not others appropriate for a maiden's costume. In this case, it does not matter whether the material, out of which these items are made, is of good or poor quality or whether they are attractive or not. Moreover, as regards this distinctive costume of unwed mothers, one has also to be aware of the item-signs themselves, since what in one village signifies an unwed mother, can be part of a maiden's costume in another village. Likewise, a married woman cannot wear the costume of a maiden even though she might consider it more comfortable or convenient. Similarly, the regional function of costumes is aimed at making them distinguishable from costumes of a different area regardless of whether they are more practical or prettier. Thus costume is characterized by an entire structure of functions.

Some functions (in a way comparable to the sails on Theseus's ship) pertain to costume, viewed as a material object (for example, the practical function) while many functions overlap with other domains. The structure of diverse functions always makes costume simultaneously a thing and a sign.

Similarly, language always fulfills several functions at the same time. Let us use a concrete example. We ask someone how to get to the railroad station and he tells us. His speech furnishes us the directions (because we understand his word-signs), but it also is a sign to us that characterizes the speaker himself, because while listening to his directions, we realize that the speaker is using dialect or argot; and, accordingly, we can determine his regional or social status. Furthermore, in a conversation we commonly adapt ourselves to those with whom we are talking. For example, if an eight-year-old child asks how to get to the railroad station, the explanation is given differently than if an adult inquires; the route is explained in a different way to urbanites than to rural people. Still other expressions are used to give directions to a stranger in town. In Gogol's *Dead Souls* there is a beautiful example showing how Čičikov, while moving among different social circles and meeting people from different social and cultural milieus, changes his behavior and language to suit the context. Something similar also takes place in connection with costume.

National costume is far more determined by the wearer than the language is determined by the speaker. By taking note of his dress—often against the will of its wearer—we can more easily determine the social position of its user, his cultural level and his taste than by taking note of his speech. Yet even costume is not determined only by the personality of its wearer, and in this respect there is a similarity with language. The wearer of a costume is concerned not only with satisfying his own personal taste but also with conforming to the costume of the region, with satisfying the norms of his environment. Everyone adjusts to his environment both in language and clothing. Ethnographers know very well that as a rule villagers who have returned to their native place from the city, stop wearing urban clothes and dress in village costume so as not to be "white crows" and stand out from the community. In the Carpathian Ukraine, married women wear the costume of the village where they live with their husbands. Even a city dweller very often dresses in accordance with how other people will be dressed at the gathering he will attend. Everyone knows how embarrassed many men get if they are dressed in informal attire where everyone is in formal attire, and conversely, how unpleasant it is to be the only one at a party in tails.

The functional method used in ethnography can not only illuminate this material but also expand it. For an ethnographer, concerned with the historical development of village life, folk costume is an indispensable object of research. If costume disappeared from village life, ethnographic fieldwork would cease. Then study would have to rely entirely on museum collections which are only more or less complete and which it is becoming more and more difficult, if not impossible, to complete or verify. A functional analysis of village costume is another matter. The function of village dress still persists even when none of the details of the old costume is present and when village and urban dress have completely merged. For the ethnographer the question then arises as to what function village dress has when its shape and material have changed and when it approaches urban dress or has completely merged with it. For example, in Russian villages during the prewar period galoshes were very much in style, but villagers, primarily young people, did not wear them in bad and muddy weather but on sunny holidays only. In the city the dominant function of galoshes was to protect the feet from moisture and mud; in the village, however, the dominant function was aesthetic. For example, there is a song that goes as follows:

All lads look fine in galoshes
but my sweetheart, even without galoshes
is neat and handsome all the time.

Thus, for an ethnographer, who uses a historical approach, galoshes are not an object of research in the area of village costume. On the other hand, for an ethnographer, who examines the function of costume, galoshes are just as interesting as the lacquered boots of the past or the decorated sandals, whose dominant function, as in the case of galoshes, was aesthetic.

The ethnographer applying a functional method can supply a great deal of information to the sociologist studying contemporary urban dress. On the other hand, the ethnographer also must constantly pay heed to the achievements in sociology. Also the study of functions and structures of other ethnographic material faces some interesting problems. Take, for example, village constructions. A village building in addition to its practical functions has other functions as well, as, for example, aesthetic, magic, regional, social, and so on. A building is not only an object but also a sign. In some regions we can determine, even from a distance, the nationality and social stratification of the household by the outward appearance of the building. Farm implements are also practical things and signs at the same time. Sometimes the aesthetic function displaces the practical, and the object, which appears to be only a practical one, becomes a sign. A striking example are the cylinders used for pressing clothes, which are covered with designs and adorned with sequins of reflective material. According to custom in some Slovak villages, the groom gives these cylinders to his bride but, in fact, they are not usable because of the decoration. There are very few village implements whose function is practical only without having at the same time also aesthetic, regional, and other functions.

In the field of folklore it is especially true that the functional approach is opening up new and broader perspectives. For example, definition of folktales exclusively on a formal basis has not proved satisfactory. Collections of folktales often include diverse types of narratives, such as historical tales that are very different from fairy-tale fiction. On the other hand, such collections often omit *byliny,* including those which are now narrated rather than chanted. However, the classification of oral folklore according to function would shed new light on folk narrative in general. For example, the study of children's tales, which have both aesthetic and practical function (the latter to calm and sometimes to lull the child to sleep), can reveal a great deal about the form of the tales themselves so that we could see them in connection with lullabies. On the other hand, a functional study of narratives reveals both fantastic and didactic elements. A structural study of various functions of folktales provides an insight into the individual functions; it clarifies, for example, many stylistic functions, once we realize that the narrative has both aesthetic and didactic functions. In folk songs about costumes, to mention another area, one must take note not only of the aesthetic function but also of various other functions such as the magical, the regional, the social, and so on. An outstanding example of structural linkage of different functions appears in incantations. Incantations have an aesthetic function, as shown by the wealth of their poetic images and figures, but the suggestive function is also very evident. The suggestive function is to induce in the sick person a state similar to that which a doctor-hypnotist would induce. Also the study of proverbs offers the folklorist a great deal of material: at different periods proverbs have different functions; often they lose their original meaning and take on a new one. This is similar to the fate of the French expression "cher ami" in Russian dialects, where it has become an insult. Thus, as these few cases indicate, a functional and structural approach provides immense possibilities. It can be relevant to many areas and open new ways for ethnography in general. To indicate these possibilities was the main purpose of this study.[4]

Notes

1. Here I take the word sign in the broadest sense. Within the concept of "sign" we should differentiate the sign itself, symbol, signal. Regarding sign and symbol, see D. Čyževsky [Tschižewskij], "Ètika i logika," *Naučnye trudy Russkogo narodnogo universiteta v Prage* [Scientific Works of the Russian National University in Prague], IV (1931), p. 231 ff. For the definition of sign, see the works of Karl Bühler.

2. V. N. Vološinov similarly and with approximately the same examples interprets the relationship of object and sign in "Slovo i ego social'naja funkcija," [The Word and Its Social Function], *Literaturnaja učeba*, 5 (1930), p. 45.

3. Vološinov (ibid.) attributes the aesthetic function to the sign. Admittedly, the question of whether this function can be attributed to the object or the sign is not clear, and therefore we leave it open.

4. See my article "Funkčno-štrukturálna metóda a iné metódy etnografie a folkloristiky" [The Functional-Structural Method and Some Other Methods of Ethnography and Folkloristics], *Slovenské pohl'ady*, 51:10 (1935), pp. 550-558.

3. Folk Song from a Functional Point of View

Petr Bogatyrev

When examining the folk songs of various peoples, what holds our attention is their distinctly marked functional character. The functions of song form a complete structure. Besides aesthetic function, song entails various other functions: magic function, regional identification, work rhythm, indication of singer's age and sex (when it is a song to be sung by males or by females), and so forth. In fact, very often the dominant function of folk song will not be aesthetic at all.

Similarly, subjecting the songs of townspeople to study by the functional method, we ascertain that the aesthetic function is not always the dominant one. Let us take the national anthem as an example. Two functions of the anthem are clearly distinguished from those of the romance. In the anthem the aesthetic function is relegated to second place. The anthem is a symbol of a particular state, as is, for example, the national flag. During the performance of the anthem, the whole audience, to whom the interests of the state are dear, shows its respect for the anthem, in turn expressing by this act its respect for the state of which the anthem is a symbol. The respect which one feels for the anthem is expressed in equal proportion to the respect shown by an individual or community for the state. One pays only insignificant attention to the aesthetic qualities of the anthem. For enemies of such and such a state hatred toward the anthem is expressed in equal proportion to the hatred felt for the state. And, in turn, enemies of the anthem pay only insignificant attention to its aesthetic qualities, which might be considerable. This is equally true regarding songs that signalize one's belonging to a particular political party. Nevertheless, nonaesthetic functions are even more frequent for folk songs than for the songs of townspeople.

Let us consider the aesthetic function of folk song first. An analysis of this function leads to the assertion that folk song, as compared with romance and urban song, is more diverse in scope. A folk song, for example, may fulfill the function of rhythmic music, that is, music whose dominant characteristics are the cadence and rhythm of dance. Such a rhythmic

"La chanson populaire du point de vue fonctionnel," *Travaux du Cercle linguistique de Prague,* 6 (1936), pp. 222-234. Translated by Yvonne Lockwood.

song could be performed with or without the accompaniment of a musical instrument.[1] The couplets of dance pieces (*pljasovye častuški*) and children's songs are often performed in dance without accompaniment. In all these songs, rhythm is dominant, and in certain cases, it overshadows the melody and particularly the words of the song. Very often in such songs, for example in couplets of dance pieces, not only the words, which often make little sense, but also the melodies are reduced to a minimum. Among the songs that have a special aesthetic function, we will mention those where the words and dramatic action are inseparable: the latter is carried out with the performance of the song.

What especially distinguishes folk song from nonfolk song is that the former is performed by all voices at the same time, whereas in the latter the tendency to separate the singer and audience becomes more and more dominant.[2] I wish to emphasize that I am speaking here of a general tendency that does not exclude the fact that within various genres of folk song, for example in the performance of *byliny* or Russian historical songs, one also notices a marked difference between the performer and the audience. On the other hand, there are urban songs performed by entire choirs, in particular songs which are performed by groups of students or soldiers.

In addition to their aesthetic function, and simultaneously with aesthetic function, folk songs often fulfill the function of historical narratives, a function that brings them closer to the functions of scientific work. Such has been the role of *chansons de gestes, byliny,* Russian historical songs, and Yugoslav epic songs. One should also include songs glorifying the adventures of brigands in this category.

Itinerant songs and songs of pilgrimage, which are very widespread in Europe, are very interesting from the point of view of the functions with which they are charged. After having sung their songs, itinerant singers used to sell the texts to listeners, and the songs spread in this manner in both town and country.[3]

One of the principal functions of these itinerant songs was to keep the rural public informed about current sensational events, such as murders, suicides, and accidents. Of this type is the Czech song, "A Murder Most Cruel," which begins with the words

Stop a moment,
Dearest Christians,
What I'm going to tell you is no lie.
This event took place in London in 1841.[4]

"The Song About Two Lovers Who Died a Cruel Death Out of Love Too Sincere," tells a story about a catastrophic love affair. Czech itinerant songs also undertake to communicate news about various disasters. A typical example is a song concerning a flood in Prague: "Listen, good people, to what I'm going to tell you of the flood that took place in Prague, Bohemia, on March 30, 1845."[5] In turn there are songs about other floods that occurred in Hungary, Vienna, and elsewhere.[6] Still further, we find a song recounting the enormous snowfalls and a terrible fire in Moscow in 1838. Another song devoted to the harvesting of potatoes begins in this way:

We give thanks to our Lord
For His great blessings,
We thank Him for having blessed the harvest of potatoes
And for having given them to us in abundance.[7]

Here is a contemporary theme, "Farewell to the *Assignats*":

How hard life is nowadays!
We cannot but believe it.
How many lamentations at the reading of the decree
Which ordered all the assignats to be burned![8]

Then, too, there are itinerant songs about wars and massacres committed by the Turks, and so on. We also find songs expressing patriotic and Slavophile sentiments.

Comparisons between itinerant songs and newspapers are easy to make. The songs as well as the newspapers indicate precisely the year, month, and day, that is, the date of the event. They cite the number of persons and the place where the event took place. The comparison can be developed still further: newspapers are obliged to relate recent acts; songs, too, purport to inform their listeners of the very latest news. Certain editions of itinerant songs and the songs of pilgrimage do not carry a date. This date can be either completely lacking or replaced by rather vague indications such as "edition of this year." The publisher of such a song did this deliberately because a song dating from several years back would have had no success with buyers anxious to get the latest songs.[9]

Particularly in the past but today as well, magical function occupies a prominent place among the various functions of folk song. The incantation song[10] had, and often still has, the same function as the incantation formula. In the examination of magical songs, as in that of magical acts, we will distinguish between those which are motivated and those which are unmotivated.[11] In the performance of a motivated magical song, as well as in a magical rite, the executant is conscious of performing an incantation while singing a song, of fulfilling via natural phenomena or via the supernatural beings which they command what the text of the song says.

The prayer song is closely linked to an incantation song when it expresses less a prayer than an order to the supernatural being to fulfill a particular desired action.

At present, folk song more often fulfills an unmotivated ritual function than a motivated one. In many cases the unmotivated song plays approximately the same role as the unmotivated magical act.

Such unmotivated ritual songs appear as an inseparable part of the ritual act and their absence, like that of other prescribed parts of a rite, removes the magical power from the latter. Peasants, for example, are aware that in a wedding it is obligatory to carry out such and such a rite, as well as to sing such and such a ritual song. At the same time, since this is in an unmotivated rite, they are not aware of the reason why the performance of a particular song should bring certain favorable results. They are aware only of having to perform this song in a prescribed manner.

For example, the song can be performed in an unknown language. Peasants are completely unaware of the connection between the text and what they want to obtain from nature or from a supernatural being, but even in cases where the text is rendered in the mother tongue of the performer it does not have any connection with what they want to obtain by performing this song.

But neither are all ritual songs and rites carried out because they bring certain favorable results. Sometimes both the song and the rite are carried out as a necessary sign of what is fitting to a ceremony. For example at a wedding, if the rites are not carried out, if all the songs are not performed, as is traditional according to the opinion of the village, no misfortune will result for the newly married couple, but without the execution of rites and ritual songs the wedding would not be regarded as it should be. Just as it is improper, for example, for a peasant to seat his guests at a table without a tablecloth, so also it is improper not to carry out all rites during a wedding and not to perform all the songs which are fitting to such a ceremony. Thus, the song here is only a sign which shows that the masters of the house know what is appropriate during a wedding ceremony.

The function of solemnity is very close to the preceding function. Songs render the rites more solemn.

Folk song appears as a revealing sign of the festival of a patron saint or family. Certain ritual songs are reserved exclusively for specific festivals. Depending on when a song is performed, we are able to determine the genre of the rite; for example, a particular rite belongs to a particular part of a wedding ceremony.[12]

The aesthetic function is in structural accord with all these previous functions.

Let us note that the songs which fulfill ritual functions are not always intended for a rite from their very origin; it often happens that they are connected to rites for which they were not originally intended. This has been the case of many lyric songs connected to wedding ceremonies.

Folk song often fulfills the function of regulating work; it marks the tempo and accelerates productivity. Regarding this topic, we refer the reader to the work of K. Bücher, *Arbeit und Rythmus,* which has attracted the attention of specialists to this question.[13] Here we are not as concerned with the problem of the origin of song as much as with the issue of song regulating work. Whatever opinion one might have on this question, it is necessary to emphasize that a whole series of songs have played, and still play today, the role of regulating work.

Let us turn now to the region-designating function of songs. Numerous examples could be cited where ritual and nonritual song are differentiated according to region. Thus, in one village only such and such a ritual song will be sung at weddings; in another, sometimes neighboring, village an entirely different song will be sung on the same occasion. The same fact applies to *rondes,* songs accompanying games, couplets (*častuški*), and lyric songs.

A different repertoire is also the mark of different religious groups. Thus, the repertoire of Catholics is not the same as that of Protestants; Russian Old-Believers used to have a different repertoire from that of the Orthodox; the same can be said for Jews, Moslems, and other groups. However, many songs having a religious character cannot be considered a sign of a particular confession. Some songs, with a biblical content or having the lives of saints as subject matter, and so forth, can be linked to songs fulfilling a historical function.

Regarding songs that identify a social group, it is necessary to note first a difference between the repertoire of artisans inhabiting a village and that of peasants. The question of differences existing between the repertoires of rich and poor peasants is a complex one. Wealthy peasants are inclined to break away from their social group and to imitate other classes. The well-to-do peasant, while living his life as a peasant and remaining attached to his milieu, will send his son to study in town; and the latter will bring changes to the repertoire that he finds in his household. It also happens that in a household of wealthy peasants the husband alone, by his manner of dress and his repertoire of songs, detaches himself from his social group, while the wife will remain loyal to the traditions of her social class.

But a contrary phenomenon is not rare. Often it is the wealthy peasants, remaining in the village where they were born, attached to their social class and proud of belonging there, who preserve the ancient traditional folk songs. Poor peasants, obliged to leave their village in order to seek work elsewhere, break away from their social milieu, forget their ancient repertoire and learn the songs sung in other villages and towns.

As we have stated earlier, song also indicates by whom it must be performed, by males or by females. Those who have collected and studied folk songs have often pointed out the differences in the repertoires of men and women. Thus, *byliny* and Russian historical songs performed by men differ appreciably from those performed by women. This difference is still more marked in lyric songs. It would be strange, for example, to hear men perform songs intended for women or vice versa. Certain ritual nuptial songs are performed by women and others by men. The same differentiation exists in the performance of couplets.

Let us cite here observations made in contemporary Russian villages: "The transcription and study of songs allows us to establish a distinction in the repertoire of males and females, particularly in the case of older peasants. Nuptial songs and *rondes* are performed by women. The song "Proščaj žis'—radost' moja" [Farewell, My Life—My Joy] has been recorded 36 times, performed 34 times by women and two times only by men. Men know and sing primarily the song "Exali soldaty" [The Soldiers Went Riding By]. It has been transcribed eleven times, ten times sung by men and once by a woman. There also are songs common to both sexes. The above demarcation is much less distinct in regard to young people. Songs of the "Komsomol" [The Young Communist League] are sung equally by young men and young women."[14]

With respect to song as an index of the marital status of a woman, there are songs performed exclusively by maidens and others by married women. This is especially striking in ritual songs and particularly in nuptial songs. This demarcation is common in many instances. Thus, in Slovakia songs that accompany the rite of the drowning of the mannequin are performed by girls. The demarcation is still more distinct for "lamentations," which are different for the mother, daughter, and wife of the deceased.[15]

It is very easy to find an indication of the performer's age in songs; from generation to generation there are songs which are sung by youths, others by adults. To the first category belong Christmas songs—these songs have always been sung by boys. On the other hand, it is necessary to distinguish songs that now are performed only by old men; however, this distinction is not constant. From one generation to another the performance may not be the same; for example, nowadays adults may sing songs which they had sung in their youth and which present-day youth no longer sing. Children's songs differ in form and functions from those of adults and are particularly interesting. We know that these songs are often incorporated into the adults' repertoire, but they adapt their form to their new functions.

The functional method applied to the study of folk song allows us to clarify obscure points in the development of folk song, for example, questions about the diffusion of literary song and romance and the modifications undergone in transition. What was not comprehensible to us in the process of transformation from literary song into folk song will be explained if we consider this process from the functional point of view. As a general rule, let us always keep in mind that the nonaesthetic function plays a much more important role in folk song than in the romances sung in town. This is one of the principal differences between these two genres. In a discussion on folk song, it is necessary to consider both aesthetic and nonaesthetic functions. We would be committing a great error if, basing ourselves on the role of functions which romance and other urban songs fulfill for townspeople, we were to try to explain why a particular song persists only in villages. It is quite natural that we forget more quickly than villagers the songs which do not meet our needs but fill other functions; we have at our disposal other activities, competing with songs and having greater success, that fulfill these nonaesthetic functions. Even if a song, which does not meet our aesthetic requirements, fulfills its historical function rather well, it will not be able to compete for long with historical works of another genre; consequently, this song will be quickly forgotten. If it tells a sensational story, we will reject and forget it as soon as more sensational news is brought to us by the press. It will not be the same in a milieu where newspapers and books exist in limited number and where song has often taken up the functions of the latter two.

With regard to *byliny* and historical songs, they undoubtedly served multiple functions, and no less so in ancient than in modern times. Their poetic function is reflected in their artistic and poetically enhanced form. But at the same time they always fulfilled and still fulfill the function of historical narratives. Early in their existence, certain *byliny* seem to have had functions analogous to newspaper articles of our time with regard to topics of domestic and foreign policy; they extolled one political faction of a Russian prince's court while discomfiting another. When they passed from the aristocratic class to the peasantry, this function inevitably had to disappear. Research in the domain of Slavic and non-Slavic epic song according to the functional method will enable us to understand a great many things which up to now have been inexplicable.

Nevertheless, in order to come up with some probable hypotheses on the functions of ancient songs, it seems preferable, from a methodological point of view, first of all to gather together all possible materials on the functions of modern songs and to specify as many laws as possible by which they are transformed. This would allow us to apply deductions made in the domain of modern song to more distant epochs. It goes without saying that when we apply an experiment carried out in the area of modern song to ancient songs, we should proceed with great caution; one must never forget that a social act can completely change in function upon entering another social structure, even when its form remains unchanged.

The same song is perceived differently by people who possess a repertoire of varied songs and by others who only know their local songs. A folk song will be perceived differently by a peasant-singer and, for example, by the composer Rimski-Korsakov, who transcribed the song exactly as the peasant sang it, but for whom the song stands against the general background of Russian and European music. Thus, one must determine first of all the position which a given song occupies in the whole repertoire of the performer and the functions that the song fulfills. At the same time one must determine the position the song holds within the totality of the song repertoire and the musical as well as poetic repertoire of the particular milieu in question. As we have repeatedly pointed out, the function of folk song is not only aesthetic. When it fulfills the function of an historical narrative, it is essential to take account of the historical knowledge of the performer and of the milieu to which he belongs. This allows us to explain how the historical element of the song is understood by the individual and by the entire group, to what degree it is comprehended in a critical manner, and so forth. Furthermore, in order to comprehend the function of folk song as a sign of region, we must render an account of regional movement and of the atmosphere of the peasant milieu. In order to understand the function of song as a sign of social class, it is necessary to know about the composition of social classes and the class struggle in the village where the song has been noted. Therefore, when we have a thorough knowledge of all structures of cultural, political, and economic life of the milieu in question, we are able to comprehend all song functions and the structure of the functions. On the other hand, songs explain many things about the cultural, political, and economic structure of this milieu.

I wish now to make a few remarks about the function of a song when it has passed from a peasant milieu into the realm of literature. We can trace this evolution on Russian territory. Up until the eighteenth century, to the best of our knowledge, the difference between the peasants' and aristocrats' repertoire of songs was insignificant. In the eighteenth century folk song was felt to be something exotic in the repertoire of literary songs. During that time, in aristocratic Russian circles, folk song primarily filled an aesthetic function, reflecting, in addition, the moral and patriarchal life of honest peasants.

During period of romanticism, the dominant function of folk song in Russian literary circles was nationalist. It was a sign of national solidarity of the people. Among the romantic Slavophiles, folk song filled the function of a symbol of the Slavophile party; it represented the Russian and Slav element, in other words the sign of Messianism of the Russian and Slavic people. At the time when he was an enthusiastic Slavophile, A. N. Ostrovskij said, "With Tertij and Prov we have reversed all of the work of Peter." (Tertij Filipov, a singer of Russian folk songs, was celebrated in Slavophile circles; Prov Sadovskij was a talented actor who played the roles of Russian types in dramas and comedies; the work of Peter refers to the work of Peter the Great and his Europeanization of Russia.) In the literary circle of the "Narodniki" the dominant function of folk song was revolutionist. For the Narodniki, folk song was a "cri du coeur" of the oppressed people. Among the symbolists the dominant function of folk song was aesthetic or mystic.

What I have just presented is a broad outline of the dominant functions which folk song has fulfilled in the course of time in different literary schools. In reality the problem is more complex. It is complicated primarily by the fact that several literary schools existed at one and the same time and each of them had its own notion of folk song.[16]

When examining various functions of folk song, we notice that some are expressed simultaneously in equal or almost equal proportion by the words and by the melody. Thus, the regional indication of a song, by which it is differentiated from songs of other regions, is expressed by its particular melody and oral text in equal or almost equal proportion. Songs as signs of class, particular castes, or different age groups have distinctive features expressed equally by melody and text.

But in certain cases, for example when songs fulfill the function of a newspaper report, the song text primarily expresses this function. Such songs are often sung to the melody of older songs that have no connection with the report song. In other cases, on the contrary (for example in lullabies), melody and rhythm serve primarily, and sometimes exclusively, to express a particular function. Their dominant function is to quiet or tranquilize a child through their melody and regular rhythm. That is why the text of these songs is usually mediocre in content. This is understandable because these songs are usually sung to an infant who is not yet able to comprehend the meaning. In cases where there is a developed text in a lullaby, it clearly plays a secondary role and does not relate directly to the individual to whom the lullaby is sung, that is, the infant, but only to the one who is singing it and who, while putting the infant to sleep, simultaneously experiences an aesthetic pleasure from the interesting words of the same song. With some modifications, the same remark should also be repeated regarding work songs, whose principal function is to produce a rhythm in work. In this case, also, the words of the song play only a secondary role.

One of the urgent tasks of contemporary musicology is the study of the musical form of song in conjunction with the modification of song function.[17] The functions of folk song do not remain fixed any more than do the functions of other social activities; they are constantly changing. Functions formerly dominant became secondary and can even disappear completely; sometimes secondary functions become primary; other times new functions appear.

The structure of song functions alter due to changes in circumstances to which songs become attached. Thus, for example, in a song regulating work the dominant function will be to determine and accentuate the rhythm of the work. When the same song is performed at a time of rest, an aesthetic function replaces the former function. The evolution of customs and way of life entails modifications in the "concept of the universe"; functions of song adapt to these changes. Thus, a song that had motivated incantation as the dominant function will pass over to the function of unmotivated incantation, and then to the function marking the solemnity of the rite. Let us take note that the changing stages are not always followed in this order; they can move in the opposite direction and sometimes even skip stages. Folk song functions are modified when the song passes from one milieu to another. The scholar should always keep this in mind while studying songs that have passed from aristocratic classes and the milieu of towns to the peasantry and vice versa. We have examined a number of diverse functions which folk song fulfills and has fulfilled. In many respects the functions of song are the same as the functions of other social activities that take place in villages. In particular a number of song functions agree with those of folk costume; both are signs of region, of age, of religion, and so on. But there are fundamental differences between folk song and costume. The latter is not only a sign; it is an object, a thing.[18] Folk song (as long as aesthetic function is taken as a sign of the social act) is only a sign. From this point of view it will be appreciably more akin to signs such as the spoken word and various genres of oral literature: tales, legends, proverbs, and so forth.

Notes

1. We see something analogous in jazz music; dance is performed to the accompaniment of song and usually also of instrumental music.

2. In Russian villages the first manner of song performance now is disappearing, as is indicated by Z. N. Kuprijanova, "Pesni derevni Pogromny" [Songs of the Village of Pogromna], *Jazyk i literatura,* 8 (1932), p. 33: "Only in the close family circle is song still performed in chorus; males sing it while working at their loom, females while spinning."

3. These songs of urban origin, nonetheless, constitute an integral part of the rural repertoire and should be studied as such. Peasants listened attentively to these songs; the songs played a considerable role in peasant life. On itinerant German songs see the interesting and well-documented article "Studien über Bänkelgesang" in the book by Hans Naumann, *Primitive Gemeinschaftskultur = Beiträge zur Volkskunde und Mythologie* (Jena: 1921), pp. 168-190. In my study, I will cite only itinerant Czech songs.

4. Dr. Karel Adámek. "Světské písně jarmarečni a poutní" [Secular Itinerant and Pilgrim Songs] , *Národopisný věstnik českoslovanský,* 15-16, p. 114.

5. Ibid., p. 143.

6. Ibid., p. 145.

7. Ibid., 24: 3-4, p. 243.

8. Ibid.

9. Ibid., 24: 1-2, p. 29.

10. See on this subject the work by Aničkov in two volumes, *Vesennjaja obrjadovaja pesnja na zapade i u slavjan* [Ritual Spring Songs in the West and Among the Slavs] = *Sbornik otd. russk. jaz. i slov.*, 74: 2, 77: 5. The author's hypothesis is that one can see in such songs the original and most ancient form of folk poetry.

11. On the difference between motivated and unmotivated magical acts, see my work "Actes magiques, rites et croyances en Russie Subcarpathique" *Travaux, Institut d'études slaves*, 11 (1929), pp. 22-24.

12. For details, see the chapter entitled "Das Lied als Zeichen" in the book by Martha Bringemeier, *Gemeinschaft und Volkslied* (Münster: i W.), pp. 107-113.

13. See Aničkov, *Vesennjaja obrjadovaja pesnja*, part 2, pp. 386-389, where the theory of K. Bücher is completed and corrected on many points.

14. Kuprijanova, "Pesni derevni Pogromny," p. 34.

15. The same differentiation exists in Russian and Roumanian laments. See E. B. Barsov, *Pričitan'ja severnago kraja* [Laments of the Northern Region], I (1872); II (1882), and Constantin Brăiloiu, "Despre bocetul dela Drăgus," *Archiva pentru ştiinta si reforma socială = Organ al institutului social român* (Bucarest, 1932), pp. 280-359.

16. On the functional differences of folk song in various Czech literary schools, see J. Mukařovský, "Vítězslav Hálek," *Slovo a slovesnost*, 1: 2 (1935), p. 80 ff.

17. There is an attempt at this kind of study in an article in Russian by Z. V. Eval'd, "Social'noe pereosmyslenie žnivnyx pesen belorusskogo Poles'ja" [Social Change in the Meaning of Harvest Songs of Polesje of White Russia], *Sovetskaja étnografija*, 5 (1934), pp. 17-39.

18. See my article "Kroj jako znak: Funkční a strukturální pojetí v národopisu" [Costume as a Sign: The Functional and Structural Concept in Ethnography], *Slovo a slovesnost*, 2: 1, pp. 43-47. The English translation appears in this anthology on pp. 13-17.

4. Semiotics in the Folk Theater

Petr Bogatyrev

National costume is simultaneously a material object and a sign—more exactly, it is the bearer of a structure of signs. National costume identifies membership in a class, nationality, religion, and so on; it indicates the wearer's status, his age, and so on. Similarly, a house is not only a thing, but also a sign of the nationality, the economic status, the religion, and so on, of its owner.[1]

What exactly is a theatrical costume or a set that represents a house on stage? When used in a play, both the theatrical costume and the house set are often signs that point to one of the signs characterizing the costume or the house of a certain personage in the play. In fact, each is a sign of a sign and not a sign of a material thing.[2] Theatrical costume and the house set can sometimes denote several signs. For instance, theatrical costume can denote a wealthy Chinese, thus marking both the sign of nationality and the sign of economic status of the depicted character. The costume of Boris Godunov denotes his being a monarch and, simultaneously, his belonging to the Russian nationality. In the theatrical production of Pushkin's "The Tale of the Fisherman and the Fish," the first dwelling is a sign of the severe poverty of the old man and old woman; the second is a sign of the old woman's aristocratic station, the third is a sign of the fact that the old woman had become the tsarina; but the scenery of all these constructions demonstrates the Russian nationality of their owners. Similar signs of signs on the stage are the command gestures of the actor playing the tsar or king, or the unsteady tread of the actor representing an old man, and so on.

However, the theatrical costume does not, nor does the house set or the gestures of the actors, have as many constitutive signs as a real house or real dress would have. Usually costume and scenery on stage are limited to one, two, or three signs. Theater uses only those signs of costume and construction which are necessary for the given dramatic situation.

I should like to make the point here that no theatrical costume, no piece of theatrical scenery, or, likewise, any other theatrical sign

"Znaky divadelní," *Slovo a slovesnost,* 4 (1938), pp. 138-149. Translated by Bruce Kochis.

(declamation, gestures, and so on) always has a *representational* function. We know the costume of the actor as an actor's costume, as such; we know the signs of the stage (curtain, footlights, and so forth) as merely signs of the stage, as such, representing nothing more than the stage. But on the stage we find not only signs of a sign of a material object but also signs of the material object itself: for instance, on the stage the actor playing a hungry person can denote that he eats bread as such, and not bread as a sign of, let us say, poverty. To be sure, the cases in which signs of signs are represented on the stage are more frequent than the cases of signs representing material objects.

On the stage are used not only costumes and scenery, not only theatrical props, which are only one sign or the sum of several signs and not a material object as such, but also real material objects. The spectators behold these real objects, however, not as real material objects, but only as a sign of signs, or a sign of material objects. If, for example, an actor, representing a millionaire, wears a diamond ring, the audience will take it as a sign of his great wealth and not care whether or not the diamond is a real or false stone. A theatrical ermine mantle is a sign of royal dignity without regard to whether the fur is real ermine or rabbit's fur. On the stage expensive red wine can be represented by real wine or by raspberry soda.

It is interesting that on the stage a real material object, for example, a real diamond, is often only a sign of a sign of a material object (for example, a sign of the wealth of the character) but not a sign of the material object itself. On the other hand at a theatrical performance the most schematic sign of the most primitive scenery can signify the material object itself. For example:

In an Altai tent stage stands a birch eternally in leaf on which there are nine notches. The notches symbolically denote the levels of the heavenly world, into which, by degrees, a shaman enters. When performing the ceremony, where he steps up along these notches, he rises in the eyes of those present from the first level of heaven to the second, whereupon he plays in each heaven a special scene.[3] (Thus, each notch denotes not only heaven as a whole but also which of its special divisions is meant: first heaven, second heaven, third heaven, and so on.)

Still another example:

The Arunts' ceremonies (performances) are held in certain places ordained by tradition: at sacred rocks, trees, ponds. With the Warramung a ceremony may be performed any place at all, but the place of action is identified by drawings. These drawings identifying the place were drawn either on the body of the participants or on the ground. The images have a certain nature; for instance, a small red circle on the back or on the abdomen of the performer denotes a pond, or they paint the earth with vermilion and, using white pigment, paint winding lines on it to signify a stream or brook.[4] (Here, also, certain signs on the body of the actor or on the ground denote the things themselves.)

Verbal scenery, that is, the traditional theatrical practice of having the actor depict the scene in words to the audience in the absence of stage scenery, must depend on the description either of a material object or of only one or several signs of the material object. We encounter such verbal scenery in the old theater of India, and it also spread everywhere in the ceremonial performances of the shamans.

All objects which are theatrical signs have, according to O. Zich, two functions: the first and most characteristic one is to give graphic depiction of the characters and the place of action; and the second function is to take part in the dramatic action.[5] Zich's characteristics are applicable not only to theatrical material objects, stage properties, but also to any material object we encounter in everyday life. Thus, a cane characterizes my taste, and perhaps my material circumstances, but I likewise use this cane: I lean on it when walking, I can use it in a fight, and so on. In the theater, however, in distinction from everyday life, each thing changes its signs much more quickly and much more diversely. Mephistofeles by means of his cape expresses his subjection to Faust and on Walpurgis night by means of this same cape expresses his absolute power over demonic forces. However, in real life one and the same dress can be a sign of the most opposite psychological frames of mind. Thus, for instance, one and the same military shirt can, unbuttoned, express the devil-may-care attitude of its soldier wearer sitting with his comrades over a bottle of wine; buttoned at every button, it expresses the careful, concentrated and accurate attitude of the wearer when he goes to report to his superior.

But besides that, on the stage things that play the part of theatrical signs can in the course of the play acquire special features, qualities, and attributes that they do not have in real life. Things in the theater, just as the actor himself, are transformable. As an actor on stage may change into another person (a young person into an old one, a woman into a man, and so forth), so also any thing, with which the actor performs, may acquire a new, hitherto foreign, function. The famous shoes of Charlie Chaplin are changed by his acting into food, the laces becoming spaghetti (*Gold Rush*); in the same film two rolls dance like a pair of lovers. Such transformed things, used by the actor in his performance, are very common in folk theater. For example, the play with things in *Poxomuškoj* fills almost the entire performance. Of particular interest are those moments when the player must demonstrate by his acting that a poker has turned into a horse, a bench into a boat, or that an old jacket tied around with a belt is, in his hands, an infant.[6]

One very complex system of signs is the language of the actor on the stage. The language of the actor on stage has almost all the signs of poetic language, and, in addition, is a constituent of the dramatic action. Later on we will take up the signs of actors' language which have the task of characterizing the personages in a play.

Practical language is a system   of various signs. A speaker not only expresses the content of his thought in his utterances, but his speech (its dialectisms, argot, vocabulary, and so on) is also simultaneously a sign of his cultural and social status, and so on. The dramatist and the actors use all of these signs as descriptive means for expressing the social or national status of the character. Also, frequently, a special selection of words and diction is used to designate a man of this or that class, or unusual vocabulary, unusual pronunciation, forms and word order are used to designate a foreigner. Similarly, a certain speech tempo, and sometime also certain vocabulary, may designate an old man. In some cases, the dominant function of the speech of a dramatic character may lie not in the content of speech as such but in those verbal signs that characterize the nationality, the class, and so forth, of the speaker. The content of speech may be expressed by other theatrical signs, such as gesture, and the like. For instance, the devil in the puppet theater often utters only certain conventional expletives that characterize him as the devil; in some puppet plays he almost never speaks but performs a pantomime on stage in place of monologue and dialogue.

The actor's verbal expression on stage normally has several signs. For instance, speech that is full of mistakes may designate not only a foreigner but usually also a comic character. Therefore, an actor, playing the tragic part of a foreigner or representative of another people, for example, playing Shakespeare's Shylock and trying to depict the Jewish merchant of Venice as a tragic character, often must abandon Jewish intonation or reduce it to a minimum, for a strongly pronounced Jewish intonation may add a comic touch to the tragic passages of the part.[7]

In folk theater we have cases where the participation of Jews, who deform ordinary speech in the way traditional for folk theater, lends comedy even to serious scenes. Here is an example from the play *Three Kings*.[8]

Herod:
Ye, who are of Law skilled knowers
And of Scripture right learned scholars,
Have ye perchance any knowledge
Or be there in Scripture some presage
Concerning the Christ, that come he can
Not ere that he be born of man?
Jews:
Vat on that point the Scripture sayth
Ve shall make known, so please Your Grace.
[They go to the table, open a book and leaf through it; then return to Herod, and the First Jew, bowing to him, says:]
First Jew:
Jabach, impich, thaic uzmrnach:
kolkoye, kolkoshe. Vich is to say:
Little town Bethlehem of Judah . . .
the race divine is born . . . this savior,
redeemer of all the vorld. And also in
another passage the true prophet . . .
Herod:
Silence!
Jews:
That pleases him not; go thou and find
something to tell him.
[They again retire to the table, leaf through the books and return to Herod]
Second Jew:
Kiroch shiroch sykorve sharke
verobím kormifel, tyberes mones.

Vich is to say: O thou, Bethlehem, little town,
Of thee werily be it known
That from thee shall a great king come
And he shall judge the Jewish kingdom.
These vords the truth do testify,
God's own prophecy prophesy.
Herod:
Silence, I say!
Jews [aside] :
Vait, I vill find yet something else
to tell him.
[They do the same as before and then say to Herod:]
Efrata betharir ipfata chayer
Bichord bochod brafe yehunda mimika,
Bitse moysil Israel
O matsazano mikodem vlan.
Vich is to say: But thou Bethlehem of Ephratah
Though thou be little among the thousands of Judah,
yet out of thee shall be a ruler in Israel;
whose goings forth have been from old,
from everlasting.
Herod:
Get ye hence, ye Pharisees,
Mine exceeding great enemies!
[Afraid, the Jews flee, and meet the three kings]
Melchior:
Tell us, Jew, if thou dost know:
Where to find the new king shall we three go?
Jews:
Go to Bethlehem, there you vill find
a young innkeeper, and old man,
a small babe, there you vill learn
the vorthiest truth.[9]

At this point comedy completely takes over. And the scene with the
Jew, who previously performed as an interpreter of the Holy Scriptures,
ends with the following routine: Caspar gives a tip to one Jew, the second
one wants half, and so they go off quarreling with one another.

Here we see one of the distinctive cases of the alternation or interweav-
ing of tragic and comic elements in folk theater. The comic figures of the
Jews have a function similar to that of the fools in Shakespeare (and other

dramatists), where the fool may express thoughts of the most serious kind, even the thoughts of the dramatist himself.

As in the matter of costume, so in that of language, the dramatist and actor select only a small part of the system of signs which practical language possesses. In practical language there are various class signs (rustic speech) that have close association with dialect, which is a regional sign of the speaking character. It is often unnecessary in dramatic works to make specific the region from which the depicted peasant originates, the actor using only certain characteristic features of the given region and sometimes even combining the characteristic features of several dialects together to create peasant speech. Such a mixture of diverse dialects contradicts reality but works effectively to depict the peasant played by the actor. In my opinion such an artificially constituted dialect has a perfect right to exist on the stage. We encounter similar phenomena in theatrical costume and scenery. Thus, in Kysela's staging of *The Bartered Bride* folk costumes from any one particular region of Bohemia were deliberately avoided, and instead a theatrical costume representing a Bohemian peasant woman in general was created.

There existed in the past and still do exist conventional dramaturgical devices for distinguishing the speech of the common people from the speech of polite society. Among them belongs, for instance, the stylistic device, used in certain periods and by certain movements in drama, of having the common people speak in prose and the nobility in verse.[10] Here too should be placed all other conventional stage dialects: for example, the tsar and boyars in Russian plays speaking in high style with an admixture of Church Slavic elements, and the peasants in low style, that is, in simple Russian; or the knights in plays of the Czech puppet theater speaking in imperfect Czech.

Conventions similar to those having to do with language are encountered in theatrical gesture, costumes, scenery, and so on. Folk theater is particularly rich in cases that vividly express the conventionality of costume and props. However, conventionality of speech does not always parallel conventionality of costumes, scenery, and so forth. On the stage conventional costumes often are, on the contrary, combined with naturalistic speech of a kind close to practical speech. For instance, folk puppeteers, working in so very conventional a theater as the puppet theater is, use many elements of the naturalistic theater. One of the best Czech puppeteers, Karel Novák, boasted to me that his puppets spoke as living people.

Were we to test O. Zich's law concerning uniform stylization in theatrical performances of various periods and styles, we would find that it does not hold up; it applies only in part for the particular theatrical movement of that period which Zich had in mind. In folk theater the simultaneous use of the most diverse styles in the same play is a widespread phenomenon, a special theatrical device of form. Besides the case already mentioned (the combining of naturalistic speech with puppet play in the puppet theater), we might also mention the joint play of live actors and puppets in folk theater. I myself saw a child acting with a puppet on the stage in Münster, Westfallen.[11] The curious simultaneous acting of people and puppets can be seen in the Three Kings play at Chodsko.

Through the villages of Chodsko walk, in imitation of the three holy kings, "three kings" from town. . . . There are always *two* persons; the *third* is a wooden figure mounted on an instrument similar to a horn; during the singing of a song this wooden king must make bows and for that purpose is animated by a handle which one of the "three kings," who is holding the horn, turns.[12]

Realism and symbolism "sometimes exist side by side in the dramatic performances of one and the same people," asserts V. N. Xaruzina; as we have already seen, they mutually interpenetrate. In one and the same play one may encounter realistic features of costume (for example, the tail worn by the actor playing an animal, the coloring of the actor's body to correspond to the coloring of the feathers of the bird he is playing), and at the same time symbolism can be very striking in the props or set designs of the scene.[13]

The folk theater is not alone in combining different styles; we often find it also in other arts. Combination of styles in architecture is a common phenomenon. Modern painters, such as Picasso and the Futurists, used to combine pieces of real things with their cubistic painting. We often see a similar montage on the covers of books. In folk art we encounter, wherever we look, the combination of the most diverse styles in the same artistic product, in one and the same narrative, in one and the same song.

Theatrical verbal expression is a structure of signs, composed not only of linguistic signs but also of other signs. For instance, speech, which is supposed to signify the social station of the character, is uttered in accompaniment with the actor's gestures and is complemented by his costume, by the scenery, and so on, which are also signs of the social station of this character. In the theater the number of fields from which theatrical signs, such as costume, scenery, music, and so forth, are drawn, is at times larger, at times smaller, but always is multiple.

Practical speech has, moreover, other specific signs, which depend on the person with whom we speak or whom we address. This plays a significant role in the theater. And changes of style of speech are often in the theater accompanied by special costuming.

Mention ought also be made of special signs of speech, such as special word order, syntax, the distribution of pauses, and other verbal means, which pervade the whole part and give it a comic or tragic coloration.[14] However, comic or tragic roles are brought about not only by verbal means but also by the costume the actor wears and by his makeup or mask. The means used for signalizing the costume of a comic character are often similar to linguistic devices, among which one of the most common is what in the Italian term are called *lazzi:* oxymoron and metathesis. We find something similar in the appearance of the costume of comic characters or in their makeup (or mask). In addition, there were and are special conventional theatrical signs in costume thanks to which instant recognition of a comic character is possible (the foolscap, the fox tail of Hans Wurst, and so on).

In almost every drama, but especially in drama of character, there is the matter of characterizing a certain particular role: the hypocrite Tartuffe, the miser Harpagon, and likewise, a many-faceted character, such as the miser, the loving father and the sly Shylock all in one role, and so on. To this end the theater uses all its available means. Here belongs, in the first place, the autocharacterization of a role; the speech of the characters in medieval mystery plays, in morality plays and also in folk plays can serve as a good example of such autocharacterization. Less clear cases occur in the tragedies of Shakespeare, Puškin, and in other dramas in which the performer delivers a monologue, acquainting the audience with the intimate aspects of his behavior. But it is not only the content of the monologue that serves as the means of autocharacterization; that end is also served by a "character dialect" (Zich's term). Let us note that finding a suitable "character dialect" for each role in the play is one of the most crucial tasks of the dramatist and the actor. We must acknowledge that in the folk theater this psychological dialect has been applied with success in many variations of folk plays. In addition to verbal means, the characterization of a role is brought about by costume (the costume of the hypocrite Tartuffe, of the miser Pljuškin in the staging of *Dead Souls,* and so forth) and still more so by the miming and gestures of the actors. Here scenery helps a great deal: the room of the lazy old bachelor in Gogol''s *The Wedding,* the study of the learned Faust superbly express the character of their occupants. In folk theater scenery generally has little significance and is not commonly used especially as a means for psychological portrayal of characters. The role of scenery here is taken over by props.

Characterization of roles is expressed not only by the means already mentioned, but also by action. The Baron in Puškin's *The Covetous Knight* not only verbally characterizes himself as a man madly in love with his wealth but also proves it by his actions on stage (his gestures, behavior, and so on). Another means of psychological characterization of a personage is the conversation of other characters about him. This characterization is aided by the costumes of the characters who are in close relationship with the personage in question, for example, the shabby clothing of the prisoners in Beethoven's opera *Fidelio* characterizes the brutal and unjust governor.[15]

In addition, various movements in the theater have had special verbal signs for representing the actor as actor—a special actor's language or "stage language" that appears not only as a matter of elocution but also as special intonation, and so forth. There are also special actors' gestures representing the actor only as actor.

An analysis of the system of signs that make up the stage language used by actors in a play proves that all these signs are found, even if only infrequently, in other genres of poetic language (the novel, the story, and so on). The difference, however, is that in the theater the sign of speech is only one constituent of the structure of theatrical expression, a structure to which belong miming, gesture, costume, scenery, and so forth, as well as language.

Such plurisignation is further increased by the fact that the part played by the actor has different signs in the case where the public is acquainted with all of the characters in the play or a large part of them. By each and every movement and intonation of his speech, Tartuffe must, to the very last scenes, appear a kind man to Orgon, but to the public a repulsive hypocrite pretending to be kind. An even more elementary case is the following: in the staging of the tale "Little Red Riding Hood," the wolf, dressed as an old woman, must seem to the granddaughter somewhat strange, of course; to the public he must appear as a wolf, who has changed his voice. The actor throughout his performance is something like a tight rope walker—he cannot play the wolf so that the audience would find it hard to believe that the granddaughter cannot recognize the wolf in him. On the other hand, he must the whole time show that he *is* wolf, otherwise the audience might, along with the granddaughter, believe that he is the old woman. In essence the actor who plays Tartuffe must do the same.

There is a special kind of plurisignation in the performance of actors in works by symbolists where, for the audience and other actors, certain characters are bearers of several signs. In G. Hauptmann's *Hanneles Himmelfahrt* there is a character who is for Hannele a teacher and for the other players and the audience is both the teacher Gottwald and a foreigner; the nun Marta is at the same time a nun and mother. We meet this phenomenon in Hauptmann's *The Sunken Bell,* in Ibsen's *Peer Gynt,* and in other symbolist plays.

The special character of theatrical signs also determines the peculiar relationship of the audience to theatrical signs, a relationship quite distinct from the relationship of a man to a real material object and a real subject. For instance, an old man's gait and gestures usually, in real life, evoke pity, while the same gait and gestures on the stage most often function comically.

We must acknowledge that theatrical productions are distinguished from all other artistic works and from other material objects, which are also signs, by their great abundance of signs. This is understandable: a theatrical performance is a structure composed of elements from various arts: from poetry, the plastic arts, music, choreography, and so on. Each separate element brings a number of signs onto the stage. Some of these signs may fall away; for example, sculpture loses one of its characteristic features—the variety of forms a work of sculpture takes examined from various visual points of view[16]—since in the theater we see a piece of sculpture only from one point of view. Similarly, works of other arts lose a portion of their signs on the stage. On the other hand, however, in combining with other kinds of art and with technical theatrical devices, they may acquire several of their elements of sign anew, for example, a sculpture under different lights can express different moods (colorful festive mood can be promoted by illuminating a piece of sculpture with bright lights, a dreary mood by the use of dim lights). Music on stage, combined with the gestures and words of the actor who plays a dying man, more concretely express sadness, and so forth. In this way, certain elements of various kinds of art in combination with others constantly acquire new signs.

This plurisignation of theatrical art is increased by the fact that different spectators comprehend the same scene differently. Take, for instance, a scene of parting in which dialogue is accompanied by music: to a musically inclined spectator music will have the dominant meaning, but for a spectator more strongly attentive to declamation the latter will be the dominant factor and music will be the subordinate one. This plurisignation of theatrical art, distinguishing it from any other art, makes it possible for theatrical action to be comprehended simultaneously by spectators of various tastes, various aesthetic standards.

Were we to compare the naturalistic and nonrealistic theaters, we would see that the naturalistic theater uses the various other arts (music, dance, and so on) less frequently than the nonrealistic theater; on the other hand, in the latter, the characters, costume, scenery, and props always have a much greater multitude of signs than in the naturalistic theater, where costume and scenery usually have only one sign; in this way conservation of theatrical means is achieved.

The actor's role is a structure of the most diverse signs: signs expressed by speech, gestures, movements, posture, miming, costume, and so forth. Moreover, to express various theatrical signs the actor makes use of various things such as costume, toupee, wig, simultaneously with his own gestures (either affected or natural), his own voice, and certainly his own eyes, and so on.

We can carry over the concept of *la langue* and *la parole* from the field of language phenomena to art. Thus, just as the hearer, in order to comprehend the individual utterance of the speaker, must have command of the language, that is, language as social fact, so also in art the observer must be prepared to receive the individual performance of the actor or of any other artist—his special speech acts, as it were—in terms of his (the observer's) command of the language of that art, its social norms. This is the point of congruence between the field of language and the field of art.

But between the processes of comprehending the signs of language and the signs of art there is a difference of principle. In the domain of language, as far as its communicative function is concerned, the process of reception works approximately this way: we hear an utterance, we screen from it everything individual and fix upon only that in the phrase heard by us which is *"langue,"* which is social fact. Were a foreigner to make such a broken statement as "he is a good girl, you daughter," we would grasp its information as "your daughter is a good girl," and the mistakes the foreigner made would not especially trouble us.

It is entirely different in the process of perceiving a work of art. An artistically executed work, an artistically performed role in drama, the performance of a musical work, song, and so forth, we perceive as a whole. If a talented actor plays Othello, it seems to us—and it is this he tries to convince us of—that everything in his performance and in the role of Othello played by him is artistically right and just, including costume, gestures, posture, voice coloration, and facial expressions, and so on. Therefore, if his performance is imitated, it is imitated in all is details— the rhythm of Othello's speech in the tradition of the famous actor, the coloration of his voice and his gestures, and so forth, and thus, in such imitation, the individual imperfections of the actor are often also imitated, since in our minds they are inseparable from   the total image of the role. K. Stanislavskij relates the following story:

A certain teacher in a dramatic school went behind the scenes after the performance of an excerpt from a student production and got quite hot under the collar: "You people never nod your heads at all. A person speaking definitely nods his head." That nodding of the head is a small story of its own. An excellent actor, who enjoyed great success and had many imitators, unfortunately possessed one unpleasant flaw, namely, the habit of nodding his head. And all of his followers, fully aware of the fact that their man was a great talent with exceptional abilities and marvelous technique, instead of acquiring from him his good qualities, which are indeed hard to acquire from another, only copied his flaws—that nodding of the head—which are things easily acquired.[17]

Stanislavskij's opposition to such slavish imitation was completely justified. There is a difference, however, between what he says and what we are saying here, namely, we are speaking only about perceiving the executed role, whereas Stanislavskij speaks about the actor's creative work. At the same time each actor in the tradition of the part must use the procedures of the famous actor, but in doing so, he must use anew his character, his vocal coloration, his movements, eyes, and so on.

Now we shall pass on to remarks about folklore. The phenomena of folklore, such as song, tales, magic formulas, and other types of folklore, approximate the phenomenon of drama. The oral folklore phenomenon like the phenomenon of actor is inseparable from the person who performs it. The hearer of such a phenomenon, in distinction from the reader of a poem or novel, cannot isolate the artistic phenomenon, as such, from the author and reciter. Therefore it is incorrect to define the text of a tale without regard to *how* it is told. What is more, the personality of the storyteller is more tightly bound up with what he narrates than the personality of the actor with his role on the stage. All that actually interests us in the performance of an actor is how he uses the dramatic means at his disposal, that is, his voice, body movements, and so forth, so as to produce a dramatic performance. The question as to whether the actor, ideally representing an evil villain or a positive hero, is a good or bad person in private life does not interest us. However, this does not hold in the case of reciting a folktale. Here the reciter not infrequently uses his own personal, real-life characteristics as artistic means. The Sokolov brothers mention the example of the reciter Sozon Kuzmič Petruševič, a target of mockery and teasing, who brings himself into the tale he tells as "Tom Fool": "There once was a peasant, and he had three sons, two were sly and one was stupid, like me, Sozon." And further on he describes the wretched looks of "Tom Fool" as being just like his own: "snotty, pimply, slobbery," and by this vivid illustration involuntarily called up in his hearers a great outburst of laughter.[18]

Likewise, the audience in folk theater continually confronts the role which an actor-peasant plays with the actor's own private life.

In the theater as in other arts, there exist signs that belong only to established artistic movements. Thus in ancient tragedy there was a special sign that distinguished main characters from the secondary characters, namely, the side of the stage from which the actor entered. In eighteenth-century opera the following system was instituted:

All soloists stand in one line parallel with the footlights at the front of the stage, at midstage are the comic characters (Chargen), and at rear stage the chorus. At front stage the order within the first row was also standardized: on the audience's left were situated the actors of the main roles, keeping places according to their importance in turn from the left to right. The hero or principal lover, in short, the "prima parte" performer, gets the honored place—first on the left, since he is the one who performs the top role in order of importance.[19]

Here, then, the places where the actors stood were signs of their parts. In the commedia dell'arte the costumes of the Dottore, of Pantalone, and others, accurately characterized these roles for the spectator.[20]

Indeed, it is not only a matter of individual periods having their own theatrical signs, which later, in another period, along with a change of the whole theatrical style, are replaced by other signs. Various players also added signs to various parts. These signs are repeated (nor could it be otherwise) by his followers until such a time as a new talented actor arrives, who reshapes the part, casting off the old signs of his predecessor and creating new ones; these are then again repeated by his followers.

We know a set of signs that were deemed characteristic of Hamlet (in costume, facial expression, gesticulations, miming, the method of declaiming certain passages, and so forth). Usually, they were created by a certain famous actor and became indispensable for his followers and also for the public raised on those signs.

Every creative performance of a role, just as every independent creation in any other art, struggles against traditional signs and strives to put new signs in their place. In the theater, then, all theatrical phenomena are signs of signs, or signs of material objects. The only live subject in the theater is the actor. Despite the fact that an actor expresses regal dignity by his costume, the sign of age by his gait, the sign that he represents a foreigner by his speech, and so on, still we see in him not only a system of signs but also a living person. That this is really the case is most easily seen when a spectator observes on the stage a person close to him—or herself, for example, a mother watching her son performing the role of a king, a brother playing the part of a devil, and so on. This special artistic duplexity acquires great theatrical effect in the folk theater where the audience knows the actors well. This same duplexity is experienced by a spectator when he sees in new roles an actor, whom he already has known on the stage a long time. To a lesser degree the spectator experiences it even when he sees the actor for the first time.

This dual perception of the actor by the spectator is of great importance. In the first place, thanks to it, all signs expressed by the actor are made animate. Second, at the same time this dual perception of the performance affirms that it is impossible to identify the player with the role he plays, that no equation can be made between the actor and the character whom he represents, that the costume and mask and gestures of the actor are only a sign of sign of the character portrayed by him. This duplexity was clearly brought out by all types of nonrealistic theater and was an obstacle to the realization of absolute naturalism in the naturalistic theater. This makes perfectly understandable the requirement of one director in the naturalistic theater that the actor should appear in public as little as possible, for otherwise many people would lose the illusion of reality when they saw him in the role of King Lear or Hamlet, and they would never be able to imagine that they see before them a real Lear, a real Hamlet, and not an actor who only plays this role.

As for the actor's acting, there existed and still exist two trends. On the one hand, actors take great pains with their makeup, their speech, and so forth, so as to be entirely different in each role; on the other hand, the actor deliberately behaves in such a manner that in each role he plays it would be possible to recognize his voice, his face on the other side of the makeup (therefore he makes up only lightly), and so on.

In the puppet theater an actor does not exist as a live person; there the movements of the puppet actor are pure sign of a sign. In the puppet theater where the puppets speak, voice is all that remains from a live person, and it is through voice that puppets approximate living persons. The analysis of signs in the theater brings us to yet one other interesting observation. We find, for instance, the following very commonly used device: an actor employs elements of a certain art for the expression of artistic emotion, which emotion rises higher and higher (for example, in a dance the tempo quickens). When the actor is no longer able to manage the expressive means of his movements, he begins to complement that that rise with exclamations. And conversely, when a singer in a crescendo no longer has sufficient vocal means, he begins to complement the rise of his singing by dance or movement. Sometimes the dance or movement is not merely complemented by the song, or the song by the dance, but they replace one another. A similar formal device is the omitting of one element hitherto structurally related to other elements of the theatrical event. For instance, the actor in the most emotional part of his speech, until then accompanied with gesture, ceases to gesticulate and only speaks or, conversely, ceases to speak and expresses his emotion only by gesture. The formal means here mentioned are at times used in other cases where the heightening of the emotional event is not at stake.

A detailed analysis of theatrical signs helps us thereby to explain other theatrical formal means.

Notes

1. Compare my article "Kroj jako znak. Funkční a strukturální pojetí v národopisu" in *Slovo a slovesnost,* 2 (1936), pp. 43 ff., and my book *Funkcie kroja na moravkom Slovensku* (Spisy Národopisného odboru Matice Slovenskej v Turčianskom Sv. Martine, sv., 1937).

2. The term *sign of sign* means here something different than R. Jakobson's "sign of a sign" in his article "Socha v symbolice Puškinově" in *Slovo a Slovesnost,* 3 (1937), pp. 2 ff., where "a sign of a sign" means that the sign from one kind of art is transferred into another art: sculpture, described in poetry.

3. V. N. Xaruzina, "Primitivnye formy dramatičeskogo iskusstva," *Etnografia,* 2: 3 (Moskva-Leningrad, 1927), p. 67.

4. Émile Durkheim, *Les formes élémentaires de la vie religieuse. Le système totémique en Australie.* 2nd edition (1925), pp. 532-53. Compare V. N. Xaruzina, "Primitivnye formy dramatičeskogo iskusstva," p. 67.

5. Otakar Zich, *Estetika dramatického umění. Teoretická dramaturgie* (1931), p. 232.

6. S. Pisarev and S. Suslovič, "Dosjul'naja igra-komedija *Poxomuškoj,*" *Krest'janskoje iskusstvo SSSR. Sbornik Sekcii krest'janskogo iskusstva komiteta sociologičeskogo izučenija iskusstva.* I. Iskusstva severa. Zaonež'je (Leningrad: 1927), p. 184.

7. Compare VI. Iv. Nemirovič-Dančenko, *Iz prošlogo* (Leningrad: 1936), pp. 180-1.

8. Jul. Fejfalík, *Volksschauspiele aus Mähren* (Olomouc: 1864), pp. 59 ff.

9. The language that the Jews read is meant to represent Hebrew. This is one of the typical cases of using a conventional language that is meant to represent a foreign language in folklore. In our case the quotations that the Jews read are perhaps basically Hebrew, but in the form that they have here it is difficult to recognize Hebrew words in them—šenke-ženku (woman), jitko-ditko (child).

10. "In the drama of the Middle Ages, for example, at times the male and female characters were distinguished by varied-syllable verse," writes K. Krejčí in his article "Jazyková karikatura v dramatické literatuře" (*Sborník Matice slovenskej,* XV, 1937), p. 388.

11. P. Bogatyrev "Puppentheater in Münster in Westfallen," *Prager Presse,* 23:8, 1931.

12. J. Baar in *Český lid,* I, 1892, p. 505, and J. F. Hruška "Tři králové na Chodsku," ibid., 6, 1897, p. 244.

13. "Primitivnye formy dramatičeskogo iskusstva," *Etnografia,* 3: 6, (1928), p. 28.

14. It thus differs from practical speech in which the comic or tragic coloration is given by the speaking character.

15. In the contemporary theater still another device helps to characterize roles, a literary, not a theatrical device, namely, the characterization of roles in the printed program.

16. Compare Jan Mukařovský, "Trojí podoba T. G. Masaryka" (Několik poznámek k problematice plastického portrétu). *Lidové noviny,* 27/2 (1938).

17. K. Stanislavskij, *My Life in Art.* [In the Russian original pp. 144 ff.]

18. Boris and Jurij Sokolov, *Skazki i pěsni Bělozerskago kraja* (1915), pp. LXIII-LXIX.

19. A. A. Gvozdev, "Itogi i zadači naučnoj istorii teatra" in the book *Zadači i metody izučenija iskusstv* (Rossijskij Institut istorii iskusstva, Academia, Petersburg: 1924), p. 119.

20. On the mixing of one theatrical declamation with another in various theatrical movements compare J. Honzl, *Sláva a bída divadel,* pp. 178-207.

5. Forms and Functions of Folk Theater

Petr Bogatyrev

One of the most important and fundamental features of the theater is *transformation:* the actor changes his appearance, dress, voice, and even the features of his personality into the appearance, costume, voice, and personality of the character whom he represents in the play. Transformation is one of the basic signs distinguishing drama from lyric and epic poetry. In lyric poetry the poet may lament with funereal weeping *his own* nearness to death, complain in song or poem about *his own* difficult fate, or he may proclaim *his own* affection for a loved one, and so forth. To be sure, in lyric poetry the poet may sing about the love of a dove and mean by that his own love, but precisely therein lies the basic difference between drama and lyric: the poet lyricist or singer does not transform himself into the dove but merely adopts from it those traits that are similar to himself, the poet. The poet may write a lyrical poem about Othello's jealousy and mean by that his own jealousy, but in drama, on the other hand, the artist must transform himself, must assume the person of Othello; in this transformation he must adopt all the signs of the character and appearance of Othello and, in particular, must demonstrate that Othello was not only a jealous man but also a courageous military leader, a good friend, and so on. He must adopt features that may not coincide with his own experience—they may even contradict them.

In pure epic poetry the narrator narrates or sings about someone else in the third person. He does not transform himself into that person but remains an objective observer of events relating to that third person or persons.

Transformation similar to that which is one of the essential elements of theater can be encountered in many situations very remote from the theater proper (compare, for example, the vivid transformation in behavior of the modest scholar who, along with the attire of gown and cap that he dons as conferrer of degrees and ceremonial orator, adopts an unusually ceremonial manner of behavior). But in all such manifestations, even

An abbreviated version of the first chapter of *Lidové divadlo české a slovenské* [Czech and Slovak Folk Theater] (Prague, 1940), pp. 9-29. Translated by Bruce Kochis.

where the dominant function is other than aesthetic, the aesthetic function still plays a significant role.

We also find transformations similar to the basic theatrical element in the carrying out of many practices, customs, and folk ceremonies that have a dominant magical or religious function. Furthermore, transformation in such activities is not restricted to the interhuman type, but also includes transformation into animals or even into material objects. Often people are transformed into animals: into a bear, goat, mare, and so on (with a change of costume). Such a transformation is characteristic for carnival festivities. In the "beheading of the rooster," however, we find the opposite phenomenon—the animal is dressed like a man. At the beheading of the rooster, performed at the first wedding in Shrovetide in Borovany, the rooster, according to Zíbrt's description "was dressed in a red cap, sometimes also in a jacket and trousers." Here the dressing up of the rooster in human guise incorporates transformation even in another respect: an accusation is brought against the rooster, a verdict is pronounced, and the sentence is carried out as if it were a man and not a fowl.

In theatrical transformation, however, neither the spectator nor the actor should have the sensation of a complete transformation. The actor must not be lost in the character into whom he has transformed himself: the action on the stage must not be sensed as reality but as theater. Alexander Tajrov relates an incident of a spectator shooting the actor playing Iago in Shakespeare's *Othello*. Clearly that spectator did not perceive the performance as theater. A child, who very much believes that a real saint is present when Santa Claus makes his rounds, does not have a correct theatrical experience. In folk theater actors deliberately disguise themselves as various animals in such a way that the spectators will easily recognize that they see before them not a real horse, goat, bear but only an actor dressed as such. Sometimes actors and spectators do experience a sensation of a complete transformation, but this sensation must be a temporary not a lasting one; it must come and go. At certain moments the spectator may forget that he beholds a stage and may perceive the performance as real life, as may the actor, as well. This alternation may be repeated from time to time in the course of the performance. However, perception of the theater as real life through the whole performance must inevitably lead to results violating the theater.

Many folk plays are connected through their origin with urban nonfolk-lore dramas, with plays of the so-called "higher strata." Many folk pieces, in fact, originated with the school plays. However, we must not forget that so-called "high" poetry and "high" drama were frequently under the influence of folklore. Instead of a one-sided theory about the drift of "high" art down to the masses (*"gesunkenes Kulturgut"*), it is necessary, in fact, to accept the more reasonable theory of a continual permutation both of "high" art and of folk art. The great step that medieval drama achieved when it relinquished the Latin text and passed gradually to dramas in the vernacular necessarily involved an approximation in style and in content of medieval drama to folklore. This folklore element found particularly forceful application in religious and school plays, and later in urban plays of a secular type, especially in comic scenes and scenes depict-ing folk life.

Once the plays of the "higher" art reached the people, they usually changed more and more in the direction of folklore, drawing away from the theatrical tradition of the "higher strata." However, the development of some plays proceeds like a curve. First they approach folklore, then withdraw from it by reapproaching the theatrical and literary tradition of the "higher strata." In this connection, let us quote Hans Neumann:[1]

"The primitive collective play (Gemeinschaftsspiel) is again almost com-pletely displaced, but even in its decline it continues to have considerable influence, and at the same time functions extensively in the decline of re-ligious drama and of the theater in general. For the most part they retain the foreign themes and, in the folk milieu, their foreign forms; but quite often they spontaneously acquire the characteristics of a primitive collec-tive play and only then does the theatrical performance become inter-esting."

Undoubtedly Neumann is correct when he points to the influence of the old folk theater on religious and secular drama, which comes to the vil-lages only from the "higher strata." However, it is not only under the direct influence of old folk plays and their original theatrical performance that religious and secular plays change in the village: they undergo funda-mental changes even where this direct influence of folk plays does not exist or is negligible. When artistic drama enters the village, it becomes a component of another structure different from the structure determined by the "higher strata." In particular, the village community, with its taste different from the city and with its tendency toward a collective participation in the creation and interpretation of folk art, profoundly influences the reception of drama and can essentially change its form and function.

As soon as the play comes to a village, it necessarily changes because the development of the plot as well as the method of acting depends on two basic theatrical factors: on the actors and on the spectators (on the stage and on the audience). The transformation of a drama within the village milieu is determined by new artistic means, by which the comic and tragic effects are attained, and by the specific artistic processes of folklore. Moreover, the whole specific social structure of the village modifies the received play in its form and function.

In folk theater, for example, the actors draw the spectators into the play, often directly provoking them, laughing at them and their environment. The community reaction may be so vigorous that it can sometimes lead to fisticuffs. How the performance of a village style of play before members of higher society may not be without a certain risk is illustrated by Ferdinand Menčík in his *Vánoční hry* [Christmas plays] :

A story is told about Count Ferdinand Des Fours, who died in 1760, that he once attended in Boskov "The Passion of Our Lord." The townsmen Václav Kurfiřt and Josef Kvand were playing Jews. Making various wild gestures in the play, they stuck out their tongues at the count and at his companion, the vicar Dušek. After the play, the count inquired as to who had played the Jews, and ordered them to appear the next day before him. Filled with fear, both proceeded to their gracious lordship, and when they had been let in, the count asked them whether it was they who had played the Jews the day before; and when they replied that they had, he rejoined: "At one time the Jews were, in fact, as ferocious as you were yesterday, and you could not have performed it better. For your performance I am giving you a bucket of beer from the brewery in Semily."

In this case, then, the count understood, or wanted to show that he understood, theatrical procedures that were foreign to him, and even rewarded the actors; but probably the fear experienced before meeting his gracious lordship compelled the actors in their next meeting with a foreign audience to refrain from those theatrical methods that were common only to the village audience.

A series of concrete examples confirms our interpretation of the modification of artistic play in the village; they show, at the same time, that the changes did not occur under the direct influence of traditional folk plays (as Neumann thinks), but also depend on the structure of folklore, distinct from the structure of so-called "high art."

Knowledge of folk play sources enable us, via the comparative method, to identify what is peculiar and original in the folk theater just as by identifying the prototypes from which the dramas of Shakespeare and Molière descend we are better able to evaluate these world geniuses. I consider as "folk" plays even those plays that originated from the artistic dramas, whether religious or secular, and, once having reached the village, became popular, were substantially changed and made proximate in their form to other folk plays; thus, they became a constituent of the structure which folklore of the particular area creates.

The specific relations between stage and audience, between actors and public, which differ greatly from analogous relations in our theater and, furthermore, a host of theatrical techniques, all these things sharply distinguish Czech and Slovak folk theater from the artistic theater and relate it to the folk theater of other European people. In the majority of cases it is possible to explain this conformity otherwise than by mutual influences. Analogous theatrical methods in the folk theater of various ethnic groups, very often separated from one another, arose independently from similar conditions, aesthetic and social. Many Czech folk plays are similar to the folk plays of their neighbors, Germans and Poles, just as Slovak plays are similar to Ukrainian and Hungarian folk plays. In some cases we can precisely establish the influence of one ethnic group on another in certain plays.

In those cases where we find the source in another culture, we cannot and should not conclude our interest with the statement that our play is not original. On the contrary, precisely here we have the possibility of comparison. By comparing it with the source from which it was taken, we can clearly ascertain within the variant its original features, conditioned by the structure of the language, the religious, social, and economic life and by the art, both "high" art and "folk" art.

In some cases where we find similar folk theatrical performances among different ethnical groups it is not possible to determine which group borrowed from which, because the plays are products of the creative work of a cultural sphere of several ethnic groups. For some plays, the sphere in question is that of central European culture; for some the cultural sphere is broader, including not only the whole central Europe but also the Balkans; for other plays the cultural sphere is even wider, encompassing all of Europe and possibly extending beyond its borders.

Note

1. Hans Neumann, *Primitive Gemeinschaftskultur* (Jena, 1921), p. 118.

Part III

6. Signs in the Chinese Theater

Karel Brušák

Chinese theater has devised a complicated and precise system of signs carrying a large and categorically diverse range of meaning. The emergence of the system was made possible by the nature of the repertoire; the number of plays is relatively small and they are familiar to most of the audience. The Chinese play is of little significance from the literary point of view; performance is paramount. The components of the structure appear simple enough, but individual elements within the structure carry numerous obligatory signs standing for referents that are often very complex.

The stage is a rectangular raised platform flanked on three sides by the audience. The rear is formed by a backcloth with two apertures. These provide the only access to the stage; the opening on the spectators' left is the entrance, that on the right, the exit. Where an actor is coming from or going to is shown by his choice of aperture. If he both enters and leaves by "the entrance," the audience knows he is going back to the same place; if two actors enter and depart by different apertures, this shows they have come from different places and are returning thence, and so forth. Court theaters, which presented numerous plays involving the appearance of supernatural beings, had their stages built on two levels, mortals figuring on the lower level and spirits on the upper. Chinese stage sets are not made up of painted scenery or architectural structures as in the West but employ only a small number of separate articles, in particular a table and chairs, which then function as specific signs according to their position on the stage. The set is further elaborated by specific elements in the player's performance. Thus equipped the Chinese stage has survived for centuries and still operates unchanged in the classical Chinese theater of today.

Until recently the development of the theater has been examined almost exclusively from the angle of literature; the significance of the text has been overestimated. Nowadays it is generally accepted that the words form only the basis of a complicated structure made up of two interrelated series, one acoustic and one visual. The visual side of any dramatic performance apprehended by the spectator can be termed dramatic space.

"Znaky na čínském divadle," *Slovo a slovesnost,* 5 (1939). Translated by Karel Brušák.

We can distinguish two qualities in it. The first is furnished by the mere existence of its members and is therefore static; the second is created and characterized only by their change and movement and is therefore kinetic. Of the static aspects of dramatic space the most permanent is the architectural element—the stage. Upon this is erected from performance to performance a variable space in the narrow sense of the word, formed by the scenery, scenic contrivances, and so on—the scene. Within this space of arbitrary duration there is formed a nonmaterial and transitory fictitious space, conjured up by the movement of actors, by the movements and color changes of light, by the moving images of a film, and so forth—the action space. In highly developed theatrical systems the stage used to have a conventional form. The Greek theater had its orchestra and proscenium; the humanist, Elizabethan and Chinese theaters had their platform; the nineteenth-century theater had a hollow cube minus the front wall, in the folklore theater the stage is formed anew for each performance. The scene may be identical with the stage if the acting is without scenery, but usually it is an independent structure built upon it. The stage, in its ideally perfect form, is an inner space, limited by the structure of the theater, and the scene is a fictitious space depicting or suggesting a real space. In the conception of the scene we must include not only the scenery and scenic contrivances but also the actors' costumes and masks. The lighting belongs to the scene only in so far as it renders it visible, contributes to the definition of place or time, or creates an impression. If it belongs dramatically in the performance, emphasizing the movements of the actors or forming an independent action, we may include it in the action space. In the same way a film, if shown as part of the scenery, belongs to the scene. But it may be shown to supplement the actions of the actors, as Piscator used to do in his crowd scenes or as an equal partner to their actions, a method invented by the Czech producer E. F. Burian and called by him "theatregraph."

Consequently, the signs of Chinese theater may be roughly divided into two groups: visual, that is, those associated with the dramatic space, and acoustic, that is, those associated with the dialogue, music, and sound effects.

The Visual Signs

This group comprises on the one hand signs related to the scene, on the other hand signs belonging to the concept of action space. Let us deal first with the signality of those elements forming the scene, namely (a) scenic articles, (b) costumes, and (c) makeup.

I The Scene

(a) Scenic Articles Articles on set are normally summarized under the general heading of stage properties. This term is, however, too imprecise in the context of Chinese theater. In addition to the usual characterizing and functional types of stage properties, we have to deal here with articles that, while resembling these, are nevertheless quite distinct in their own right; they function as elementary signs, symbols standing for referents composing the scene.

The hierarchy of articles on set can be determined if they are considered in terms of their various functions. The most significant, dramatically active, are those that participate in the player's performance, for example, swords, goblets, and so forth; they represent a point of transition from scene to action space and can be termed *scenic articles* in the proper sense of the word. After these come articles not brought into active use; their function is passively to complement the character of the scene or dramatis personae (for example, boulders, trees, armor, accoutrement, rings, and so on); they particularize the place of action (in time, history, society, and so forth) and are closely allied to scenery—these are *complementary articles.* As two distinct functions are involved, the borderline between the two types of article is clear enough. Nevertheless, an article on set may combine both functions; scenic articles may be and usually are also complementary articles (chairs, and so on) or, alternatively, articles previously considered as merely complementary may enter the play at some point as scenic articles. The latter is a less common occurrence and therefore dramatically extremely effective. The signification of these two types of articles on set is self-evident. An object may appear on set either in reality or in representation. If the object itself is displayed, it presents, both as a whole and in its individual qualities, the same series of signs as in real life (for example, a specific piece of furniture may be, in relation to its owner, a sign of his social standing, taste, upbringing, state of health, habits, and so forth). While in real life the utilitarian function of an object is usually more important than its signification, on a theatrical set the signification is all important. A real object may be substituted on the set by a symbol if this symbol is able to transfer the object's own signs to itself. To satisfy this condition, it is sufficient for the symbol to possess only a few of the basic characteristics of the represented object. The article on set as a theatrical sign of the object itself takes on the sign duties of the object represented; thus articles on set are theatrical signs of signs and frequently very complex.

Chinese theater however possesses articles of a special kind, exceptional in their relationship to actors and set. These are *object signs,* able to represent all aspects of the scene alone and unaided. On a stage without scenery or lighting effects these serve to denote the locale of the play. They are elementary theatrical signs and, as such, distinct from scenic articles and complementary articles, that is to say, they are neither signs of signs nor a structure of signs; they are signs not of particular objects but of objects in general.

The most important of these are a table and chair that are almost never absent from the Chinese stage. If the table and chair are standing in the usual manner, then the set is an interior. On the other hand, a chair placed side on the ground or on its back signifies an embankment or earthwork; overturned it signifies a hill or mountain; standing on the table, it signifies a city tower. Apart from the table and chair the Chinese theater uses articles that, while resembling the scenery of Western theater, differ in that they remain the same for each play they are required for and are consciously interpreted as theatrical signs. A mountainous or desolate area is sometimes represented by a board with a stylized drawing of a mountain; city battlements are represented by a length of blue material held by theater assistants; sometimes a gate and wall masonry are depicted on it, and sometimes it is simply a plain rectangular piece of cloth, unadorned by drawing.

These object signs are also used in the Chinese theater to portray natural phenomena. Black pennants waved by theater assistants are a sign

for wind; a hammer and mirror signify a thunderstorm; a sign for blizzard
is confetti falling from black pennants that unfurl as the assistants wave
them. Chinese theater does not alter the brightness or color of the lighting; the onset of dusk and night is marked by a theater assistant carrying
on a lit lamp or lantern. An object, pennant, or piece of material showing
the stylized drawing of a wave and fish is a sign for water; the actor playing a drowning person leaps between the assistants bearing these signs, and
all go off together.

The Chinese theater does, however, also have objects on set which we
have termed scenic articles; for our purposes we shall distinguish articles
that are adjuncts to the actor's performance and articles that are signs
characterizing his dramatic personality.

The elaborate system of signs evolved has enabled the Chinese actor to
give a comprehensible portrayal of the most varied actions without having
to re-create reality on the stage. He is able to manage with a few props,
chiefly relying on his own performance. For example, to act riding on
horseback he uses a whip that represents the horse. The color of the whip
denotes the color of the horse. Thrown at random on stage, the whip
represents a horse grazing. Riding by carriage is indicated by an assistant
carrying a banner on both sides of the actor, usually a yellow banner
marked with a circle, the sign of a wheel; to indicate alighting, the assistant raises the banner. To indicate a trip in a boat, it is enough for the
actor to carry an oar with which he performs a great variety of exactly
defined motions while walking about the stage. If an execution is to be
enacted, a packet encased in red silk signifies the severed head; the man
executed runs off the stage, and an assistant displays the packet to the
audience.

Characterizing signs are those articles worn visibly and continuously by
the player; they form a point of transition to costume and generally comprise banners, coils of silk, pieces of material. The use of scenic articles
linked to costume comprehensibly delineates the character of the personage while obviating the necessity for explanatory passages in the dialogue.
Spirits are revealed by black or red veils or paper tassels, a sick person is
marked by a stripe of yellow material tied round the head and running
down onto the back, a captive wears a long silk cord round his neck. The
sign for the rank of general is a collection of triangular shaped bannerets,

usually four, embroidered with dragons, flowers, and phoenixes, fastened on the actor's back; a special banner is reserved for a general in command, another for a general on concluding peace. Special coils of yellow silk denote an imperial order or imperial safe-conduct, and its bearer may enter places forbidden to others; a board cased in yellow silk denotes an official seal, and so forth.

(b) Costumes Four types of character are most frequent on the Chinese stage: i. heroes of shining character, loyal and honorable men (shēng), ii. villains, cruel and faithless men, coarse soldiers, servants (jìng), iii. clowns, dancers, and acrobats (chǒu), iv. female characters (dàn). All these roles admit of many nuances according to age, situation, and so on; the second group (jìng) is distinguished from the first (shēng) by its actors wearing makeup on their faces. Religious reasons prevented women playing in the Chinese theater; female parts were formerly distinguished only by the actor playing a woman wearing a blue tulle band around his head, but later this simple sign was replaced by a more elaborate form of dress, makeup, and hairstyle.

Each of these types wears a costume appropriate in material, color, cut, and design to the character's meaning. Chinese theatrical costume observes strict conventions, but in contrast to Chinese object signs, which are elementary signs, it is a complicated structure of signs. It differs from Western theatrical costume not only by its plurisignification but also by the nature of the referents. It reveals not merely the wearer's social status, age, and so forth, but his worth, character, and so on. This purely theoretical aspect has its practical consequences. It reveals an interesting interdependence between aesthetic outlook and questions of technique. For the costumes used are always made from high quality, expensive materials painstakingly put together to fulfill to perfection the demands of stern convention, while at the same time upholding the immutability of that same convention by their own durability. Chinese theatrical costume, however, has another important task to fulfill—that of forming the scene. The object signs are very restrained; besides, the Chinese classical theater is without lighting effects. This gives rise to the magnificence of Chinese theatrical costume, whose variegated colours, sophisticated cut, and intricate embroidery are the most splendid in the world.

We may distinguish three types of costume according to cut and design: ceremonial garb (mǎng), everyday wear (diéz), and military uniform (kǎikào). Any of these may be worn by either male or female characters, situation being the only determining factor. Alongside these, however, there exists a large series of separate items of dress which function as distinct autonomous signs. Chinese costume in its function as sign adopts those elements of ordinary dress which are signs standing for specific referents but simplifies or adapts them. Thus, for instance, the beggar's costume stems from its counterpart in everyday reality but is converted into an autonomous theatrical sign; the beggar in the Chinese theater wears an everyday silk dress (diéz) spangled with multicolored silk patches. A mandarin is distinguished by his long coat and thick-soled shoes, and so on. Occasionally the meaning of the sign varies according to situation; a cape worn early in the morning betrays the fact that the character returned home late at night, worn later in the day, however, it indicates the wearer's laziness and slovenliness. A woman's skirt signifies dress that is not too clean and as such is common with women of the lower class; if worn by a wealthy woman, it shows either that the person in question is on a journey and unable therefore to care for her appearance or that we are dealing with a disguise.

(c) Makeup An actor is still more closely identified with the character represented by his makeup. Makeup in Chinese theater is used as a sign that sets apart complex and exceptional characters. Not all players are given makeup, only those acting second or third group parts (jìng and chǒu); honorable men (shēng) and women (dàn) are never made up. The makeup used is unimitative and independent entirely of matters of physiognomy; it forms a self-contained, artificial sign system. It is strikingly similar to the ancient war mask of the Chinese; theatrical make up was evidently derived from it when evil and cruel personages were being represented and the need arose to find some way of clearly marking them apart from other characters. These masks, portraying spirits and demons intended to overawe the enemy in battle, had a long tradition behind them and boasted a suitably strict symbolism, but they were too stiff and rigid to be suitable in themselves for the flexible and constantly changing dramatic space of the Chinese theater. This most probably gave rise to the idea of painting them directly on the skin of the face, which was then still able to use its expressive resources beneath the colorful abstract patterns of the makeup. Pattern and color of makeup are signs of the character of the personage represented by the actor. In the course of time, though, signs, which in the original system had universal validity and permitted of random combination, grouped themselves into schematic units, ideographs, connected with specific heroes of individual plays; within these schemes, however, the signs retained their original values. The scheme painted on the actor's face is, in fact, a chart of the moral qualities of the dramatic persona.

The patterns employed are several and diverse in meaning. Most widespread is a form of makeup dividing the actor's face into three sections, roughly in the shape of a Y, consisting of the forehead and both cheeks; the chin is generally covered with a beard and has no special function in this regard. Old men are characterized by evenly painted eyebrows extended to the ears. The wounded have their face covered with irregular drawing and multifarious colors. The parts of clowns are marked by makeup distorting the features, with irregular placing of nose and eyes, or alternatively the forehead is painted with a triangle with its point on the bridge of the nose.

Colors fulfill a much more precise sign function. It is comparatively rare to find the whole face made up with one color, white, black, red, and so forth, these indicating either unambiguous characters or supernatural beings. Black means simplicity, sincerity, courage, and steadfastness; red denotes loyalty, honesty, and patriotism, crimson is used with old men as a sign for the calm of old age and prudence allied to these qualities; blue expresses obstinacy, cruelty, and pride; yellow indicates ruthlessness, slyness, and wiliness, white stands for hypocrisy, irascibility, baseness, and viciousness. The extent of the colored area on the actor's face corresponds to the extent of the moral quality in the character of the dramatis persona. Thus, for example, there are many degrees in the use of white, from a face totally white except for the eyebrows to a mere white spot on the nose. In the first case the spectator is informed that the dramatis persona has no other qualities than those having white as their sign; that is, he is an utter villain (usually of noble birth). In the second case the moral qualities signified by the white color form only a very small part of the character of the dramatis persona; that is, he is an honest man with a few light moral blemishes (usually a simple soldier). Makeup serves also besides costume to set apart supernatural beings; green is reserved for spirits and devils, gold for gods.

The use of false beards and mustaches, of which there are more than a dozen kinds is also subject to convention. Their shape and mode of wear are nonrealistic; they are fastened with wires behind the ears, and their styles, which are often very bizarre, are signs of the wearer's age, status, and personality.

II The Action Space

The second type of visual signs are those belonging to the action space. Every motion, gesture, and facial expression of the actor are signs that, as in Western theater, serve both to expound the character and to indicate its relationship to others. As well as these, however, the Chinese theater provides abundant examples of signs realized within the action space, which have representative function and stand for referents outside persons; they represent nonexistent components of the scene or scenic articles. Every routine, whatever its particular significance, has been evolved through long tradition into an obligatory convention. Its present shape has been affected not only by the attempt to devise a sign at once simple and comprehensible but also by constant emphasis on aesthetic function. The Chinese player's actions were subjected to precise rules that allow no basic deviation. Perfect mastery of technique is enabled by educating the actor in these rules from a tender age, and by having him play the same part throughout his career. The conventional *action signs* never aim at imitation of reality. They naturally take this as their starting point, but in most cases they are so constructed as to divorce themselves from realism as much as possible. The player for example suggests the action of drinking tea by raising an imaginary cup to his lips, but in order to avoid being realistic, masks the hand executing the gesture with a special movement of the other hand. To illustrate someone sleeping, he does not lie down but sits leaning the fingers of one hand lightly on his temple. An action sign thus owes its final form to a tension between the aesthetic function and other functions, communicative, expressive, and so on. The relationship of action signs to reality is variable; conventional sequences of movements which relate to the scene even at their most artificial are in fact in closer contact with reality than actions expounding thought processes and character relationships. The Chinese actor evokes the action space with the full gamut of elements of movement, gesture, and facial expression at his disposal. Movements are here taken in the narrower sense of body movements. One special mode of expression is the use of various motions performed by means of pheasants' plumes attached to the player's headgear. These are very long, and the actor may bring them into gyrating or nodding motion by turning or drooping the head or he may move them by hand. The Chinese actor's gestures differ profoundly from those of the Western actor. The primary gestures are made by the hands, which are seldom left free but are generally cloaked in long flowing silken-cuffs fastened to the sleeves. The gestures carried out by the actor with these sleeves are rich in signification. Though the facial expressions are not in general distinct from the Western kind, they are more diversified and specific. Movements of the facial muscles are conventionalized; binding stipulations govern which facial expression should be used to express a given emotion relative to character type and age and the nature, intensity, and duration of the feeling. Generally, movements and gestures in the wider sense are conveyors of signs substituting for the scene, while sleeve gestures and facial expressions together express the thoughts and emotions of the dramatis persona.

A great proportion of the actor's routine is devoted to producing signs whose chief function is to stand for components of the scene. An actor's routine must convey all those actions for which the scene provides no appropriate material setup. Using the applicable sequence of conventional moves, the actor performs the surmounting of imaginary obstacles, climbing imaginary stairs, crossing a high threshold, opening a door. The motion signs performed inform the onlooker of the nature of these imaginary objects, tell whether the nonexistent ditch is empty or filled with water, whether the nonexistent door is a main or ordinary double door, single door, and so forth. To show a person entering a dwelling of the poor, the actor carries out the proper motion in a bent position, for the poor live in low-ceilinged basements; if appropriate, the regulations avail him of the opportunity to show himself hitting his forehead on an imaginary lintel. The player's actions are particularly complicated when involving objects or animals; here the actor sometimes bases his routine on residual parts or fragments of the imaginary articles. When speaking about scenic articles, we have mentioned the use of an oar to represent a trip in a boat; if the actor arrives with his oar on an empty stage by the "exit" doorway, this means the whole stage is water; he may receive other persons on board his boat of fantasy and row to the "entrance," which stands for the shore. An unusually involved routine is used by the actor to suggest actions with a horse, mounting, riding, trotting, galloping, dismounting, leading, and so on. The signification of all these movements is so intricately devised that it allows the spectator to imagine even the nature of the imaginary horse. In one play the actor representing a servant has eight imaginary horses on stage; the audience can tell from his behavior that one horse is exceptionally beautiful, another bites, another bucks, another is sick, another worn with age, and so forth. The servant saddles the horses, leads them to his master's residence, and announces to the company that they are in readiness. The knights come out, pretend to mount the imaginary horses, and ride off at a trot. The same degree of detail marks the stipulations governing the representation of diverse types of work and activity: weaving, sewing, thread making, writing, and so on; each dispenses with stage props.

Signs connected with the psychology of the dramatis persona are usually sleeve gestures carefully worked out to fit each individual instance. The "raised sleeve gesture," in which the long sleeve is thrown upwards and hangs out, expresses despair or revolt. Another sleeve gesture signifies a weighty decision; the "decisive sleeve gesture," carried out by the right hand circling slowly upward and quickly downward, signifies that the person has made some fateful decision, sacrificed someone's life, and so forth. To show dejection, for example, frustration of plans, the Chinese actor is not permitted to let his arms dangle by the side of his body, since this gesture does not comply with Chinese aesthetics; the actor lowers only one arm, but this he holds in front of him and presses somewhat to the body, gripping it under the elbow with his other arm, bent. This "gesture of repose," a set position in fact, is observed not merely by actors expressing fatigue but equally by those portraying spirits. Another standard position, to show the poverty or unreality of the dramatis persona, is the "drooping sleeves gesture"; the actor playing a poor man or a spirit allows his sleeves to droop from his arms, held somewhat forward from the body. Gestures performed with the hands alone are also used to signify emotions. If the concept cannot be expressed by a sleeve gesture, the actor tucks up his sleeve in order to have his hand free and covers it again after completion of the gesture. Hand gestures may replace sleeve gestures only in the case of signs representing emotions but some hand gestures cannot be replaced by sleeve gestures. Hand gestures are signs of illness, feelings of heat, cold, powerlessness, disappointment, pain, pity, contemplation, and so on. The gesture of protest may serve to show their complexity. The hand is partially clenched into a fist, the thumb rests on the middle joint of the middle finger, the index finger is curved across the thumb and at the same time the tip of the little finger is made to touch the third finger, to avoid the shape of an ordinary fist. Whereas gestures never signify joyful emotions, body and feather movements have no other function but to express joyful emotions. Military roles contain many motions expressing strength and ardor. A sign of vigor is a movement that the actor performs using his left leg while standing erect on his right; he raises his left thigh and bends his leg at the knee into an obtuse angle. The "dragon's turn" at the waist has the same meaning. Keeping his arms on his hips, the actor rotates his trunk, stretching out deeply in all directions. In one play the actor in this leaning pose uses his teeth to seize a glass of wine from a tray proffered by a servant on his right, leans back, as if to quaff the cup, and returns the glass to the tray, now held by the servant on his left side. The most extreme signs of levity and gaiety are dancing movements with feathers, most often performed by one of the female characters (dàn).

Finally, the last but most important theatrical signs belonging to the concept of action space are those that reveal the relationship of the person performing the routine to another character. Here we have to deal with signs displaying the social relations of individuals, dramatic signs in the true sense of the word, for it is these that express conflict most often. Some have transferred themselves to the Chinese stage straight from the ceremonial of social intercourse, acquiring still greater complexity and lexicality. They concern the salutation and welcome of a guest. The "sleeve gesture of respect" is a sign of a highly courteous greeting; it is performed by a crossing of the arms. If the actor wishes to present his respects or request attention or a hearing, he carries out the "sleeve gesture of address"; he raises his left arm to beneath his chin, letting the sleeve dangle, lightly touches the latter with the fingers of his right hand, leaving out the index finger, and greets the person accosted. This gesture and sign of respect, however, are also performed by the player when uttering the name of a person not present whom he loves or cherishes. An actor acknowledges a greeting or show of respect by performing the "sleeve gesture of attention"; he places his right hand beneath his breast letting the sleeve drop, at the same time bowing. These motions are a sign replacing the verbal wish that the other desist from his greetings. Another series of signs concerns the greeting of a guest. Together with the usual salutations, the actor welcoming a guest performs other gestures; he conveys the dusting down of the chair by a movement of the sleeve right, left, and right again, first with the right arm, then the left, and last the right again. The affectation and significance of this ceremony as carried out on similar lines in everyday life enabled it to be adopted with only minor alterations by the action space. Similar lexicalized routines for greeting a guest, including dusting the chair, are also known in some country districts in Bohemia and had their own importance in a series of ceremonies, for instance matchmaking. The action space of Chinese theater has also elaborated signs expressing disagreeable feelings. Anger, repugnance, or refusal are conveyed by the "sleeve gesture of aversion"; with a circling motion the player hurls his sleeve in the subject's direction and simultaneously twists his head the other way. To send a person away, the actor carries out the "sleeve gesture of refusal." By means of bending movements of the wrists he hurls both sleeves out from the body once, twice, thrice, stepping back at the third gesture. The "sleeve gesture of concealment" indicates that the actor is obscuring his action or words from the other person on stage; its meaning is thus close to the aside of Western theater. If the player wishes to communicate to the audience some secret that must remain hidden from the other persons, or if he wishes to express a private thought, he raises his right-hand sleeve to the level of his face; this gesture denotes an opaque wall between the other characters and the actor, who then points to them frequently with his other hand. The actor may hide himself behind a still more perfect imaginary wall when in a dilemma or afraid of discovery by using the "sleeve gesture of hiding." Here the arm is bent in an obtuse angle to the brow, and the sleeve flows down across the whole face.

The Acoustic Signs

The second group of Chinese theatrical signs are characterized by the signs of theatrical speech, song, and music. The language in the Chinese theater has special signs that distinguish it from ordinary speech. The composition of Chinese plays is not in most cases dramatic in the Western sense; it generally lacks the tension reflectable in dialogue. Chinese drama is a structure made up of verse, prose, and music; these elements intermingle and always appear. Theater speech was formed by an artificial mixing of various dialects and its signification stems also from a special mode of declamation employed. The declaiming of individual words is founded on a strictly adhered to system of four tones which prevents possible errors in comprehension due to the homonymous character of Chinese vocabulary and also serves to heighten the musicality of the speech; at the same time, however, each of the tones is a sign and expresses the speaker's inner state of mind. The spoken word must always blend with the rhythm of movement, whether it be prose or verse. Verse dialogue or monologue is composed of quatrains; the first two lines are delivered in a monotone, the third line rises and slackens off, and the fourth is delivered slowly and quietly. If, on the other hand, the actor raises his voice on the last line, this announces the imminence of music and dance.

Music in the Chinese theater follows convention. It is played at the beginning of a play, at actors' entries, and at certain identical situations in the course of the play. The most important instruments of the theater orchestra are two-string violins, three-string guitars, reed organs, horns, flutes, drums, gongs, cymbals, and clappers. For centuries the music played and written has been based on a five-note scale derived from the ancient Chinese flute, and the classical Chinese theater remains faithful to this tradition. For the principal situations conventional themes are prescribed which always enter at the reaching of these points in the play; otherwise there is no music or simply improvised music. The themes are stated either by a singer or solo instrument and are then recapitulated in unison by all instruments. Arias are sung in an archaic almost incomprehensible form of language; thus certain features are signaled by the music alone, since the themes are precisely defined, either in conjunction with the action space or in isolation. Occasions where music functions as a sign are, for example, anger, hatred, horror, surprise, anxiety, sadness, meditation, love, joy, drunkeness, the toilette, fray, flight, and so on. Often the circumstance in question is conveyed by the music alone, for instance if drunkeness is to be represented; its realistic imitation, common on the Western stage, is forbidden to the Chinese actor on aesthetic grounds.

By examining the signification of individual elements in the Chinese theater, we find a structure generally homogeneous, a stock of several systems of lexicalized signs, systems which though autonomous in their own right develop spontaneously one from another. The shaping of these systems, the stability of whose entire structure depends on the maintenance of virtually inviolate lexicons, evidently owed something to external, extra-theatrical influences (religion, traditions of social intercourse, and so forth) but the influence of the scene itself was highly important. Articles on set standing for referents composing the scene grew into special theatrical signs, adopting new functions and bequeathing their original ones to the action space. The latter could discharge only its own role by transferring certain of its sign functions to the remaining elements of the structure, chiefly the music. In Chinese, as opposed to Western theater, a dramatic work does not envisage realization in some form dependent on numerous chance shaping factors ranging from a producer's conception to an actor's diction. Production of single established plays in the ancient Chinese theater are finalized beforehand down to the last ingredient. They persist in the abstract as uninterrupted series, familiar already to the entire cast in each and every cross section, and are merely reevoked from time to time without any serious structural change. The structure is to a certain degree sure in itself, so that there is not even any need for a producer to supervise its unity.

7. Dynamics of the Sign in the Theater

Jindřich Honzl

Everything that makes up reality on the stage—the playwright's text, the actor's acting, the stage lighting—all these things in every case stand for other things. In other words, dramatic performance is a set of signs.

Otakar Zich expressed such a view in his *Aesthetics of Dramatic Art* when he advanced the notion that "dramatic art is an art of images and is so, moreover, in absolutely every respect."[1] Thus the actor represents a dramatic character (Vojan represents Hamlet), the scenery represents the locale where the story unfolds (a Gothic arch represents a castle), bright lighting represents daytime, dim lighting denotes nighttime, music represents some happening (the noise of battle), and so forth. Zich explains that though the stage certainly involves architectural constructions, still it cannot, in his view, be consigned to the domain of architecture because architecture does not want to stand for anything and, hence, does not have image function. The stage has no other function than to stand for something else, and it ceases to be the stage if it does not represent something. To comprehend Zich's assertion better, we may put it into other words and say that it does not matter whether the stage is a construction or not, that is, whether the stage is a place in the Prague National Theater or a meadow near a forest or a pair of planks supported by barrels or a market square crowded with spectators. What does matter is that the stage of the Prague National Theater may perfectly well represent a meadow, or the meadow of an outdoor theater clearly represent a town square, or a section of square in a marketplace theater represent the inside of an inn, and so on. Zich, however, does not discount the architectural nature of the stage. Whenever he speaks of the stage, he always has in mind a stage inside of a theater building. But we may, nevertheless, venture to infer from Zich's argument the conclusions, already mentioned, as to the nondependence of the stage's image function on its architectural constructedness.

Moreover, from this instance of the semiotic character of the stage we can draw an analogy to other aspects of theatrical performance. It has already been maintained that although the stage is usually a construction, it

"Pohyb divadelního znaku," *Slovo a slovesnost,* 6 (1940), pp. 177-188. Translated by I. R. Titunik.

is not its constructional nature that makes it a stage but the fact that it *represents* dramatic place. The same can be said about the actors: the actor is usually a person who speaks and moves about the stage. However, the fundamental nature of an actor does not consist in the fact that he is a person speaking and moving about the stage but that he *represents someone, that he signifies a role in a play.* Hence it does not matter whether he is a human being; an actor could be a piece of wood, as well. If the wood moves about and its movements are accompanied by words, then such a piece of wood can represent a character in the play, and the wood becomes an actor.

We have freed the concept of "stage" from its constructional restrictions, and we can free the concept of "actor" from the restriction which claims that an actor is a human being who represents a dramatic character in a play. If acting merely consists in representation of the dramatic character by something else, then not only can a person be an actor but so can a wooden puppet or a machine (for example, Lisicky's, Schlemmer's, and Liesler's mechanical theater using machines) or anything at all (for example, the advertising theater of Belgian cooperatives where a bolt of material, a spider's leg, a coffee grinder, and the like were dramatic characters).

And if simply a voice, heard from the wings of a stage or over the radio, properly signifies a dramatic character, then such a voice is an actor. Precisely such an acoustical actor appears in Goethe's *Faust:* in the usual performances of this play we perceive the role of God in the prologue merely as a voice. Finally, in radio plays, voice and sound represent not only dramatic characters but also all other facts that make up the reality of the theater: the stage, scenery, props, and lighting.

There are acoustic signs for all aspects of the theater on the radio. These acoustic signs are referred to as acoustic scenery and are exemplified by the sound of the tapping of typewriters used to denote an office, the rattling of pneumatic drills and the rumbling of wagons to represent a coal mine, and the like. A glass as a prop may be represented by the pouring of wine or by a clinking sound, and so on.

Zich limits his discussion of dramatic character to the conventional forms of theatrical performance. He speaks solely of "plays and operas performed in a theater" and takes into account only actors and singers who perform on the stage of theaters. But now that he has lifted the restrictions that bound the stage specifically to architecture, the way has been opened for all other aspects of dramatic performance to reach a similar freedom. Liberation awaits dramatic character, up to now closely associated with human gestures and motions, as it also does the playwright's text, hitherto *verbal* text, and so on for the other devices of dramatic art. And much to our amazement, we are discovering that stage "space" need not be spatial but that sound can be a stage and music can be a dramatic event and scenery can be a text.

First of all, let us deal with the stage and those signs that denote it. We may say that the stage can be represented by any real space or, in other words, a stage can equally well be a structure or a town square surrounded by spectators or a meadow or a hall in an inn. But even when a stage is such a space, it need not be denoted solely by its spatial nature. We have already used the example of a radio stage (a business office, a coal mine, and so forth) that is denoted acoustically. However, even the conventional theater can provide us with examples of a nonspatial denotation of a stage, for example, sound representing a stage. In the last act of Čexov's *The Cherry Orchard* it is precisely the orchard that plays the main role. The cherry orchard is on the stage, but in such a way that we cannot see it. It is not represented spatially, but acoustically, as the blows of axes cutting down the orchard are heard in the last act. In such a manner, a playwright and a director can denote the stage by those features of reality as best correspond to their intention and as best and most effectively promote understanding between themselves and the audience.

The facts that we have mentioned so far resulted from the observation and evaluation of concrete artistic work and are not merely scientific deductions. Zich's notion has the stage always still in a theater, in the architecturally denoted place "where plays and operas are performed." It was precisely concrete artistic work that dared to move into the areas where the theory of theater had not yet entered even though it had already pointed in that direction. Modern theater has had the effect precisely of freeing the stage from its previously permanent architectural constants.

Cubo-futuristic theatrical experiments turned our attention to stages and theaters other than those built for the tsarist ballet, the box displays of high society, or for the cultural activity of the small-town amateurs.

Through these experiments we discovered the theater of the street, we became fascinated by the theatricality of a sports field and admired the theatrical effects created by the movements of harbor cranes, and so on. Simultaneously, we discovered the stage of the primitive theater, the performances of a barker, children's games, circus pantomimes, the tavern theater of strolling players, the theater of masked, celebrating villagers. The stage could arise anywhere—any place could lend itself to theatrical fantasy.

With the freeing of the stage, other aspects of theatrical performance were released from their confinements. Scenery of wooden frames and painted canvas awoke from its spell. Stylized theater from as early as the time of Théâtre d'Art in France, or G. Fuchs and A. Appia in Germany, the Society of New Drama in Russia, and of Kvapil in Bohemia adhered to scenic signs that might be called scenic metonymies. A Gothic arch was used to represent an entire church (Kvapil's staging of *L'Annonce faite à Marie* by P. Claudel), a green square on the floor meant a battlefield (Kvapil's Shakespearian cycle), and the English coat of arms on a silken arras was enough to represent royal halls (in the same cycle). A part represented the whole. But a part could indicate several different wholes: a Venetian column and a flight of stairs sufficed for almost all the scenes in the *Merchant of Venice,* excepting scenes in Portia's or Shylock's rooms or in the garden. The column and the flight of steps were used not only as scenery for the street but also for the harbor, the square, and the court of justice. The attributive scenery of the stylized stage always sought to use devices of one single meaning whenever possible. True, a Venetian column could be placed on a square or in a street or made part of a house. But in each and every case it meant a Venetian building, and nothing but a Venetian building, of which it could be a part. With the advent of cubo-futuristic theater new materials appeared on the stage, and formerly undreamed of things acquired various representative functions. The theater of Russian constructivism used a construction made of planks to represent a factory yard, a garden pavilion, a wheat field or a flour mill. The question can be asked, which part or what property of these planks carried the representative function? It was not color or colored shapes, since such constructions were made of raw, unvarnished wood or were uniformly colored. Constructivism excluded the use of picture or color signs on the stage (at any rate, is the constructivism of Popova and Meyerhold). However, very often even the arrangement of the construction failed to create an unambiguous theatrical sign. Meyerhold's construction for *The Death of Tarelkin* was simply a crate combined with a cylindrical object of the same material whose circular end faced the audience and could have suggested any number of things, but none of them without ambiguity. Perhaps the most definite idea it conjured up, in this case, was that of a meat grinder. But it could equally well have indicated a circular window or a round cage or a huge mirror, circularity being its most striking feature. Since "circularity" is so richly suggestive, one could have interpreted that cylindrical object as a sign for a great many things. Therefore the question arises as to what property of a stage construction can have semiotic function when such a function is not carried by either color or shape.

Some time ago, while writing about Tajrov's presentation of *Giroflé-Girofla,* I pointed out that we cannot tell what a contraption on stage is supposed to signify until it is used by an actor. He has first to sit on it or rock on it or climb out of it. It is only when Giroflé and Marasquin sit down that we realize that a certain prop is a love seat hidden away in a shadowy corner of a park. But during the aria this same seat sways rhythmically from the impact of oars propelling a little boat over a calm lake. Or when a band of fierce pirates jumps on this same prop, we know by the way they straddle it and shift the weight of their bodies from one leg to the other that this is a part of a deck—the ladder leading to the bridge. The sign (representative) function of the scenery and props is determined solely by the movements of the actor and by the manner in which he uses them, but even then their representative function is not entirely unambiguous.

Let us return to the example of the set used in Meyerhold's staging of *The Death of Tarelkin.* It is only when we see the actor pacing back and forth in the cylindrical structure like a prisoner and clutching its slats like bars that we realize the function of this stage prop: it is a cell. Simultaneously, however, there remain in our minds all the associations of form that originated during our first glance at the said prop. The idea of a "meat grinder" in combination with the idea of a "prison cell" acquires a mutual polarization of new meanings.

If we examine other stage sets used by Meyerhold in his stagings of that period, we frequently see a system of suspended planes, staircases, and props whose meaning as sign is completely indeterminate. The critics of these performances and sets often spoke of "abstract scenery." Neither Meyerhold nor any other stage artist was concerned with abstract scenery. His stage sets had very concrete tasks and functions. Indeterminate in shape and color, they became signs only when used for the actor's actions. It can be said that *a representative function was not expressed by means of form or color, but by the actor's actions* on the stage construction, on the bare floor, on the suspended planes, on the staircases, on the slanting surfaces, and so on.

However, this does not bring us to the end of our inquiry into the changes undergone by scenic signs on the stage. That structure of signs, which is every theatrical performance, has to retain its internal balance in every situation, whether favorable or unfavorable.

If the constancy of the key points of the structure is assured, transformations in its complex ground plan can be effected without substantial changes. If we remove a single pillar, however, basic changes on the plane of the structure as a whole are necessary. Examples of structural stability are of course theaters with a centuries old tradition such as the traditional Japanese Nō theater, the more recent tradition of the Japanese Kabuki theater, the old Chinese theater, our puppet theater, folk theaters, the theaters of primitives, and so on. The constancy of a structure causes theatrical signs to develop complex meanings. The stability of signs promotes a wealth of meanings and associations. In the Chinese theater every step taken by the actor is imbued with meaning, every lifting of the arm is a different form of address. A step toward the left stage exit indicates a "return" and acquires a different meaning in each particular situation. We may imagine that in one instance this step indicates a battlefield to which a wounded hero is returning, while in another instance it signifies the longing that recalls a lover to mind.

Were we to take the example of puppet theater, the puppets' movements are similarly lexicalized into signs. For instance, the entry of a puppet from above the stage indicates "a sudden apparition," the disappearance of a puppet through the floor symbolizes "death or departure for hell . . . ," and so on. Assessing the wealth of expression in theatrical performance we find that the immutability of the structure's key points does not necessarily impoverish its expressivity because within this traditional structure subtler and finer changes can take place. The spectator is sensitive to even the slightest vibrations of a tightly drawn structural base. At this point an admonition should be addressed to those people who would like to use the ancient traditional theaters as models to counter the restless spirit of ever-searching artists: the impressions of the spectator are brought about precisely and solely by *changes* in the structure. The firmer the structural base, the more finely will the textural strands weave patterns and pictures that captivate us with their beauty.

Here I should like to quote from P. Bogatyrev's "Folk Theater":

A characteristic feature of the audience of folk theater is the fact that they do not hanker after plays of new content, but year after year watch the same Christmas and Easter plays, as for example the play about St. Dorothea, and so on. . . . The spectator watches these plays with extraordinary interest although he knows them more or less by heart. And it is herein that lies the basic differences between the spectator at a folk theater and the average visitor to our theater. . . . In view of the fact that the spectator of folk theater is well acquainted with the contents of the play being performed, it is not possible to surprise him with the novelty of plot development, that novelty which plays such an essential role in our theatrical performances. For this reason *the focal point of a folk theater performance lies in the treatment of detail.*

The desire for freedom of expression and technique is a tendency that has constantly had determinative effect on art. The theater brought about by the cubo-futuristic revolt "for fresh air" introduced new theatrical devices and dispensed with many others. Russian constructivism rid the stage of scenery, wings, overhang, and backdrops. As a result the stage lost the possibility of localizing an action through the use of painted signs indicating an interior or exterior. That was not all, however. Not only did directors reject scenery, stage front and rear, overhang and wings, but they also departed from the bare stage that remained after their revolt. They even rejected the five walls that enclosed the space displayed in front of the auditorium so that every spectator could see it. However, the directors who succeeded them (Oxlopkov, Gropius's theater design) did away with a

stage completely or, more precisely, placed the stage among the spectators
so that any free place in front of, above, next to, or behind the audience
could be a stage. Thus they consigned to oblivion all those rare and precious stage mechanisms that, in obedience to a single command by the
director, lowered a section of stage or piece of scenery or a prop or even
an actor from the heights of the rope gallery, rotated the rear part of a
stage set to the front, shifted prepared scenery from the wings, raised up
whole stage areas with scenery intact through trapdoors, and so on. The
wizard of the theater was deprived of all the mechanisms with which he
performed his magic. All that was left to him were his bare hands. To
represent or signify the spatial location of a play became problematical
with the abandonment of many of the conventions established between
stage and auditorium by long-standing tradition.

Furthermore, a stage situated among the spectators completely lacked
the possibility of erecting scenery signs. Such a stage could not even use
constructions whose representative functions were far more indeterminate
than that of scenery and yet afforded the possibility of situating and organizing the stage space by means of flights of steps, variously located surfaces, inclined planes, contraptions, mechanisms, and so on. Out of its
former stage mechanisms, the only thing left in Cetnerovich's and
Oxlopkov's theater was the floor. Of course, there was still the actor,
lighting, and sound.

When the foundations of theatrical structure are shaken in this way
measures must immediately be taken to adapt to new modes of operation.
If one of the muscles in the set muscles that move the forearm in a living
organism is paralyzed, then that organism is safeguarded by the fact that
one of the coordinated muscles will take over the function of the one
paralyzed. One theatrical function is to locate a play spatially: to signify
a lawn or barroom, to represent a cemetery or a banquet hall. This is an
essential function of the stage which must be implemented just as much
by a stage using constructions as by a stage using scenery, and, just as
much by a stage located in the midst of the spectators as by one that is
traditionally located. Signs whose function is to promote the spectators'
understanding always involve the designation of a space. It is precisely
this designative function that constitutes the stability of these signs. In all
other respects these signs retain the greatest possible dynamics. The fact

that the signs are supposed to designate the space in which an action takes place does not mean that they must be spatial signs. We have already shown that space can be designated by an acoustic sign or by means of a light sign. On the centralized stage possibilities are extremely limited for the placing of objects, large pieces of furniture, or scenery signs. While the constructivist stage concentrated on the actor's actions, the centralized stage is often solely dependent on the actor per se. Oxlopkov's theater has acquainted us with a number of superb instances of the *actor* becoming a sign for spatial location. Here one found not only actor-scenery and actor-set, but even actor-furniture, actor-props.

Oxlopkov created an *actor-sea* by having a young man dressed in a neutral manner (in blue, that is, "invisible," coveralls with a blue mask on his face) shake a blue-green sheet attached to the floor in such a way that the rippling of the blue-green sheet expressively replaced the waves of a sea canal. He created *actor-furniture* by having two "invisibly" attired actors kneel opposite each other and stretch between them a tablecloth into the quadrilateral shape of a table. An *actor-prop* originated by placing next to the actor playing the role of the captain, another actor dressed in blue coveralls who held up the handle of the ship's horn the moment when the captain, pulling the handle, blasts a signal to the sailors.

To the three typical examples, quoted above, of transfer of stage functions to the functions of the actor, I could add many equally or even more interesting examples such as actors indicating the phenomenon of a snowstorm. Or another example: a theater, of course, possesses various acoustical devices for indicating a storm; but in a presentation by Oxlopkov, a metaphor of a storm was shown by an invasion of carnival merrymakers. Boys and girls (actors in blue coveralls) threw confetti at one another while jumping about and generally making noise. This metaphor of a storm—this carnival whirlwind—was not an *act* in Oxlopkov's production of *The Aristocrats,* not part of the actors' performance, but spatial scenery, a means of depicting the environment of the action—the sign of a storm.

Every student of the theater immediately saw analogies between Oxlopkov's staging procedures and the methods employed by ancient Chinese and Japanese theaters. The ancient Chinese theater has a primitive stage, and its spatial restrictions affect all other stage factors. Here, too, we find "invisible" men (dressed in black) who assist in changing scenes, for instance, by covering the bodies of the dead warriors with a black cloth. The battlefield disappears and the plot can continue elsewhere. Similarly, the Japanese stage uses all the techniques of dramatic performance for spatial location of the given plot. Here, too, space need not be indicated by a space, sound by a sound, light by lights, human activity by an actor's acting, and so on. In this case it also happens that "we see tones" and "hear the open countryside" or learn from an actor's costume what in the European theater we would hear from the actor's lips. I recall the following illustration of the change of devices in Japanese theater:

Yransuke leaves the besieged castle. He moves from the background into the foreground.

Suddenly the rear backdrop, depicting a life-size door, rolls up and we see another backdrop on which there is a small door indicating that the actor has drawn away some distance.

Yransuke continues on his way. A dark green curtain is lowered over the rear backdrop which indicates that Yransuke can no longer see the castle.

A few more steps. Yransuke sets out on the "path of blossoms." In order to indicate this still greater distance he begins to play his samisen (a kind of Japanese mandolin) behind the scene.

First withdrawal: a *step* in space.

Second withdrawal: *a change of painted scenery.*

Third withdrawal: a conventional symbol (a *curtain*)—which nullifies the visual stage device.

Fourth withdrawal: *sound.*

Here the changing of stage devices, which successively take up the same function, is interpreted as the gradation of one dramatic action: the walking of Yransuke, his drawing away from the castle.

With equal justification we could, in this case, interpret the actor's step away from the painted backdrop as a function of spatial location. The stage artist "paints" either with the step of the actor or the sound of his mandolin. He uses different devices to specify the location each time. However, we can add to these two interpretations still others. We could ask whether the change of the rear backdrop with the castle door is not an artistic replacement of the playwright's text, that is to say, the words of the actor saying: "I left the castle." Or whether the melancholy sound of the samisen is not a substitute for the verbal expression: "I have set out on a long pilgrimage." Yet, if we were to seek other interpretations we still would not arrive at the essence of the matter. We would not be able to decide which of them are fundamental and we would not be able to deny the justification of the others.

It would be wrong, however, to think that this changeable method of dramatic expression is a speciality of the Chinese or Japanese theater or of a Russian innovator from the year 1935. Similar methods of dramatic expression can be found in many Czech stage performances. I should like to mention my own production of *The Teacher and the Pupil* (by V. Vančura) in cooperation with the painter Jindřich Štýrský at the Municipal Theater in Brno in 1930.

The fourth act of the play is situated at the edge of town. In order to indicate this fact we made use of a *dramatic mask.* But we took this dramatic mask from the face of the actor, relocated it, and applied it as a spatial *sign on the stage.* Projected across a wide area of the circular horizon was a face whose lower part was covered with a scarf in the manner of highwaymen. This face, with evil eyes below a forehead covered by a hat, arched above the stage and shaded that area in which the spectator usually sees a sky with floating clouds.

Through relocation, the dramatic mask acquired new meaning.

In the same play there also was a dramatic mask, projected on the stage in a magnified manner, that carried out another function. In this case, *the scenery became an actor.*

The pupil, Jan, whose home confines him like a musty prison, adamantly maintains an intention to run away. He resists the pleas of his aunt and the threats of his teacher. Through the walls of his home he stares "into the brilliant and glowing abyss of the world which opens up before his eyes." He forges his resolve in a long monologue.

By making the stage almost completely dark and thus concealing the presence of the actor on the stage, we allowed the actor's words to be heard in such a way as to create the impression that they were being spoken by the projected enlargement of the actor's face which gazed fixedly on an imagined goal.

In my production of *The Executioner of Peru* (Ribemont-Dessaignes) in 1929, a duplication of devices was used: an actor's face was projected on the stage, and the actor's real face was visible.

In my production of Apollinaire's *Tiresias's Breasts* (in 1927), the poet's words were changed into a painter's images. We transformed the actors into letters that then moved like figures about the stage. The different combinations of the letters created different verses.

In the production of Goll's *Methusalem* (1927) *stage props* (bread, a bottle, and so on) appeared in the play as characters who rebel against Methusalem.

Many other examples could be brought in to show the special character of a theatrical sign whereby it changes its material and passes from one aspect into another, animates an inanimate thing, shifts from an acoustical aspect to a visual one, and so on.

We have already stated that in the theater it is not possible as a rule and in every case to decide that what is normally called the actor's acting will not be entrusted to the scenery, just as it is not possible to foresee that music will not take over what is a phenomenon of the visual arts;

Indeed, precisely this changeability, this versatility of theatrical sign, is its specific property. And through it we explain the changeability of dramatic structure.

It is the changeability of the theatrical sign that the main difficulty of defining theatrical art lies. Definitions of this concept either narrow down theatricality to the manner of expression of our conventional drama and opera theaters or expand it to such an extent that it becomes meaningless.

It is on the basis of changes of the theatrical sign that we explain yet another theoretical confusion that hinders research of the problem of who or what is the central, creative element of dramatic expression. If we say that it is the playwright, then we are certainly correct as regards numerous cases and examples. However, we still would not grasp the essence of many historical examples of theater and could not prove that in all cases it is the word of the playwright that represents the axis of theatrical art. The entirely free theme or wholly unthematic character of improvised Italian comedies and similar forms shows that even the playwright and his text are susceptible of the changes we have discussed earlier. Similarly, we cannot regard as completely true the statement that the main bearer of theatrical art is the actor. As a proof of this I have in mind that static positioning of actors on the stage (characteristic of many dramatic styles of both past and present) which converts theater into a dialogue recital carried out by stationary figures (Théâtre d'Art, stylized German theater, Meyerhold) or anesthetizes the actor into a puppet with prearranged stilted movements, thus changing his traditional acting function into a function of a stage prop or structure. And should a modern director say that he himself is the center of dramatic creation, we can agree with his statement only in the instances whereby he demonstrates this to us. Should he speak of the theatrical art of past times when there was no director, then we cannot but disagree with him.

We do not mean by this to prove that the text, actor, and director are auxiliary or dispensable factors that merely affect the balance of theatrical structure. We wish to show only that every historical period actualizes a different component of dramatic expression and that the creative forces of one factor can replace or suppress others without decreasing the strength of the dramatic effect. We could also prove that certain periods directly demand such shifts in the balance of the dramatic structure. After all, there exist or existed theaters without authors (or without authors of note), there exist or existed theaters without actors or without great actors, and there exist and existed theaters without directors. However, if we go into the matter more deeply, we find that the actor's function is always present even though it may change into, or appear in the guise of, another function. Similarly, we must allow that what we call the organizational force of the director was present in every historical period of the theater, even when there was no director as such.

The extraordinary and contradictory statements that an actor participates in the theatrical performance even in the case of theater without actors, that the word is always an essential component of theatrical art even in the case of "wordless" theater, and that the so-called "scenic function" finds application even in theater without scenery—all such statements are justified by the specific character of the theatrical sign, dramatic structure, and dramatic material. I believe that in the preceding explanation we afforded sufficient proof of the changeability of the theatrical sign, which passes from material to material with a freedom unknown to any other art. Indeed, there is no music without tones, no poem without words, no painting without colors, and no sculpture without physical substance. Expressed more clearly, painting is not painting if words are used instead of colors, music is not music if harmony is composed of materials other than tones, and so on. Naturally, there are cases in which an artist borrows devices from another sphere of art if his own material does not achieve the desired intensity of expression. For example, Beethoven brought the musical expression of the finale of his Ninth Symphony to such an extreme that the listener finds tones insufficient and can be satisfied only by *words*. In the field of poetry, we could mention as an example of a change of device Apollinaire's *Calligrams* or the so-called "pictorial poems" invented in Bohemia. We could also seek similar examples in painting (cubism that paints with newspaper cuttings and inscriptions), and other arts. However, such examples are always the exceptions that confirm the rule about the unchangeability of material in the various other arts. As we have seen, however, in theater this changeability is the rule and the specific characteristic of theatrical art.

A number of theories of theater built around changeability have been advanced in the effort to organize or unify the multiplicity of dramatic material, devices, and procedures. The best known of these is undoubtedly Wagner's concept of theater as "collective art" (*das Gesamtkunstwerk*).

Multiplicity of devices is organized by "collective art" (*Gesamtkunstwerk*) in such a way that individual components unite in a result, provide a "collective effect." Thus the dramatic character is present not only on the stage, but also in the orchestra; we experience its inner state, development, and fate not only from words and actions we see on the stage but also from the tones we hear. Here it is a matter of the parallelism of the musical stream, the dramatic action, the words, scenery, props, lighting, and all other factors.

In his *Parsifal,* Richard Wagner was not content solely with the effect of scenery: a spring landscape on the stage was not only expressed through scenery but also by the orchestra. For the author of *Der Ring des Nibelungen,* the stage props had multiple implementations. Siegfried's sword is given a special place on stage; it is, moreover, illuminated with light and also made to glitter in the clear musical tones of the sword "leitmotiv." Wagner's dramatic characters always enter upon the stage not only as actors but also as "leitmotivs." A character's gesture is repeated in the orchestra (the pain resulting from Beckmesser's beating causes the music to limp), and the magnificence of the costumes and scenery that characterizes the guests' arrival at Wartburg is also reinforced by means of music. In every case, one could illustrate the principle of parallelism which unifies a number of dramatic devices in the sense that it brings them into parallel relationship.

This principle of "collective art" (*Gesamtkunstwerk*) assumes that the intensity of dramatic effect, that is, the strength of the spectator's impressions, is directly proportional to the *number of perceptions* that synchronically flood the senses and mind of the spectator at any given moment. The task of the dramatic artist (in the Wagnerian sense) is to equalize the effects of various dramatic devices in order to produce impressions of the same impact.

Thus, this theory does not recognize changes of theatrical sign which can use different materials for its implementation. On the contrary, Wagner's *Gesamtkunstwerk* theory indirectly claims that there is no specific, unitary dramatic material but that there are diverse materials which must be kept apart and treated side by side. Accordingly, there is no dramatic art as such, but there are music, text, actor, scenery, stage props, and lighting, which collectively make up dramatic art. Thus dramatic art cannot exist by itself but only as a collective manifestation of music, poetry, painting, architecture, histrionics, and so on. Dramatic art results as the sum of other arts.

With regard to the spectator and to the psychology of perception, I am of the opinion that this theory is incorrect. Uppermost is the problem of whether the spectator perceives acoustic and visual signs simultaneously and with the same intensity or whether he concentrates on one aspect only in the course of perception. When trying to solve this question, we must also bear in mind the fact that it is a matter of the perception of *artistic signs* and that this is a special case of perception. If the spectator's mind has to concentrate in order to understand the semiotic value of certain facts, it can certainly be presumed that it also concentrates on perceptions of a particular kind, visual or acoustical. However, should the concentrated attention of the spectator perceive both visually and acoustically, we cannot speak even in this instance of a *sum* of impressions but only of a special relation of one kind of perception to the other, of the *polarization of these perceptions.*

After all, we encounter among spectators people who visit a theater to listen to music or to a poet or to see the performance of a certain actor, and so on. However, even persons without special interests find themselves, when attending a theater, listening only to the music at one moment and captivated by the actor or enchanted by the poetic text at another moment. I would say that nearly all theatergoers fall into this category. At the same time, however, the interest of the spectator does not pass from one device to another merely by chance; it does so deliberately. If we observe the audience at a theater we see that its members turn their eyes to the same spot on the stage, that they all have the same interest in a single actor at one moment or interest in the observation of the scenery at another moment. The psychology of the spectators' perception thus prevents us from accepting the assumptions of the Wagnerian theory of "collective art."

Moreover, this theory does not recognize the fact of the development of theatrical art, about which I have already spoken and from which I have drawn examples. Theatrical art has existed without music, there have been theaters without scenery, directors have produced theater without actors, the commedia dell'arte was a theater without authors, as well as without so-called dramatic plot. Nevertheless, they were dramatic manifestations that by no means left a void in the soul of the spectator. If it were true that dramatic art is the sum of various arts (*Gesamtkunstwerk*), there would, for example, be no theater of artistic expression whose sole means would be the actor himself, that is, an actor without stage, words, music, scenery, and so on. And indeed recognition as a theatrical performance must be accorded even to a pantomime that is conducted in an empty circus ring solely by the actions of a player. There are numerous examples (such as the famous clowns Grock, Fratellini, and others) that the actor's actions by themselves can captivate the audience.

I would say that the Wagnerian theory conceals rather than reveals the essence of theatrical art: it surrounds theater with so many other arts that the special quality of theatricality dissolves and disappears. We lose sight of it.

However, it is not our intention to revive the dispute over *Gesamtkunstwerk*. I chose this matter merely as an example of the problems that arise as soon as we fail to understand or to take into account the special property of the material and devices of dramatic expression about which I have been speaking. Apart from the dispute over *Gesamtkunstwerk,* one could also mention other theories of theatrical art which are similarly confused because their authors, unable or unwilling to understand the special character of dramatic material, too uncautiously transferred the relations of poetry, painting, music, and other arts to dramatic art.

I commenced my study with a quotation from Zich and I should like to conclude by returning to Zich's views. We saw that even Zich, at the beginning of his *Aesthetics of Dramatic Art,* could not give a satisfactory definition of dramatic art. Although no adherent of *"Gesamtkunstwerk,"* still he did not have the audacity to maintain unreservedly that dramatic art is a *"single* art and not a *combination* of several arts." According to Zich the specific character of theatrical unit is the *combination* of "two simultaneous, inseparable, but *heterogeneous,* components, that is, visual components (optical) and audible components (acoustical)."

However, even this "combination" does not prevent us from seeking and finding a unity in dramatic art, from declaring that it is a single, integral art. The binary character of the materials, that is, the visual and acoustical character of dramatic devices, does not negate the unity of the essence of theater art.

Since the acoustical and the visual can change places on the stage, it may happen that one of the components submerges below the surface of the spectator's conscious attention. For example, the meaning of heard dialogue may push the spectator's perception of dramatic gestures, dramatic appearance, scenery, lighting, and so on, into the background, or conversely, it may happen that witnessed dramatic action nullifies acoustical perceptions (words, music, murmuring, and so forth).

Let us note, furthermore, that the silent film was also once called visual *theater* and that the radio play could be called acoustical *theater.* Thus the specific character of theater art does not lie in the division of its devices into acoustic and visual one. It is necessary to seek the essence of theater art elsewhere.

It is my belief that with our analysis of the changeability of the theatrical sign we have undertaken a task that can test the trustworthiness of many definitions of theatrical art and decide whether those definitions make provision for the old and the new types of theater that have originated in different social structures, in different historical periods, under the influence of different poetic or dramatic personalities, as the result of many technical inventions, and so on. I am also of the opinion that we should restore respect for the old theory of theatrical art which sees its essence in *acting*, in *action.*

In this light, the theatricality of dramatic character and that of place and that of plot will not appear to us as things permanently separated from one another. Moreover, the relationship among these three components of drama will not appear to us as a relationship among three *separate and individual theatrical arts* that are parallel without touching one another and amount to a "collective theatricality" whose success intensifies the greater the number of autonomous arts participating in its structure. One should recognize the invalidity of the notion of the "relative nonparticipation of the scenic image" in the dramatic whole, a notion that could "even maintain that the scenic image (dramatic place) is *not* a fundamental component of a dramatic work, for the reason that it can be reduced from extreme elaborateness down to the minimum of *pure space* merely demarcated architecturally."[2]

Action, taken as the essence of dramatic art, unifies word, actor, costume, scenery, and music in the sense that we could then recognize them as different conductors of a single current that either passes from one to another or flows through several at one time. Now that we have used this comparison, let us add that this current, that is, dramatic action, is not carried by the conductor that exerts the least resistance (dramatic action is not always concentrated only in the performing actor) but rather theatricality frequently is generated in the overcoming of obstacles caused by certain dramatic devices (special theatrical effects when, for instance, action is concentrated solely in the words or in the actor's motions or in offstage sounds, and so on), in the same way that a filament fiber glows just because it has resistance to an electric current.

Of course, we can speak of the relative nonparticipation of place (that is, scenery and sets) in drama and in dramatic art, but this nonparticipation should not be regarded as a permanent property of every instance of dramatic place but precisely as the property of a *certain type of theater,* a particular drama, a particular method of direction, and so forth. The action value, that is, the theatricality, of place in the English theater of the Elizabethan dramatists consisted merely in changes indicated by inscriptions hung on the stage: the terrace below the castle; the throne room;

a chamber; a cemetery; a battlefield.   The dramatic action of place consisted solely in such announcements.   It is true, that our theaters have not deviated from this method of indicating dramatic place, since it is all the same (precisely with regard to action as an element of drama) whether a change of scene is indicated by an inscription or by a costly stage set of a terrace, throne room, cemetery, battlefield, and so on.

Modern theater begins the very moment scenery is evaluated according to the function it fulfills in the actual dramatic action.   The fact that the Théatre d'Art in the nineties restricted its scenery to "a backdrop and a number of movable curtains" has to be explained, from our viewpoint, as a recognition of the real function of stage scenery in plays whose theatricality and action are created verbally (Maeterlinck).   If the German Shakespearian stage was limited to a Gothic arch or column against a blue backdrop, it was the result of the awareness that a stage set participates in a Shakespearian play solely as a simple scenic sign informing the spectator of the change of scene.

The new limitations in stage art resulting from Russian constructivism spring from the idea of dramatic performance which is manifested by *the player's movements* and everything that serves these movements: acrobatic props or contraptions, a movable wall or floor, and so on.

From the viewpoint of dramatic action the theatricality of music can be evaluated solely according to the part it has in *the acting out of the play.*   Thus, scenic musical forms are either *musical scenery* or *music as action.*   All the difficulties that arise for the modern composer of opera and for theories of opera stem from the inability or impossibility of recognizing their division, of defining music action.

The examples I have employed show clearly that there are no permanent laws or invariable rules for the unification of dramatic devices via the flow of dramatic action.   In its autonomous development, which is an integral feature in the development of every art, the theater actualizes different aspects of theatricality at different times.   For example, Maeterlinck's symbolism actualizes the verbal text as the bearer of dramatic action (Materlinck's play *Les Aveugles is acted out* through the dialogue of immobile actors conversing on stage).   Russian constructivism, on the other hand, *acts* by means of the dance or the "biomechanical" movements of the actor.

The changeability of the hierarchical scale of components of dramatic art corresponds to the changeability of the theatrical sign. I have attempted to throw light on both. I wanted to demonstrate the changeability that make stage art so varied and all-attractive but at the same time so elusive of definition. Its protean metamorphoses have sometimes even caused the very existence of a theatrical art to be doubted. Existence as an autonomous art was attributed to the dramatic poem, to histrionics, to painting and to music—but not to "theatrical art." It was only a combination of separate arts. Theater had not located either its core or its unity. I have shown that it has both, that it is one and many like the Triune God of Saint Augustine.

Notes

1. Otakar Zich, *Estetika dramatického umění* [Aesthetics of Dramatic Art] (Prague: 1931), p. 45.

2. Otakar Zich, ibid., p. 45.

8. Dramatic Text as a Component of Theater

Jiří Veltruský

This paper proposes to analyze one of the fundamental components of theatrical structure, the dramatic text. It does not seek to examine all the aspects of its theatricality—that would be impossible within the limited space of a single article—but rather to focus on those features of the play which in a general way determine its place in the structure of theater.

The fact that at present many stage directors take great liberties with the written text will be disregarded here. Theory can derive little benefit from the polemics provoked by this practice, which have centered especially around the so-called avant-garde directors. It is too often forgotten that Stanislavskij, too, used to interfere with the work produced by the dramatist.[1] And we just do not know how the problem was dealt with in the past—not even how Shakespeare the actor treated his own plays.

In any event, the theoretical implications of those practices we do know about are so enormous that they would require a special study. Suffice it to say that sometimes by tampering with the text the stage director and the actors bring out points that the author himself then perceives as defects in his drama, even as a literary work. The present form of *R.U.R.,* for instance—established in its second edition—differs in many respects from the first edition because Karel Čapek adopted all the changes made in the first theatrical performance. Only two factors are relevant for the present study. On the one hand, the dramatic text performed in theater belongs to the dramatic genre, whether it is or not identical in its direct speeches with what the dramatist wrote (if the stage director's changes have replaced its dramatic structure by a narrative or lyric structure, it no longer falls within the scope of what is to be examined here). On the other hand, the text exists with all its structural features before the other components of the theatrical structure are created; the fact that it may undergo further modifications in the course of their creation is of minor importance.

"Dramatický text jako součást divadla," *Slovo a slovenost,* 7 (1941), pp. 132-134. Translated by Jiří Veltruský.

Drama as Literature and Its Performance in the Theater

The unending quarrel about the nature of drama, whether it is a literary genre or a theatrical piece, is perfectly futile. One does not exclude the other. Drama is a work of literature in its own right; it does not need anything but simple reading to enter the consciousness of the public. At the same time, it is a text that can, and mostly is intended to, be used as the verbal component of theatrical performance. But some forms of theater prefer lyric or narrative texts to drama; theater enters into relation with literature as a whole, not just with the dramatic genre.

Dramatic dialogue and the plurality of actors

The primary distinctive feature of drama as a literary genre is that its language is rooted in dialogue, while lyric and narrative derive from monologue. As a result, the semantic construction of a play relies on the plurality of contexts that unfold simultaneously, relay, interpenetrate, and vainly strive to subjugate and absorb one another. Each one of them is associated with a different character.

The theatrical counterpart of the complicated relationship between the semantic contexts is very simple: each character is usually enacted by a different actor. It may seem that this goes without saying and is due to simple technical reasons. But it is not so. Much more often than not, only one character speaks at any given moment because in dialogue the speakers alternate. It would be feasible for one actor to enact them all. That is what actually happens in some forms of theater. For instance, in folklore, certain tellers of traditional tales put on a solo theatrical performance, impersonating the characters of the tale, miming their gestures and even complicated actions, constantly moving from spot to spot and changing the pitch, the loudness, and the speed of the delivery in the course of the dialogue in accordance with the alternation of speakers.[2]

When a separate actor stands for every character, the spectator continuously perceives all the participants in a dialogue, not just the one who says something at a given moment. This leads him to project each semantic unit into all the competing contexts immediately, without waiting until the other characters react one way or the other to what is being said. Yet this is precisely what distinguishes dramatic dialogue from the ordinary kind.

The mere presence of the actors representing all the participants signals the coexistence of several contexts. Moreover, in this arrangement, dramatic action is rarely limited to the current speaker. Significantly, the simultaneous representation of more than one character by a single actor can usually be found in the performance of a narrative, rather than a dramatic, text. Narrative dialogue differs from the dramatic chiefly in that it emphasizes the succession of speeches rather than the simultaneous unfolding and interplay of the contexts from which they spring.

Direct speeches, author's notes, and their transposition
One of the fundamental oppositions within drama as a literary work is between direct speeches and author's notes and remarks, usually though somewhat misleadingly called the stage directions. In theatrical performance, these notes are eliminated, and the resulting gaps in the unity of the text are filled in by other than linguistic signs. This is not an arbitrary process but essentially a matter of transposing linguistic meanings into other semiotic systems. Yet, even where it endeavors to be as faithful as possible, it necessarily brings about important modifications in the meanings themselves. The whole semantic structure of the work is recast. The extent of the change depends mainly on the number and weight of author's notes in the text, that is to say, on the importance of the gaps created by their deletion.

In so far as such gaps disrupt the continuous flow of meanings, the play tends to disintegrate into separate roles or parts and to abandon those parts to the actors as mere components of the stage figures they are to create. The less pronounced such gaps are, the more the language tends to keep its unity. If this tendency gets the upper hand, the creative freedom of the actor is confined within fairly narrow limits; the stage figure he constructs is much more absorbed by the language of the play than his lines are absorbed by the stage figure. Maeterlinck's plays, especially the early ones, are an outstanding case in point. Significantly, it was in his production of Maeterlinck's *La mort de Tintagiles* that Meyerkhold for the first time achieved, to his own satisfaction, the "stylized theater" of which he had been dreaming; incidentally, in the whole of the first two acts of *La mort de Tintagiles,* not a single speech is interrupted by a stage direction.

The relative weight of direct speeches and of author's notes in the dramatic text is also reflected in various types of relations among stage figures (and characters) that arise on stage. Where the deletion of the notes does not open really important gaps, these relations tend to remain chiefly on the plane of pure meanings, characteristic of language as a semiotic system: the simultaneous and successive interplay of semantic contexts, their reciprocal tensions, their striving to decompose each other's unity of sense. All variable relations between characters are more or less perceived against the background of constant relations that give them a broader perspective; that, of course, does not prevent such constant relations from drawing their own concreteness from the variable ones as the play unfolds. More important gaps open the way for what might be called material relations, that is, for action in the narrow sense of the word. When such relations among stage figures prevail over the purely semantic ones, all that is variable in them becomes more important than what is constant. Single physical acts multiply and attract so much attention that they overshadow the basic, less variable but immaterial relations between semantic contexts. The momentary superiority of one character over another, which shifts from one situation to the next, almost totally obscures the general hierarchy of all the characters which remains constant for the whole play.

Dramatic text and theatrical space

All the relations between stage figures and characters are projected into space. They constitute the so-called dramatic space, a set of immaterial relations that constantly changes in time as these relations themselves change.[3] Of course variability is possible only against the background of something constant. Where the purely semantic, immaterial relations between whole contexts are veiled by the variable material relations between stage figures or, to put it differently, where the balance of dramatic space is not maintained by the constant forces deriving from the linguistic component of the performance, dramatic space must draw its stable forces from somewhere else. That is the function of scenery or scenic objects that are semantically independent signs—the stage set does not substantially change during a given situation. Wherever the dramatic space contains a constant element of this kind, it may itself expand, through its variable components, beyond the limits of the stage (I am referring to the interplay between the actor and the spectator on the one hand and the so-called imaginary stage, that is, the audible off-stage action, on the other). It can also restrict itself at given moments to small parts of the stage. So the existence and importance of the scenic set, too, depend on the structure of the dramatic text or, more precisely, on the extent to which the continuity of meaning is disrupted by the deletion of author's remarks. The more adequate the constant relations between semantic contexts are as a background to the variability of the dramatic space, the more semantically vague can the scenic set become. In an extreme case, it may even lose all independent meaning of its own, receiving different meanings as they are bestowed upon it by other theatrical components (compare the localization through dialogue in Elizabethan theater). The meanings the set receives in this way are not of course as constant as its own, independent meaning. The set merges with the stage, a delimited, semantically unspecified playing area.

The construction of the stage, its shape and location, is determined by the needs of the performance. Like all other components of theater, the stage depends, though in a variable degree, on the structure of the dramatic text; since the auditorium is inseparably connected with the stage, we can say that the arrangement of the entire theatrical space depends to some extent on the structure of the dramatic text. In Elizabethan theater, for example, the use of the upper stage, not radically different, it seems, from certain spectators' rooms, corresponded to the intimate relationship the plays tended to set up with the audience. The presence of some spectators on stage—as well as the strict separation of the boxes from the galleries, and especially from the pit—corresponded to the same tendency, since it turned the spectators on stage and in the boxes into something like performers in relation to the other spectators, especially those standing in the pit. Similarly, the immense dimensions of the auditorium in classical Greek theater satisfied the striving of tragedy to make language predominate over the actor and to make the stage figure, as created by the actor, so abstract that it remains under the threshold of consciousness as merely a fairly irrelevant carrier of a function.

The idea that the stage and the entire theatrical space are partly dependent on the dramatic structure seems to conflict with the experience of many avant-garde stage directors. They condemn the picture-frame stage because they feel the relations between actors and audience need to be thoroughly recast. Yet in most cases this condemnation remains purely theoretical; buildings with a different stage and auditorium are not available. With very few exceptions, however convincingly he may write about the need to reorganize the whole theatrical space, the stage director must, in practice, use the traditional picture-frame stage. Even detailed projects for a new theater, such as Gropius's and Piscator's Total Theater[4] or Burian's and Kouřil's Theater of Work,[5] remain on paper for lack of financing. However, the contradiction may be more apparent than real. A theatrical performance is ephemeral by its very nature, while the construction of a theater building is, usually, a long-term venture. Therefore, it takes time for the theatrical space to adjust to the requirements of the dramatic structure. Such a time lag must often have occurred in the history of theater, especially when a new dramatic structure emerged gradually. And as regards avant-garde theater, nobody could claim that it is a new structure which has already taken shape; by its very vocation, it is experimental and widely diversified, each initiator pushing his experiments in a different direction.

Moreover, a negative proof that theatrical space is more dependent on dramatic structure than the other way round was given when a new theater, which could have satisfied all the ambitions of Meyerkhold Tajrov, Vaxtangov, Piscator, Schlemmer, Honzl, E. F. Burian, and all the others, was constructed in Paris in the hope that it would give rise to work comparable to theirs. It did not stimulate the development of a new structure, nor attract stage directors, and it had finally to be converted into a cinema.[6]

Dramatic text and music

So far, little attention has been paid to the intricate problems of the semiotics of music. Therefore, I must limit myself to a few observations.

As a component of theater, music has its starting point in the dramatic text. This applies both to vocal music and to musical accompaniment of the spoken word. In both functions, the musical structure is connected with the sound structure of the text. The possibilities of setting a dramatic text to music or of composing music to be played during its declamation are delimited by the phonic line—*ligne phonique*—of the text itself.

The manner and the degree of that delimitation are variable, depending on the nature of the phonic line. For instance, the text may require to be set to music and, at the same time, impose little limitations upon the musical creation. Such is especially the case of a text written in what is called sung verse.[7] But the phonic line of a text can also be of a nature and intensity such that a composer attempting to set the text to music must make a strenuous search within the repertory of musical means in order to discover those that come closest to the phonic line concerned. He may even be obliged to infringe certain canonized musical norms, for instance consonance (cf. Leoš Janáček's transcriptions of the intonations of speech into musical tones). There are also cases where the phonic line of the text resists its being set to music.

Therefore, the possibilities of theatrical music are, one way or another, determined by the language of drama. That is also attested by the special difficulties that arise when the libretto of an opera is translated into another language, as well as by the many textual modifications which some composers make. On the other hand, even if the dramatic text is its starting point, music, especially operatic music, often tends to eliminate it from the theatrical structure altogether. The observation Meyerhold made in connection with his staging of Wagner's *Tristan and Isolde,* namely that opera is much closer to mime than to the performance of drama, is relevant here. In so far as that is true, theatrical music is outside the scope of the present study.

In any event, theatrical music is not as closely bound up with the dramatic text as the actor's performance. Even when they sound the most alike, the components of music and the sound components of the text belong to two entirely different semiotic systems. By contrast, the same sound components of the text enter right into the stage figure, becoming part of the actor's voice performance.

Predetermination of the Stage Figure by the Text

Independent movements
Semantically independent movements are transpositions of the meanings conveyed by the author's notes, remarks, and comments. Apart from that, they are often directly called for, therefore predetermined, by

the dialogue that refers to them while they are being carried out, for example:

Hamlet: Come on, sir.
Laertes: Come my lord.
(They play.)
Hamlet: *One.*
Laertes: No.
Hamlet: Judgment!
Osric: A hit, a very palpable hit.
Laertes: Well, *again!*
King: *Stay, give me drink.* Hamlet this pearl is thine; *Here's to thy health. Give him the cup.*
Hamlet: I'll play this bout first; *set it by awhile. Come.* (They play again.) *Another hit.* What say you?
Laertes: A touch, a touch; I do confess't.
King: Our son shall win.
Queen: He's fat and *scant of breath. Here, Hamlet, take my napkin, rub thy brows. The queen carouses to thy fortune, Hamlet* [. . .]

(William Shakespeare, *Hamlet,* V, 2)

Elsewhere, there is a gap in verbal communication, and the speech following it reacts to the physical action which occurred in the meantime. In the following example, the last verse reacts to the movement ordered in the stage direction, which is itself really redundant.

Laertes: [. . .]
Hold off the earth awhile,
Till I have caught her once more in mine arms.
(Leaps in the grave.)
Now pile your dust upon the quick and the dead [. . .].

Whether a movement is determined by the dialogue or by the author's notes, the actor is given considerable leeway in his choice of the specific means by which to carry out the movement, since only its global sense, never exactly transposable from language into the action of the muscles, is imposed on him.

Accessory movements

The actor also complements the dramatic text by the kind of movements that help to shape the meaning of the speeches. Movements belonging to this second category are often numerous and important even when a play with few authorial notes is performed. They, too, are far from being completely at the actor's discretion. They are there to convey meanings contained in the written text but hardly conveyable by the vocal resources on which spoken language relies:

1. The emphasis marked by the italics in the following speech from Ibsen's *John Gabriel Borkman:* "You deserted the woman you *loved!* Me, me, me!" cannot be created by intensity, since the peak of loudness is reached at the end of the triple exclamation that follows. The meaning of the graphical sign will almost automatically be transposed into a gesture.

2. The ironical meaning of a word, which may be signaled by quotation marks, cannot be adequately expressed by voice coloring when the phonic line of the speech is dominated by the continuous undulation of intonation, because an abrupt change in voice coloring would break up the continuity of the intonation; so the irony must be signified by a gesture, a grimace, and so forth.

3. Gestures are also quite often used to mark the articulation of a syntactically complicated sentence, signaled by diacritics in the text but perhaps beyond the scope of the actor's vocal resources.

4. Some meanings have no signifier of their own in the written text because they derive from the sense of the whole context, as, for instance, when a speech is addressed to a specific character who is not explicitly indicated in any way. The reader recognizes the addressee because of the overall sense of the speech concerned, though perhaps only at the end of the speech or when the addressee responds. In the theater, the actor must usually face his addressee from the very beginning of the speech. All this comes out more clearly in the frequent cases where a character first replies to what another said and then immediately, within the same speech, speaks to a third.

5. Deictic gestures also belong to this category, especially when they accompany such deictic pronouns or adverbs as reveal the reality to which they refer only in conjunction with the context of the speech or with the extralinguistic situation. What I have in mind here is utterances like: "He

was the one." In the written play, this needs no authorial note when the reader already knows who the culprit is. In theatrical performance, it would be very odd—indeed it would be a striking artistic device behind which we should perceive the hand of the stage director—if it were not accompanied by a deictic gesture.

6. Lexicalized gestures often accompany linguistic clichés, as when a glass is lifted to the words: "To your health."

7. Instinctive movements that in fact are physiologically conditioned but function for the audience as signs underlining the meaning of the speech they accompany (distortion of the face in a scream, and so on).

Since the accessory movements receive their meanings from the speech that they accompany, and since they mostly have little or no independent meaning of their own, their specific form adapts itself to the speech, especially to its phonic line.

Movements and voice performance
The dominant position of a sound component manifests itself through its free evolutions, which are independent of the intrinsic tendencies of the others. Three sound components—intonation, voice coloring, and intensity—are in this respect particularly important for the construction of dramatic dialogue because they correspond to the three fundamental types of dialogue:

1. *Intonation* in a dominant position tends to undulate continuously. It also tends to loosen the direct relation of single language units to the realities they refer to, to make speech flow smoothly; this enables the meanings to enter into complicated mutual relations. In dialogue, the undulation of intonation freely crosses the borders between successive speeches. This reveals unexpected semantic shifts and brings into focus hardly perceptible connotations because such shifts throw the usual meaning of the words out of balance. It generates all kinds of faint and fleeting connections between the words.[8] The author interrupts the continuity of intonation as little as possible by his notes. Indeed, dramatists as different from each other as, for example, Maurice Maeterlinck, Oscar Wilde, and Karel Čapek, the outstanding common aspect of whose plays is the dominance of intonation, all make an exceptionally sparing use of author's notes.

Finally, intonation aims to restrict semantically independent move-ments—actions in the physical sense—because they perturb its free and smooth undulation. It gives scope mainly to such movements as follow its own lead, without usurping attention either by the wealth of their own meanings or by their striking materiality—in other words, to movements that are considerably stylized,[9] to more or less lexicalized conventional gestures and to deictic gestures.

2. *Voice coloring* or *timbre* tends, by its frequent and abrupt changes, to break up speech into a multitude of independent segments that are sep-arated from each other by what might be called semantic hiatuses. Every speech is hermetically sealed off, as it were, from those before and after it. Moreover, it is generally divided into separate segments, each of which points directly to some psychological feature or momentary state of mind of the character who says it. The cohesion of each semantic context is relegated to the background by a rapid sequence of emotional responses. The dialogue frequently turns into physical activity which is largely arbi-trary and unforseeable, since it is motivated by purely emotive causes. The author's notes and remarks are numerous because the concrete changes in voice coloring cannot be predetermined by the construction of the speech alone and so must be explicitly indicated by the notes.

But this means that it is not the sound components of the literary text that give rise to the specific voice components of the stage figure. These spring rather from elements transposed from a different material: the emotive qualities of the direct speeches on the one hand and the directions given in the author's notes on the other.

3. *Intensity* in a dominant position markedly divides the speech into segments ordered in a clear hierarchy of expiratory stresses. The borders between successive speeches are underlined by striking intonational cadences which end nearly all of them. The distinctions between single contexts tend to be very pronounced and every single speech is formulated in such a way as to recall the context to which it belongs.

In theatrical performance, the relationship between language and physi-cal movement varies, as does language itself, depending on the combina-tions into which intensity enters with the other sound components of the text. The movements may be numerous, in which case they tend to be semantically independent of the speeches, or they may be extremely limited in scope and number. Especially important in this connection is whether it is voice coloring or on the contrary intonation that comes closest to the dominant intensity in the hierarchy of sound components. But as a rule physical movements tend to be strongly typified. In periods when intensity dominates the sound structure, the actor's movements are not infrequently subjected to a convention and even to some degree of lexicalization.

Constant components and features
The sound structure of the dramatic text also tends to predetermine the set of so-called constant components or features of the stage figure, such as the name of the character, the actor's physical constitution and characteristics, the costume, the actor's face or mask, the general pitch, loudness, and color of his voice, and so forth, as well as certain more or less permanent features of the variable components, for instance a given actor's characteristic gestures or voice inflections, the way he articulates certain words, and so on. They have the double function of unifying all the variable components of the same figure and distinguishing it from all the others. In fact, it is this double function, not the constancy, that characterizes them. They need not all be really constant. Indeed, certain theatrical structures make them as variable as possible and reduce the opposition between constant and variable components to that between components which vary occasionally and those which vary all the time.

The semiotics of these components has not yet been really studied, so I can give just a few indications:

1. The name of the character, which comes from the text, may be semantically poor, serving merely to indicate the character's sex (Mary, Charles); or it may not even do that, as is often the case in Maeterlinck. However, the name can also be used to convey a variety of meanings, such as the nationality of the character (foreign name), the main features of his personality (Sir Toby Belch and Sir Andrew Aguecheek in *Twelfth Night,* the conventional characters in *commedia dell'arte*), etc. It can even assume a whole cluster of precise meanings and shades of meaning (the name of a real person intimately known to the audience or the name of a famous and much discussed character like Electra, Antigone, Faustus, St. Joan).

2. The physical constitution and characteristics can best develop their semiotic potential in the performance of difficult and exacting movements and when the body is partly or wholly stripped. If these elements are to assume a heavy load of meanings, the costume takes a subordinate position: it must not hamper the actor's movement, nor distract attention from his body. Many illustrations of this principle can be found in Tajrov's work. But the costume can also have the contrary function, to conceal the actor's body. It may serve, for instance, to prevent the body from attracting undue attention when it is the text that is to dominate the whole dramatic structure (classical Greek tragedy).

3. When it is subject to strong convention, the costume can convey very rich and diversified meanings. Convention may link a specific costume with a traditional or famous character. Harlequin's or Pierrot's costumes have perpetuated that link far beyond the *commedia dell'arte.* Another, though in many respects different, case in point is Hamlet's black costume, certain modern stage directors deliberately produced a shock by the mere fact of dressing him otherwise. However, convention may also operate in an entirely different way, as in Chinese theater, where costume is composed of a great number of lexicalized signs.[10]

Costume can also acquire a great semantic charge without the help of any convention whatever. An interesting case is reported by Stanislavskij. After watching a performance of *The Seagull,* Čexov asked him to play Trigorin in torn shoes and checked trousers. Here is Stanislavskij's comment:

Trigorin in *The Seagull* was a young writer, a favorite of the women—and suddenly he was to wear torn shoes and checked trousers! I played the part in the most elegant of costumes—white trousers, white vest, white hat, slippers, and a handsome make-up.

A year or more passed. Again I played the part of Trigorin in *The Seagull*—and during one of the performances I suddenly understood what Čexov had meant.

Of course, the shoes must be torn and the trousers checked, and Trigorin must not be handsome. In this lies the salt of the part: for young, inexperienced girls it is important that a man should be a writer and print touching and sentimental romances, and the Nina Zarachnayas, one after the other, will throw themselves on his neck, without noticing that he is not talented, that he is not handsome, that he wears checked trousers and torn shoes.[11]

As one of the constant components of the stage figure, the face presents certain problems which distinguish it from all the others. This is mainly due to its inherent semiotic quality which is very strong, both in its variable and in its constant features. The movement of facial muscles is one of man's most effective resources in expressing his personality and state of mind. At the same time, the face is by the far the most important of the characteristics by which we recognize an individual. Its features are more often than not interpreted as signs of a person's mentality, personality, intelligence, temperament, even his way of life, background, and so forth. Finally, what a speaker does with his facial muscles significantly complements his speech. None of these semiotic qualities of the face can be ignored in theater. They must be either exploited or neutralized. Since they draw on the variable features of the face as much as on the constant ones, there are certain problems inherent in using it as one of the constant components of the stage figure, as may be illustrated by the effects obtained by "sculpting" the actor's face with a kind of putty: this may increase the constant semiotic potential of the face but it immobilizes certain facial muscles and therefore reduces the expressive potential of their movement.

To neutralize the semiotic qualities of the face, an immobile mask is used in some forms of theater. That was probably the main function of the mask in classical Greek tragedy; it was the dramatist's word rather than the play of facial muscles that gave the face its specific meanings. But in other dramatic structures, the mask is used to increase the role of the face among the constant components. On the other hand, in the many periods when makeup is systematically used, the fact of leaving the face bare may be a means of reducing, or even neutralizing its semiotic potential because it signals that no importance is to be attached to the face and its movements; bareness produces the opposite effect with respect to the actor's face than with respect to his body.

Through theatrical convention, the face can be made to convey an enormous variety of meanings, some of which are entirely unrelated to its semiotic qualities in everyday life. Particularly rich material of this kind can be found in Chinese theater where highly complicated makeup, the uniform coloration of the face and the lack of makeup, all three lexicalized, are combined with the play of facial muscles.[12] It would not be altogether surprising if further study revealed that here the semiotic function of the dynamic play of the muscles has been dissociated from that of the face as one of the constant components.

5. As regards the constant voice features, the particular relationship that exists between voice coloring and intonation is especially important. Wherever intonation prevails, the color of the voice is relegated to the lowest place in the hierarchy of sound components and vice versa. In this most subordinate position intonation asserts itself mainly as the general pitch of the voice, coloring as its constant, characteristic color. The sound structure of the text determines the component that will take this position but does not determine the concrete quality of that component. It determines, for instance, that the pitch of each figure will be relatively immobile but not that this or that figure will have a high, low, or medium pitch, let alone a specific register; it determines that each figure's voice will keep approximately the same color during the whole performance but not whose voice should be raucous, whose squeaky, whose melodious, and so on; that may, however, be indicated by the nature of the parts.

The general color of the voice is capable of carrying a considerable semantic load; it can denote the character's sex, age, some features of his mentality (for example, tenderness, rudeness, shyness), and so forth. Therefore, in a play dominated by intonation, even the set of constant components can be dominated to a large extent by linguistic means. By contrast, since the pitch has a very low semantic potential, the dominant position of voice coloring in the text makes it necessary to draw heavily on extralinguistic components in constructing the constant features of the stage figure.

Stage figure as a structure of signs
The stage figure is a complicated structure of signs which includes all the components, whether linguistic or extralinguistic, whether constant or variable, and so on. But, though integrated, it is a structure of structures. All the movements of a figure also compose a structure of signs whose parts are all interrelated and hierarchically arranged. So do its constant components and features. And so do its voice components. They are struc-

tures within the structure. The whole structure of the stage figure is made up of links by which they are connected. But there is a fundamental difference between the structure of the voice performance and the others. In its general outline, the voice performance is a direct translation of the sound contour of the text which exists before any theatrical performance. This enables the text to predetermine, though in a variable degree, the stage figure in all its aspects.

The fundamental relationship just mentioned exists even where the actors improvise, as for instance in folk theater, Chinese theater, *commedia dell'arte,* and so forth. Improvisation is only a different way of performing a play. As a rule, the actor's freedom in the choice of both the verbal and the nonverbal means he may use in his improvisation is restricted by stringent norms.[13]

The actors's creation can never fully escape the obligations imposed on him by the dramatic text. It is true that he alone creates all the extralinguistic components of the stage figure. But even here, his scope is not unlimited. He is very restricted in his creative freedom when the voice performance is strongly dominated by a component such as intonation, which is already so concretely shaped in the text that relatively little can be added in the performance. The actor must adapt himself and mold the extralinguistic resources accordingly, so that they do not disrupt the sound dominant. In practice, this means that he must limit them as much as possible, so that they do not deflect attention, because of their striking materiality, from the subtle meanings conveyed by the movements of the dominant sound component. On the contrary, when the sound structure is dominated by a component such as voice coloring, the movements and specific shape of which are predetermined by the text only in a very general way, the actor's freedom to choose his means increases. Language is subordinated to the extralinguistic resources at his disposal. An infinite variety of combinations can be found between these two extremes.

As a structure of signs, the stage figure is not only a structure of structures but also an integral part of that broader structure of signs, the whole performance. There lies another source of its predetermination by the dramatic text.

The Dramatist, the Stage Director, and the Actor

Because of the unity it presents despite its great diversity, every artistic structure appears not only as an object but also as the act of a subject.[14] This problem is far from simple at the best of times. But it is particularly complicated with regard to theatrical structure. It cannot be fully outlined, let alone analyzed, within the scope of this paper. I shall limit myself to a few, rather sketchy, remarks concerning the way in which the characteristics of the dramatic text affect the position of the subject in theatrical performance.

The characters engaged in the dialogue are subjects, let us say operative subjects. But they are subjects only in a certain degree because there is also the author. He, too, is a subject—and indeed an operative subject as well—albeit on a different level. In contrast to the characters, the author is the central subject—the subject behind the characters, the maker of all the semantic contexts to which they are respectively linked, of all the situations, of all the speeches, etc. So we have a double complication in drama as regards the subject of its structure: on the one hand, there is a plurality of subjects, let us say partial subjects, linked to the plurality of semantic contexts; on the other hand, there is a definite antinomy between these partial subjects and the author, who is the central subject.

However, drama is not only dialogue but also plot. In the plot, all the intrinsic contradictions, reversals, and modifications of the dramatic conflict are unified into a single whole. Just as the interpenetration of the semantic contexts gives rise to semantic shifts and reversals, so the plot provides all those semantic changes with a single motivation.

When they are viewed in the light of the plot, all the semantic shifts that abound in drama converge to a single point from which the whole structure can be seen in perspective, so to speak. It is on this spot that we find the one central operative subject of the dramatic structure. Though it remains in the background, this central subject always makes its presence and its operation felt as the conveyor of the plot and the source of its "proportionality," momentum, and unity.

When it comes to the theatrical performance of the text, the dramatist may or may not retain this key position. That will be determined mainly by the structure of the text itself. Naturally, much will depend on whether, in theatrical performance, this structure makes the linguistic components predominate over the extralinguistic, or the other way round. But the problem has other aspects as well.

The dramatist will, for instance, be perceived as the principal orginator of the theatrical structure when the way the dialogue unfolds appears necessary, inevitable. This happens particularly where the spontaneity of the characters is restricted while the differences in their basic attitudes are emphasized—in such cases fortuitous elements are generally eliminated from the dialogue and each segment of the dialogue contributes to the progression of the plot. The lack of spontaneous decisions on the part of the characters points to the dramatist as an invisible force above them, as the subject whose intention manifests itself in the orderliness of both dialogue and plot. Sophocles's tragedies provide a typical example.

The operation of the dramatist may also be emphasized when characters in specific, unique situations make statements of more general application than their immediate setting warrants. This tends to project whatever is said and done on stage onto a different plane and to relate it to certain general "truths." The speeches convey a kind of wisdom to be expected from somebody observing the action from a distance, rather than from persons directly involved, with the result that they are, to some extent, perceived as being formulated, and put into the characters' mouths, by the central subject. Many examples can be found in Shakespeare's plays.[15]

In plays which bring the emotions of the characters into the forefront, the situation of the dramatist is different. The single, partial, subjects appear to be more or less emancipated from their immediate dependence on the central subject and the dialogue looks like a chain of spontaneous reactions which reveal the characters' minds and dispositions much more than their attitude to reality. Dialogue based on momentary moods appears to progress in an extremely haphazard and tortuous manner, so that the audience largely ceases to be aware of its being organized; consequently the operation of the central subject tends to sink under the threshold of consciousness. Naturally, in drama as literature, the author makes his presence felt in such plays through frequent notes and remarks. But those are absent in the performance.

The sound structure of the text is also relevant to the problem under discussion. In the performance of a text dominated by intonation, single characters tend to dissolve in the dialogue and the author to remain continuously present in the minds of the audience.

His presence also tends to be strongly felt where intensity predominates, though here he remains more in the background and tends to manifest himself through the characters. Since every speech is quite clearly related to specific context to which it belongs, emphasis is put on the definite philosophy, purpose, or permanent psychological profile of the character. Shaw's *The Devil's Disciple* provides a good illustration. The plot is organized in such a way as to give prominence to two reversals in the hero's situation: the first comes when, in the most critical moment, he acts in a manner contrary to what all the characters expect of him; the second, when the devil's disciple turns into a minister of the gospel. But since the phonic line of the play is dominated by intensity (though in certain scenes the changes in voice coloring come fairly close to taking the upper hand), there are no reversals in the semantic context composed by Richard Dudgeon's lines. In his confrontations with the other characters, the hero reacts very clearly from first to last as "a Puritan of the Puritans," to use Shaw's description.[16]

The situation is entirely different when abrupt changes in timbre dominate the voice performance of the actors: the characters are in the forefront and the dramatist remains more or less hidden behind them. Moreover, to perform this kind of drama also raises numerous problems that are not solved in the text; the text merely indicates the direction in which the solution should be looked for.

This is where the stage director takes over from the dramatist. In the first place, he must choose actors whose constitution, physical qualities, and voice correspond to the requirements of the parts. He must also participate in the choice and molding of semantically independent movements that are numerous and very important here while the text determines them only in a very general way. He must influence and concert the intentions of individual actors in their choice of specific timbres and gestures, so as to create an integrated "psychological situation." Finally, he must direct their interplay and coordination, because the relationships between the characters keep shifting, and create the "proportionality" of the whole performance, because the proportionality of the plot tends to recede into the background under the impact of the emotionally charged dialogue and the materiality of physical action.

In the performance of a text relying mainly on timbre, the actor's freedom increases as well. The many semantic gaps in the direct speeches enable him to shape his independent movements as he sees fit. The text predetermines only their global meaning, the starting point and the outcome of every movement, not the specific means by which it is to be carried out. However, when the emancipation of the actor's performance goes beyond a certain limit, a qualitative change sets in. The stage figure becomes an independent sign and tends to clash with the semantic requirements of the text. Various inhibitions begin to afflict the actor; for instance, he keeps forgetting his lines. That is why the tendency to develop the actor's own creativity as much as possible may call for the constant intervention of a strong stage director. The decisive contribution of Stanislavskj, as a stage director, to the dominant position of the actor in the Moscow Art Theater Is a classical case in point.

Some texts seem to give the actor a considerable degree of freedom in the selection of linguistic as well as extralinguistic means and confine themselves to predetermining only the global sense of the dialogue and action. Yet even in such an extreme case as *commedia dell'arte,* the theatrical structure was predetermined by the text. Indeed, in addition to the general sense, the text in fact also prescribed the whole set of specific means that the actor had at his disposal. It did so in two different fashions. First, the name of each character designated a standard type to which a fixed set of devices was attached by convention. Second, each situation, as indicated by the text, was marked by a certain set of specific devices governed by convention too. It was only choice within these repertoires that was left to the actor's discretion. Finally, the relations between the standard characters were fixed by convention as well, so that the name of a character, as given in the text, also predetermined the character's relation to each of the others. All this goes to show that even when the actor predominates over the other operative subjects of the theatrical structure to the highest possible degree, he does so not in defiance of the text but in conformity with it.

Conclusion

Drama brings intense pressure to bear upon all the other components of theater. But none of these yields to that pressure entirely nor ceases to maintain a certain degree of resistance. This is so because each one is an integral part of an independent art: acting, music, architecture, and so on. At each moment of its development, an art can break new ground in more than one direction. But the number and the nature of these openings are not infinite. Therefore any single component of theater can respond to the requirements of drama only up to a certain point; if it went beyond this point, it would cut itself off from the art to which it belongs.

Consequently, the individual arts in their turn influence the development of dramatic literature through the intermediary of theater. Indeed, when he writes a play, the dramatist is not unaware of the existing theatrical structure and of the various openings it presents to new developments. This is true even though the play is a self-sufficient work of literature which does not necessarily require theatrical performance; the creating subject usually feels, though often unconsciously, the possible applications of his work.

We have seen, however, that the dramatist can assign to certain components of theater such a place in the dramatic structure that they will appear as pure meanings, deprived of their specific material—as, for instance, in the verbal localization of the action in so far as it eliminates the use of material scenery. Even then theater is a synthesis of all the arts because the contribution of a given art to its structure is noticeable even when that art is present only potentially.[17]

There is only one art whose participation in the theatrical structure cannot be reduced to the degree of mere potentiality. That art is acting, for, as far as we know, without acting there is no theater, at least no drama-performing theater. Craig's dream of theater without actors remained confined to his programmatic writings, while as stage director he did not go beyond reforming the actor's style. He actually anticipated that difference between program and practice even in his famous essay, "The Actor and the Übermarionette."[18]

In theater, the linguistic sign system, which intervenes through the dramatic text, always combines and conflicts with acting, which belongs to an entirely different sign system. All the other components, such as music, scenic sets, and so forth, can be eliminated by the text itself; by the same token, the intervention of the sign systems to which they belong can be reduced to "zero degree"—unless they reenter the theatrical structure through the intermediary of the actor. Therefore, the general function of drama in the shaping of the semiotics of theater can be brought out only by means of confronting the two sign systems that are invariably present, that is, language and acting.

Of all the characteristics of the semiotics of language, the most important in this connection is that meaning is so tenuously tied to sensory material—the sound components on which the linguistic meaning relies are to a large extent predetermined by the meaning itself. This enables the linguistic meaning to create the most complicated combinations and relationships. The exact opposite is true of the semiotics of acting. Here, the material bearer of the meaning—the actor's body in the most general sense—absolutely predominates over the immaterial meaning. In theater, the sign created by the actor tends, because of its overwhelming reality, to monopolize the attention of the audience at the expense of the immaterial meanings conveyed by the linguistic sign; it tends to divert attention from the text to the voice performance, from speeches to physical actions and even to the physical appearance of the stage figure, and so on.

No other semiotic system intervening in theater attains either of these extremes. Let us take the signs that make up the stage space. However they are chosen and molded, they have neither the same semantic potential as the speeches nor the same degree of reality as the actor. The meanings they convey are limited in their evolutions by being tied down to the material that bears them. In its turn, this material does not display the same degree of reality as the actor because it is an artifact.

Since the semiotics of language and the semiotics of acting are diametrically opposed in their fundamental characteristics, there is a dialectical tension between the dramatic text and the actor, based primarily on the fact that the sound components of the linguistic sign are an integral part of the voice resources drawn upon by the actor. The relative weight of the two poles of this antinomy is variable. If the linguistic sign prevails, there emerges a tendency to strip the sign embodied by the actor of its materiality, or at least some of it; that explains why Maeterlinck, Craig, and many others were so fascinated by puppets. If, on the contrary, the linguistic sign is outbalanced, its semantic potential diminishes. However, both sign systems not only check but also enrich each other. The actor gives more weight and punch to the language he voices and, in return, receives from it the gift of extremely flexible and variable meanings.

These characteristics of the sign systems which combine in theater determine what may be called the basic, and in a sense constant, structure of the components. This basic hierarchy may never materialize. But it is perceived by the audience as the background of a specific structure into which the components may be grouped in a given performance or in a given period or style. Therefore, the variability of the theatrical sign, which Honzl regards as its distinctive feature,[19] must be seen in its dialectical unity with its opposite, the stability of that sign. Though extremely variable, the theatrical sign is at the same time extraordinarily stable in that its basic, "unmarked," structure is strongly pronounced.

Notes

1. See Constantin Stanislavskij, *My Life in Art* (New York: 1956), pp. 498 ff.

2. See I. V. Karnauxova's description of a performance by Russian folktale teller P. J. Belkov, as reproduced in Petr Bogatyrev, *Lidové divadlo české a slovenské* [Czech and Slovak Folk Theater] (Prague: 1940), pp. 17 ff.

3. Otakar Zich, *Estetika dramatického umění* [Aesthetics of Dramatic Art] (Prague: 1931), p. 246.

4. Erwin Piscator, *Das politische Theater* (Berlin: 1929), pp. 122 ff.

5. Miroslav Kouřil, *Divadlo práce* [The Theater of Work] (Prague: 1938).

6. Jindřich Honzl, *Sláva a bída divadel* [Glory and Misery of Theaters] (Prague: 1937).

7. See the analysis of sung verse in old Czech in: Roman Jakobson, "Verš staročeský" [Old Czech Verse], *Československá vlastivěda*, vol. III (Prague: 1934), pp. 429 ff. Some remarks on what is likely to be a form of sung verse in modern Czech can be found in my article "Zpěvní kultura obrozenské doby" [The Song Culture of the Period of the National Revival], *Slovo a slovesnost*, VI, 1940.

8. See Jan Mukařovský, "Próza K. Čapka jako lyrická melodie a dialog" [The Prose of Karel Čapek as Lyrical Melody and Dialogue], *Kapitoly z české poetiky*, vol. II (Prague: 1948).

9. See ibid.

10. Karel Brušák, "Znaky na čínském divadle" [Signs in the Chinese Theater], *Slovo a slovesnost*, 5, 1939. The English translation appears in this anthology on pp. 59-73.

11. Constantin Stanislavskij, *My Life in Art*, pp. 358 ff.

12. See Karel Brušák, "Znaky na čínském divadle."

13. See my "Notes Regarding Bogatyrev's Book on Folk Theater"; Pierre Louis Duchartre, *The Italian Comedy* (New York: 1966), pp. 33 ff.; and Karel Brušák, "Znaky na čínském divadle."

14. The concept of subject is used here in the same sense as in modern philosophy (for example, in Ernst Cassirer's *Philosophy of Symbolic Forms*, particularly in its third volume), that is to say, as a member of the antinomy object-subject. In this sense, the subject perceives the object, acts upon the object, makes the object, and so on. The subject in this sense is that to which all mental representations or all operations and actions are attributed. Unfortunately, in the English language there is a danger of confusion. Although common usage knows such derivatives as "subjective" and "subjectivity," the term "subject" is mostly used, when there is question of art, semiotics, and so forth, in the sense of "subject matter." This danger of confusion cannot be avoided. The concept is too important to be replaced by circumlocutions or by terms that are only partly synonymous. For instance, it would be tempting to avoid the language difficulty by replacing the antinomy object-subject by the antinomy "it"—"I." But that would be misleading because it would conceal the antinomy which is inherent in the concept of subject itself: the subject can be not only "I" but also "thou"—it can be not only the first-person subject but also the second-person subject. Because of its psychological connotations and of its intrinsic paradoxicalness, the antinomy "Ego"—"other Ego" cannot help either. [Author's note to the English translation.]

15. In order to avoid any possible misunderstanding, it should be pointed out that what is discussed here is an artistic device, not the question whether or not maxims used by Shakespeare's characters reflect the sentiments, the ideas or even the *"Weltanschauung"* of the dramatist. [Author's note added to the English translation.]

16. Bernard Shaw's preface to his *Three Plays for Puritans*.

17. See Jan Mukařovský, "K dnešnímu stavu teorie divadla" [Concerning the Present State of the Theory of Theater], *Program D 41*, pp. 229 f.

18. Edward Gordon Craig, *On the Art of the Theater*, London, 1911.

19. Jindřich Honzl, "Pohyb divadelních znaků" [Dynamics of the Sign in the Theater], *Slovo a slovesnost*, VI, 1940. The English translation appears in this anthology on pp. 74-93.

9. The Hierarchy of Dramatic Devices

Jindřich Honzl

It has been, and likely will continue to be, the common case that when the dramatic works of classical antiquity are presented on the modern stage they lose their essential foundation and thus appear distorted with respect to the principal means whereby their original performance was accomplished; that is to say, they appear minus that relationship the ancient theater had with poetic language. A test for basics in the matter of staging plays is how the hierarchy of theatrical means of expression is arranged. Every adaptation of the verbal design of an ancient play to the modes of performance and dialogue techniques of a modern play inevitably contravenes the integrity and balance of the old work. What "acting" is for the modern drama and what a present-day theatrical director considers "dramatic action" are substantially different than in ancient drama, for not only have the means of expression in the modern play and modern theater changed (song, music, and dance have acquired a different function, the chorus has been eliminated, the performance of the actors is different), their relationship to one another has changed, as well.

Every handbook on the art of drama concurs with Aristotle in stating that Greek tragedy derives from the Dionysian dithyramb and from a specific innovation introduced by Aeschylus—the addition of a second reciter (a second actor) to the original chorus and single reciter. Aeschylus "restricted the role of the chorus and made dialogue the most important part" (Aristotle, *Poetics*). Nevertheless, the introduction of new devices did not automatically mean the transformation of the dithyramb into drama. The dithyramb initially embarked on its development toward drama (a process set in motion by the introduction of new devices) when the progenitor of tragedy "made dialogue the *most important part.*" The supremacy of *dialogue* over *recitation* meant the supremacy of *action* over *narration* and meant turning already existing, familiar devices to a new purpose. Through their new purpose the traditional devices also acquired a new meaning. Although the poetic devices adopted by drama from the dithyramb appeared to remain unchanged, they in fact did alter their mode of existence

"Hierarchie divadelních prostředků," *Slovo a slovesnost,* 9 (1943), pp. 187-193. Translated by Susan Larson.

by assuming a new function. And even though Aeschylus had to shift the emphasis from the chorus (the choral chant) to dialogue in order to establish the foundations of dramatic poetry, the chorus still remained an indispensable component of Greek drama and preserved the most salient features of its dithyrambic prototype. But while we still do discern dithyrambic features in the performance of the chorus, the shift in emphasis to *action*, to *acting*, amounts to a fundamental shift of function.

My crutch the faltering tread of leaden feet sustains;
My voice is plaintive like the aged swan's.
What am I but the merest murmuring of feeble lips,
The sheerest phantom of a dream?

(Euripedes: *Heracles Mad*)

This lyrical choral chant, which narrates to the audience and, simultaneously, describes an action ("My crutch the faltering tread of leaden feet sustains"), is a *dramatic* component by virtue of its function. Incorporated into the plot, inserted into the concrete device that served as the basis for the theatrical staging of Athenian tragedy, this choral dithyrambic element is the means by which the ancient tragic dramatist specified the dramatic action. In selecting his devices the Greek dramatist possessed a degree of freedom similar to that exercised by modern dramatists who prefer not to leave a single phenomenon on stage go unnoticed and who make anything visible to the audience a vehicle for their thoughts and ideas. Though the Greek poet was bound by historical precedent and tradition in the verbal expression of the dithyramb, this did not preclude the option of introducing new uses and functions for dithyrambic devices. A modern dramatist would be inclined to question the necessity of verbally specifying "faltering tread of leaden feet" for describing old men walking with the aid of a crutch if the dramatic action on stage already demonstrates this to the audience. Whether due to the structural exigencies of Greek tragedy or the concrete context of the ancient stage and style of acting, the audience had to be provided with a sound (verbal) image of what was, in fact, a visual percept. But neither does the modern playwright eschew applying verbal deixis (for that is strictly what the case in point here is) to a visual percept when he considers it necessary. Thus, for example, often in the modern theater an actress is a "devastating beauty" only because the dramatist indicates so in the dialogue or we observe "an enigmatic quality in the way she walks" only because the dramatic text refers to it. It is invariably true of both the ancient and the modern theater that for the audience only those things exist on stage which are specified by the dramatic action or by the elements of the theatrical realization; moreover, only those things exist which the audience's interpretative activity apprehends under the influence of the dramatic action. Everything else visible or potentially audible on stage remains "below the threshold" of the audience's consciousness. It is not there, it doesn't exist! The psychological ability of a spectator to focus his exclusive attention on a specific thing includes, as well, the ability to eliminate from his conscious awareness anything extraneous to the object of his concentration. For example, to be blind to the sackcloth dress of an actress around whose neck are wound strands of tinsel that glisten gold, red, and blue on her young bosom and indicate the role of a Semiramis or a Cleopatra; or to be blind to the real fact of a torn peasant shirt and focus all one's visual power instead on its brilliant whiteness that transforms anyone attired in it into a messenger from heaven, into the Archangel Gabriel or any other of the heavenly host just as benign and powerful; to be blind in this way is neither a deficiency in the human observer nor an indication of his naiveté, but rather proof of his psychological capacity for concentration, for focusing intense attention along lines designated by the drama and by the interpretative fantasy of his, the spectator's own, imagination. Therefore, we must consider the capacity for concentrated attention and the capacity to exclude from it everything extraneous to be polar attributes of one and the same perceptual faculty of the spectator. Precisely this kind of attention and perception has been assumed as normal and necessary from the standpoint of the theater and the dramatist and has been implied in all the basic techniques of staging and performance, whether in the ancient amphitheater or on the stage of a village theater. On the other hand, the so-called realistic theater at the turn of the twentieth century assumed in the spectator an *inability to see and interpret reality* through the prism of his imagination, and this necessitated, as far as staging was concerned, the presentation of *stark* reality, of reality *alone,* of *whole and complete* reality (a requirement bound to come to grief in ambitions beyond human capacity and the possibilities of the stage)—that is to say, nontheatrical perception was assumed. Dramatic verbal deixis of the type used and cultivated in particular by the ancient drama, whose dithyrambic origin made it possible for a lyrical or epic utterance to become the vehicle for the dramatic action, such verbal deixis serves as a semantic filter that enables the dramatist to create an image of the world and of people from the limited repertoire of things and the few artistic resources that the ancient actor and ancient stage technology were able to provide. Thus, for example, the fixed tragic mask of grief the actor wore and the unchanged setting of the royal palace on stage could be dramatically changed by the word, which, like a sun at the center of the poet's universe, either illuminates the stage, the actor, and the dramatic events or, conversely, casts over them a shadow of invisibility. Such a semantic filter, which does not admit images undesired by the dramatist, alters the profile of those real elements out of which the representation of a human being and his behavior is created in a play. Actions and deeds are realized visibly on the ancient stage only by means of a verbal reference to them.

Go slower, pray! Do not yourselves fatigue,
And have a pity for my ancient limbs,
Lest you fall a-laboring like a horse
That gallops up a slope with heavy load!
Whose foot is feeble, let him hold
Another by the robe and by the hand.
Let the eld give eld support.

(*Heracles Mad*)

The second excerpt from Euripedes' *Heracles Mad* is presented here to illustrate the oscillation between the dithyramb and the drama from the opposite side. If the first excerpt, in and of itself, is a lyrico-epic dithyramb changed into dramatic action by functional incorporation into the structure of the tragedy, the second excerpt, likewise in and of itself, is a dramatic apostrophe, a part of the dramatic dialogue, but which serves as an epic deictic reference within the drama. Without its imperatives the entire excerpt would belong within parentheses, as part of the "stage instructions," or belong to *description* of an action which the dramatist assigns to an actor. Still, even minus parentheses, the words of the chorus remain a *narrative* of an action performed by a player. But in the structure of an ancient play (and that means in the structure of its implementation, as well) the words acquire dramatic justification through *verbal deictic reference to action on stage,* which deixis was for Euripedes, Sophocles, and Aeschylus a basic compositional device.

For the Hellenic dramatist, no deed or action was dramatic by itself. A turn of events or action on stage became dramatic only by poetic verbal reference, which in ancient drama was an essential prerequisite for the audience's apprehension and interpretation of the play.

Behold him: on the start his head he wildly tosses,
And uttering no sound, rolls eyes ablaze with madness.
Now with mighty breath he snorts like a bull about to charge
And in a ghastly, bellowing voice calls upon the fiends of Tartarus.

(*Heracles Mad*)

In these words Euripedes has the goddess Lyssa (Madness) describe Heracles as he sets out from his home in a deranged state of mind. If this section of Euripedes' drama were to be staged in the manner that is common to modern theater, the actor who portrays Heracles would be obliged to act out the changes prescribed by the author in the text: the shaking head, the wild, blazing expression of the eyes, the labored breathing and snorting—the actor might even attempt to articulate a terrifying roar that would make both theater and stage quake. We are all familiar with stagings that have interpreted the function of the verbal expression of the ancient dramatist by actually having the actor perform narrative references to events, changes, actions, with the result that the unity of the text was destroyed or disrupted by the shouts, roars, hisses, and miming acrobatics used in realistic or expressionistic styles of acting, or by stage decor, lighting, and sound effects. Such theatrical stagings testify to the fact that the hierarchical order of the dramatic devices in ancient drama was not accounted for and that the difference in the underlying basis of ancient and modern dramaturgy was not discerned. The poem (which is what ancient tragedy has always been) was transformed from a dithyramb into drama by a device that Aristotle characterized as "action, not pure narration." But the means for realizing that "action" remained within the domain of the dithyramb, and speech retained its dominant position within the hierarchy of these devices. The dramatic action unfolded through the word, and any changes in the dramatic situation likewise were manifested through the verbal medium. In this way, then, it was possible for the word to become a device we sometimes interpret as performance and at other times as a change of scenery. It is precisely the flexibility of the dramatic sign that enables the word to become "actor" or "scenery," to take upon itself functions of other poetic devices of drama.

The Greek poet did not utilize the word to refer to something that already was being performed or shown on stage. He did not describe the action on stage, that is, he did not verbally double the stage performance. The deictic references, about which we have been speaking, were not designed to draw a parallel between the dramatic reality and a narrative about that reality. Duplication that seeks merely to achieve as close a parallel as possible diminishes the impact of the impression precisely because an exact parallelism is never attained. Discrepancies in duplication make for more of a hindrance than would a case of complete dissimilarity or total contrast. Extraverbal reality alone would have a more forceful impact on the audience than it would if accompanied by an inexact or partial verbal account, just as a verbal message produces a more vivid impression alone than with an imperfectly matching piece of extraverbal reality. The Greek theater operated on the basis not of parallelism but of polarity of impressions. That is why the ancient actor's wholly unchanged expression and immobile mask are a fitting accompaniment for Euripedes' text where it speaks of the rolling eyes, the wild, blazing expression, the labored breathing and other mimetic alterations through which the homicidal frenzy of Heracles is manifested.

The pleasure of theatrical perception always arises on the basis of an opposition between mental representation and reality. This opposition is a basic prerequisite. It is not at all to be understood as a result, because what is involved is a *synthesizing* of the opposition. Theatrical perception comes about by virtue of this opposition being overcome, by virtue of the fact that the opposition between mental representation and reality is synthesized in the spectator's act of interpretation which transforms both the representation and the reality in a flash of emotionally charged "seeing."[1]

Just as Euripedes' text refers to something *not demonstrated* by the actor, so also, in Aeschylus, for example, reference may be made to something which is *not present* on the stage but which is, nevertheless, present
in the mental representation of the spectator under the spell of the poetry:

The words have been fulfilled and now are deeds.
The earth trembles.
A rumble of thunder resounds from the sea
And fiery flashes cover the sky.

Dust swirls in the rising tempests.
Winds battle winds,
Furious with darkness.
Sea and sky have merged together.

Thus does Zeus' wrath upon me fall
And bodes me terrors I cannot escape.
O holy Mother, o Aether,
Whose all-seeing flame all things illuminates,
Thou seest me here unjustly suffering.

(Aeschylus: *Prometheus Bound*)

Poetic reference to something that does not transpire on stage we may
call *phantasma-oriented deixis,* since it specifies a dramatic action that is
realized solely in the spectator's imagination. That this "phantasma-
oriented deixis" is one the principal devices in Greek dramaturgy is evi-
denced by the fact that the deeds of highest tragedy do not, as a rule,
take place on stage but are realized either through just such a deictic reference or through aural signs (for example, shouting or calling offstage).
Agamemnon's murder and the slaying of Aegisthus and Clytemnestra (in
Aeschylus's *Oresteia*) are "hidden" in this manner from the direct view of
the audience. Sophocles' Oedipus (*Oedipus Rex*) and Haemon (*Antigone*),
who blind themselves, and Euripedes' Heracles and Phaedra (*Hippolytus*),
who slay their own children, "perform acts" through the word, through
the lamentations of the chorus who narrate an account of the deeds to the
audience. This of course does have some connection with Greek attitudes
and customs, but that is by no means all that is involved.

Actions and deeds performed on stage before an audience allow of multiple meanings and interpretations. The tragic, comic, or emotionally

neutral quality of any particular act, be it of the most horrendous or in-sipid kind, does not inhere in the act as its objective, fixed characteristic, but rather is a matter of subjective interpretation. The spectator who sees Shylock sharpening a knife on the sole of his shoe to cut a pound of flesh from Antonio's body closest to the heart, bursts out laughing in the midst of Shylock's bloodthirsty preparations and Antonio's anxiety. Roles in Shakespeare's plays did not exclude the possibility of contradictory inter-pretations on the part of the audience. In Greek drama such a possibility was excluded. And all classical periods in the evolution of the theater con-formed in this respect to ancient Greek drama. When a tragedy was per-formed, nothing but a tragic interpretation of what took place on stage was admissible. The tragic aspect of such plays is not dependent on the action or deeds, since the actions and deeds were deliberately situated by the author outside the visual field or were so situated as to be hidden from the audience. Actions and deeds are represented by a verbal exegesis that, like every verbal designation, is not a pragmatic fact open to a variety of mean-ing and interpretations but belongs within the domain of semantic and evaluative structures rigorously differentiated according to a set of poetic, ethical, and esthetic norms.

Also, the acting of the players—especially, no doubt, that of players in the ancient Greek theater—was an aesthetic system of vocal and gesticula-tory signs, and the techniques used by the players were, no doubt, differ-entiated as to use in tragedy or comedy. When, with respect to some particular piece of stage action, the ancient Greek dramatist gives the word predominance over other devices, that very fact serves as evidence of the hierarchical superiority of the word, which is used because it engages the imagination more strictly and directly into the sphere of tragedy.

It might appear that the aim of our inquiry has been to dissolve the conceptual distinction between "action" and "narration," and that we are seeking to interpret something that is basically an epic message as the dy-namic component of dramatic action. Not at all. We know that even in Greek drama, particularly in Euripedes' plays, pure narration is a recurrent compositional device. But that is not the point here. Our aim is to dem-onstrate that a narrative, while remaining in and of itself a narrative, may become a dramatic act when we view it as an integral part of the play, specifically when we have in mind a definite hierarchy of dramatic devices—and not solely of linguistic but also of staging devices. It is precisely this flexibility of the dramatic sign that makes it possible for the dramatic text in Greek tragedy to form a bond with stage presentation (in both the positive and negative sense).[2] And if we arbitrarily divide that which was originally conceived as a single structure into two separate structures, we have not properly understood the function of either linguistic or stage devices. If we wish not to get bogged down in meaningless theoretical schemes and if we wish not to use words that are mere abstractions and devoid of any substance, it is essential that we link Aristotle with the Greek poets in order to grasp the real meaning of what they considered "action, not pure narration." A theoretical construct of the art of the drama and the theater cannot be formulated in isolation. Theory and practice mutually influence and determine each other. Definitions are enlightening only if we have in mind concrete instances of practice.

We wish to conclude this critical inquiry by saying that contemporary presentations of ancient dramas will achieve higher efficacy and dramatic value not by arbitrarily destroying the given hierarchy of dramatic devices or by substituting for this hierarchy one of more recent vintage but rather by attempting to apprehend the essence of the original hierarchy, so that the *poem*—which is basically what a Greek tragedy remains—be the primary consideration of every theatrical presentation.

Notes

1. The fact that our critical inquiry is limited to literary illustrations from Greek tragedy does not imply that we would necessarily find different norms and laws governing theatrical creativity and perception in other periods during the historical evolution of the theater. On the contrary. We are aware of the fact that our hypothesis could be substantiated equally well by examples from medieval mystery plays, from the Symbolist theater at the turn of the twentieth century, and from the theater of other epochs and other movements.

To show that the medieval actor did not seek a concurrence between the verbal message and his own expression, it perhaps will suffice to quote from an essay by W. Golther (included in a book of selected essays, *Der Schauspieler,* ed. by E. Geisler, Berlin: 1926): "Every player is to step to the center (of the stage), turn to all sides, even to the rear of the stage where Christ stands. . . . (During the course of the play) the movements are clear and measured *throughout the pauses, whereas during the singing and speaking parts the actor stands still,"* (italics and parentheses my own, J.H.).

We will forgo illustrations from the Symbolist theater since they are, I trust, already well known. Indeed the very designation of the Symbolist theater as "the theater of the static" proves the thesis about a conscious reordering of the theatrical devices such that the specifically motor and gesticulatory aspect of the actor's performance was deliberately suppressed.

And finally, even the theater based on the unity and integrity of the actor's performance achieved its best results from the ignescent polarity of the opposition between the mental representation evoked by the text and the action performed by the actors. As evidence we may cite the method employed by the most successful director of the realistic theater. The specific term he coined for describing the disparity between the verbal message and the dramatic performance—to play the subtext—proves to us that this disparity was viewed as one of the underlying bases of the dramatic method of the realistic theater. Thus, our hypothesis about the essence of theatrical perception, which we view as a synthesis of the opposition between the mental representation evoked by the word and the pragmatic reality projected on stage via the actors' performance or the stage setting, appears to be an enduring law of theatrical creativity and perception.

2. See my discussion in *Slovo a slovesnost,* 6 (1940). "Dynamics of the Sign in the Theater" (pp. 74-93 of this anthology).

10. Basic Features of Dramatic Dialogue

Jiří Veltruský

Dialogue is a verbal utterance delivered by two or more alternating speakers; as·a rule, they address their speeches to each other. Dialogue, therefore, differs from monologue in that it unfolds not only in time but also in space. Every single unit of dialogue is situated at a unique point of intersection of the continuum of time and the continuum of space or, to put it differently, in a specific "here and now." This "here and now" keeps changing, just as in every discourse the present continuously turns into the past and the future into the present. The constantly changing "here and now" may be called the extralinguistic situation of the dialogue.

The second characteristic of dialogue follows from the first: unlike monologue, dialogue is always integrated in the extralinguistic situation. This comprises not only the material situation, that is, the set of things that surround the speakers, but also the speakers themselves, their mentality, intentions, knowledge pertinent to the dialogue, their mutual relations, the tensions between them, and so on—in short, what may be called the psychological situation.

The relationship between the dialogue and the extralinguistic situation is intense and reciprocal. The situation often provides the dialogue with its subject matter. Moreover, whatever the subject matter be, the situation variously affects the way the dialogue unfolds, intervenes in it, brings about different shifts or reversals, and sometimes interrupts it altogether. In its turn, the dialogue successively throws new light on the situation and often modifies or even transforms it.[1] The links with the extralinguistic situation contribute as much to the actual sense of the individual units of meaning as their integration in the linguistic context.[2] The intense relationship between the dialogue and the extralinguistic situation is reflected in the vocabulary of the dialogue and in the various ways it uses certain elements of language.[3] However, the intensity of that relationship is highly variable.[4]

The third characteristic of dialogue is a specific kind of semantic construction:

"Základní vlastnosti dramatického dialogu," *Drama jako básnické dílo* in *Čtení o jazyce a poesii,* ed. B. Havránek and J. Mukařovský (Prague: 1942), pp. 414-423. Translated by Jiří Veltruský.

In dialogue, several, at least two, contexts interpenetrate and alternate, whereas monologue has a single and uninterrupted context. Of course, dialogue cannot do without semantic unity either, but that unity derives from the subject matter, the theme, which at any given moment must be the same for all the participants (. . .). The context is something other than the theme, it is given by the sense the speaker introduces the theme, i.e., by the attitude he adopts toward the theme and his assessment of it. Since in dialogue there are more participants than one, there is also more than one context: the speeches of each person, although they alternate with those of a second one (or of the others), form a certain unity of sense. Because the contexts, which in this way interpenetrate in dialogue, are different from, and often even opposed to, each other, sharp semantic reversals occur at the borderline between individual speeches. The livelier the dialogue and the shorter the individual speeches, the more noticeable are the shocks between the contexts; that brings about a special semantic effect for which a term has been created by stylistics—stichomythia.[5]

This third characteristic of dialogue is linked to the second. Indeed, the attitude of each interlocutor towards the subject matter, which determines the context made up of his speeches, depends mainly on his place in the extralinguistic situation. Furthermore, if the interlocutors can understand each other and grasp each other's standpoint only when they speak about the same thing, this is not a unilateral relation. Often the addressee can understand what the speaker is talking about only if he knows his attitude toward that subject matter or, what amounts to the same thing, only if he knows the sense that unifies the context to which the speech in question belongs. A mistake concerning a very slight element of the psychological or material situation may lead to a far-reaching misapprehension of what the whole discussion is about.

Dialogue, then, becomes semantically unified on two distinct planes. One is the subject matter and the other the extralinguistic situation. As a rule, the respective shares of the two in the semantic unification of the dialogue are uneven—either one or the other is in the foreground. If it is the subject matter, the dialogue looks more or less like a gradual clarification and elaboration of it. If it is the situation, the dialogue comes closer to interaction between the participants, to a chain of actions and reactions. In any case, however, the unification proceeds on both planes because it cannot be achieved on either one alone. Both aspects of dialogue, elaboration of the theme and reciprocal action, are therefore always present. One does not exist without the other; they form a dialectical antinomy. Their dissociation disrupts the dialogue, unless it is used as a literary device. In dramatic dialogue, the whole matter is still more complicated than in an ordinary conversation. Like any other literary work, a dramatic text relies on language as its only material. Therefore, it contains no extralinguistic situation; that situation is merely imaginery, suggested by its language. Even dramatic dialogue is, of course, associated at every moment of its unfolding with a specific situation. In this case, however, the situation is not an objective reality external to the language; it is an immaterial meaning generated by the language itself.

The semantic construction, too, is more complicated in dramatic dialogue. Unlike the ordinary dialogue of everyday life, dramatic dialogue is both a sequence of alternating utterances made by several speakers and an utterance made by a single speaker, the author. In dramatic dialogue, the speakers themselves, like all the other components of the imaginary extralinguistic situation, are pure meanings deriving from the language of the play. The speeches attributed to each character are constructed in such a way as to be intelligible not only to the other character but also to the reader—and more or less in such a way as to enable the reader to grasp how they are understood by the different characters. This intrinsic antinomy of dramatic dialogue takes different forms in specific plays, bringing the dramatic dialogue closer to, or on the contrary removing it further from, everyday dialogue. This depends on the manner in which various linguistic resources are used. The reader perceives dramatic dialogue as a homogeneous utterance addressed to him by the author because the language is used and the sense constructed in the same manner throughout all the speeches, irrespective of the alternation of speakers: a play in which the speeches of one character are dominated by the undulation of intonation and those of another one by the gradation of intensity, for instance, does not exist; the interlocutors may differ in their vocabulary but not in the general technique of denomination, which is the author's own technique; they may differ in the functional languages they respectively use, but then the speeches of all are constructed in such a way as to allow for the functional differentiation of language.

The impression that dramatic dialogue is a homogeneous utterance by the dramatist is stronger in those plays where those linguistic resources that by their nature promote the continuous flow of language rather than its division into distinct segments predominate. When emphasis is put on the continuity of the discourse, the borderlines between the alternating speeches tend to be blurred; when emphasis is put on its segmentation they are sharply marked, precisely because they are the most effective means of cutting up a dialogue. On the sound level, for example, the predominance of intonation makes the dramatic dialogue appear more clearly as the dramatist's own utterance than the predominance of intensity because the continuity of the language is carried primarily by the undulation of intonation and its segmentation by the grading of intensity. Here are two contrasting examples:

[Intonation:]

Chasuble: Was the cause of death mentioned?
Jack: A severe cold, it seems.
Miss Prism: As a man sows, so shall he reap.
Chasuble [raising his hand] : Charity, dear Miss Prism, charity. None of us is perfect. I myself am peculiarly susceptible to draughts. Will the interment take place here?

(Oscar Wilde, *The Importance of Being Ernest,* II)

[Intensity:]

Richard: What danger?
Anderson: Your uncle's danger. Major Swindon's gallows.
Richard: It is you who are in danger. I warned you—
Anderson [interrupting him good-humoredly but authoritatively] : Yes, yes, Mr. Dugeon; but they do not think so in town. And even if I were in danger, I have duties here which I must not forsake. But you are a free man. Why should you run any risk?

(George Bernard Shaw, *The Devil's Disciple,* II)

This distinction concerns all the planes of language, not only its phonic aspect. For instance, in the examples just quoted, the tendency to endow the dialogue with unity and continuity also appears in the coordination of syntactic units (in other cases, the same tendency can produce an accumulation of mutually unrelated subordinations of different sorts which cancel the very principle of subordination). On the plane of meaning, all the units tend to carry about the same semantic weight; the insertion of phrases like *it seems* or *dear Miss Prism* serves to reduce the semantic charge of such units before or after them as would stand out in comparison with the others. On the contrary, the tendency to divide the language into segments finds its expression in clear-cut syntactical subordination (*It is you who are in danger* or *And even if I were in danger, I have duties here which I must not forsake.*) and in the gradation of the semantic weight given to the different units of the same sentence or cluster of sentences (for example, more semantic weight to *uncle's* than to *danger,* to *Swindon's* than to *major,* to *gallows* than to *Swindon's,* and so forth).

Among the linguistic resources that cut the discourse up into segments, a distinction must be made between those which serve the structure of the discourse itself and those which spring from the extralinguistic situation; the first category, as a rule, does not tend to jeopardize the unity of the discourse while the second may tear it to pieces. That is what marks the difference between intensity, which behaves mainly in accordance with the syntactic construction, and voice coloring or timbre, which corresponds to the emotions of the speaker. For illustration, the dialogue in which intensity predominates, as quoted above, may be compared to the following one which is dominated by marked changes in timbre:

Abbie [in her most seductive tones which she uses all through this scene] : Be you—Eben? I'm Abbie—[She laughs] I mean, I'm yer new Maw.
Eben [viciously] : No, damn ye!
Abbie [as if she hadn't heard—with a queer smile] : Yer Paw's spoke a lot o'yew. . . .
Eben: Ha!
Abbie: Ye mustn't mind him. He's an old man. [A long pause. They stare at each other.] I don't want t' pretend playin' Maw t'ye, Eben. [Admiringly] Ye'r too big an' too strong fur that. I wan t' be frens with ye. Mebbe with me fur a fren ye'd find ye'd like livin' here better. I kin make it easy fur ye with him, mebbe. [With a scornful sense of power] I calc'late I kin git him t' do most anythin' fur me.
Eben [with bitter scorn] : Ha! [They stare again, Eben obscurely moved, physically attracted to her—in forceful stilted tones] Ye kin go t' the devil!

(Eugene O'Neill, *Desire Under the Elms,* I/4)

Real semantic gaps are noticeable between the segments that differ from each other in the timbre of the voice, even within the same speech. Between the successive speeches, where they are deepened by the change of speaker, the gaps become unbridgeable. On the syntactic level, the language is markedly choppy and elliptic or, to put it differently, fragmented. On the semantic plane, units of meaning are largely isolated and mutually independent. The thematic plane is full of obscurities because the dialogue keeps jumping from topic to topic. All these features help to disjoint the language. The dialogue itself tends to break up into single speeches, so that its unity and homogeneity are scarcely perceptible (yet the accentuation of those means which disrupt the continuity of the language remains the same throughout the play, so that it, too, betrays the hand of the dramatist).

The impression might arise that because it is also the utterance of a single speaker—the author--dramatic dialogue comes closer than the ordinary dialogue to monologue. The opposite is true. Those features that distinguish the semantic construction of dialogue from that of monologue are particularly emphasized in dramatic dialogue, precisely because it has that specific feature.

Notes

1. See Jan Mukařovský, "Dialog a monolog" [Dialogue and Monologue] , *Kapitoly z české poetiky,* 1 (Prague: 1941), pp. 151 ff.

2. See Roman Jakobson, "Beitrag zur allgemeinen Kasuslehre," *Travaux du Cercle linguistique de Prague,* 6 (1936). [In Jakobson's terminology, "linguistic and extra-linguistic context."]

3. See J. Mukařovský, "Dialog a monolog," p. 152.

4. Ibid., p. 155.

5. Ibid., p. 151 ff.

11. Construction of Semantic Contexts

Jiří Veltruský

Context is a dynamic unit of meaning, in the sense that its meaning emerges gradually, in time. That is what distinguishes context from the static unit, such as the denomination, whose meaning is given all at once.[1] Therefore, the language context is fundamentally governed by the same principles as any temporal object, to borrow a term from Husserl who undertook a penetrating study of the problem in his 1904-1905 lectures.[2]

Husserl differentiates the consciousness of the past into successive phases, which enable him to explain how an entire temporal object is perceived as a unity in spite of its continuous flow. At any given moment in the duration of a temporal object, only one of its phases is actually present, and it immediately starts receding into the past, to be replaced by the next phase. But the elapsed phases are still retained by the perceiver. That is why he is conscious of all the phases from the outset to the given moment as being present or, to put it differently, of one and the same temporal object as now persisting. Retention unites the present phase with those that have elapsed. On the other hand, as it recedes into a more and more distant past, each elapsed phase undergoes gradual modification.[3] Husserl himself illustrated this process by the following diagram (O is the starting point of the temporal object, E its final point, and P any point inside it; the horizontal line represents the sequence of phases, the diagonal lines their elapsing into the past:

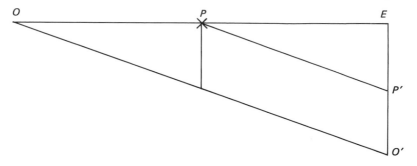

"Výstavba významových kontextů," *Drama jako básnické dílo, Čtení o jazyce a poesii,* ed., B. Havránek and J. Mukařovský (Prague: 1942), pp. 434-442. Translated by Jiří Veltruský.

the vertical lines indicate the direction of the retention and represent the continuum of the phases, which Husserl also calls the "horizon of the past"; the prime added to the letters representing the phases that have elapsed indicates the modification they undergo while sinking into the past.)

The diagram could easily be made more intelligible, for instance by marking more than one point inside the sequence between O and E and by adding further primes to represent the degrees of modification which correspond to the degrees of the sinking into the past:

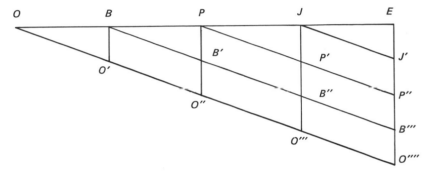

In any event, however, when applied to the semantic context, the diagram betrays a definite one-sidedness in Husserl's conception. The diversity of the temporal object has been sacrificed to its continuity. Except for the beginning, the end and some arbitrarily chosen point or points in between, the static units that compose the dynamic unit are disregarded. This is in full agreement with Husserl's statement that: "With respect to the elapsing phenomenon, we know that it is a continuity of ceaseless transformations, which forms an indissoluble unity, indissoluble into independent spans and indivisible into independent phases, into the points of the continuity."[4] This one-sidedness is undoubtedly due to Husserl's choice of the tone as his example of a temporal object; a tone is a single unit, not a real context, even when it is very long.

A more complete conception of the dynamic unit was worked out by Vološinov who based it on the study of language utterance. Vološinov recognizes that static units exist and that they convey meanings.[5] Yet, even his conception is marked, though to a lesser degree, by the same onesideness as

Husserl's. Indeed, according to Vološinov, "the meaning of a word is determined entirely by its context" and "there are as many meanings of a word as there are contexts of its usage," while "the word's unit is assured by (. . .) that factor of unity which is common to all its meanings"[6]—which amounts to denying that the static unit has a general meaning and reducing this general meaning to some sort of common denominator of its particular meanings. This conflicts with a fundamental principle of semantics. In fact, each component of language which is endowed with meaning has a general meaning; this general meaning comprises hierarchically ordained particular meanings that are variants of it.

The dialectics of the dynamic unit was described by Mukařovský. He emphasizes that the relationship between the static and the dynamic unit of meaning is reciprocal, that they depend upon, and conflict with, each other.[7] This difference is reflected in the diagram designed by Mukařovský, which corresponds to Husserl's in its symbolism—except for the primes—but inserts letters into the different lines to signify the static units of meaning:

$$a - b - c - d - e - f$$
$$a \quad b \quad c \quad d \quad e$$
$$a \quad b \quad c \quad d$$
$$a \quad b \quad c$$
$$a \quad b$$
$$a$$

Mukařovský has established three fundamental principles of the semantic construction of the context: the unity of sense of the entire context, the accumulation of meanings, and the oscillation between the semantic statics and dynamics.[8]

The unity of sense is something that imposes itself upon the addressee or the reader as soon as he begins to perceive a series of meanings as a context: he tries to grasp the total sense of that context although it remains merely potential as long as the context is not finished. The role of this principle in the semantic construction of the sentence and of higher categories of context has also been stressed by Ingarden.[9]

The accumulation of meanings consists, on the one hand, in that the units of meaning which make up the context are perceived as a continuous succession of meanings, irrespective of any syntactical links, subordinations, and so on, and, on the other hand, in that each of these units is perceived against the background of the preceding ones—so that, when the context is finished, all the units of which it is composed are present in the addressee's or the reader's mind in the order in which they were uttered. In Mukařovský's diagram the horizontal line a - b - c - d - e - f represents the succession of the units in the context while the vertical columns under each letter represent the accumulated units as a background against which every new unit is perceived.

The accumulation of meanings is the same process as the one that Husserl analyzed. Unlike Husserl, however, Mukařovský does not speak of the gradual modification that every unit undergoes as it recedes farther away from the "now" point; that is why the primes are missing in his diagram. To some extent, however, this highly important aspect is implied in Mukařovský's statement that "even in the final accumulation of the units of meaning of a sentence, the order in which this accumulation took place is relevant." This, indeed, can be explained only by the modification each unit gradually undergoes as it sinks into the past because each layer in the "horizon of the past" is marked by a definite degree of such modification. In Mukařovský's diagram unit b in the horizon of unit c, for example, is marked by the same degree of modification as unit c in the horizon of unit d, while in the horizon of this same unit d a stronger modification already marks unit b, and so on. In other words, if horizontal lines were drawn at all the levels of the diagram, each of them would symbolize the same degree of modification. The reason why the order in which the units accumulate remains the same in the final accumulation is simply that it is reflected in the grading of their respective modification.

The oscillation between the semantic statics and dynamics springs from the interdependence of the context and of the units of meaning of which it is made up. As Mukařovský put it, "the dynamic unit is not merely 'composed' of the static ones because it transforms them, and, in its turn, the static unit does not behave passively toward the context but puts up a resistance to it, in that, through its associations, it exerts pressure on the direction in which the semantic intention of the context points; it even strives to emancipate itself completely."[10] The active relationship between the units of meaning and the context was also pointed out by Ingarden.[11] However, unlike

Mukařovský, Ingarden did not conceive this relationship as an antinomy.

Dramatic dialogue, naturally, is governed in its semantic construction by the same three principles as any other type of linguistic context. But their operation here has certain specific features which cannot be found elsewhere.

The reader of dramatic dialogue is oriented toward the unity of sense of each context because all the speeches of a given character are united by that character's name. This unity may also be stressed by a use of language characteristic of all the speeches which belong to it—such as an unusual frequency of certain words or phrases, syntactic peculiarities, the use of a dialect or functional language, and so forth. On the other hand, in dialogue the semantic unification of each context is hampered by the fact that the different speeches of the same person, through which the context becomes explicit, are not continuous. As already mentioned, in its explicit parts, each context is fragmentary; it is up to the reader to establish the links between the fragments, with the help of the other characters' speeches that separate them. These are the objective prerequisites of the reader's search for the unity of sense in each of the interacting contexts. The total sense of each one is determined by the place which the character associated with it occupies in the extralinguistic situation of the dialogue.

In a specific dialogue, the accumulation of meanings proceeds in the same way for all the contexts; they all comprise the same units, arranged in the same order. That is because each context is composed not only of those units of meaning which make up the speeches of its bearer but also of all those that are uttered by the other interlocutors and are merely perceived by the character concerned. However, each unit of meaning uttered by one speaker enters the context of the addressee through a new act which modifies its meaning and may even modify the word that appears most suitable to convey that modified meaning. This shift is due to the total sense of the context into which the perceived unit enters and to which it must adjust. Therefore, the single contexts differ from each other not in the accumulation of the units of meaning but in their respective total sense and in the modification this total sense imposes upon the units of meaning. This can be schematically represented by the following adaptation of Mukařovský's diagram (x and y designate the total sense of each of the two contexts in a dialogue and the corresponding modification of their—common—units):

Context x:

$$a_x - b_x - c_x - d_x - e_x - f_x$$
$$a_x \quad b_x \quad c_x \quad d_x \quad e_x$$
$$a_x \quad b_x \quad c_x \quad d_x$$
$$a_x \quad b_x \quad c_x$$
$$a_x \quad b_x$$
$$a_x$$

Context y:

$$a_y - b_y - c_y - d_y - e_y - f_y$$
$$a_y \quad b_y \quad c_y \quad d_y \quad e_y$$
$$a_y \quad b_y \quad c_y \quad d_y$$
$$a_y \quad b_y \quad c_y$$
$$a_y \quad b_y$$
$$a_y$$

This, however, is only the first phase in a complicated process. In fact, the shift the meaning of a unit undergoes when it enters the context associated with the addressee intervenes also in the context associated with the speaker, insofar as the speaker anticipates the addressee's interpretation of his utterance. Let us recall that in dialogue the various points of intersection of the homonymic and the synonymic series in which the same unit of meaning is located not only alternate in the flow of time but also enter into play simultaneously. What really diversifies the same unit of meaning in different contexts is that it acquires different, more or less conflicting values that cannot eliminate each other. In reference to the preceding diagram, the units accumulating respectively in Context x and in Context y could be more accurately presented by the following symbols: a_{xy} - b_{xy} - c_{xy} - d_{xy}, as opposed to a_{yx} - b_{yx} - c_{yx} - d_{yx}.

Moreover, all this applies only in so far as all the interlocutors take part in the whole of the dialogue. Yet in drama they mostly change in the course of a dialogue: some come in the middle, others leave and possibly come back before the dialogue is over. The segment of a dialogue during which the interlocutors do not change may be called a scene.[12] The fact that some interlocutors remain the same and others change from one scene to the next is used by certain dramatists as an important device. Since different characters participate in different scenes, the accumulation of meanings is no longer the same for all contexts. For instance, the context a - b - c - d - e - f may be confronted with the context a - b - e - f and with the context b - c - d - e.

The third principle of the semantic construction of the context, the oscillation between semantic statics and dynamics, is strongly affected by the plurality of contexts in dialogue. Every single context is undermined in its cohesion and unity by being obliged to take in units stemming from the other contexts, whose meaning often cannot be easily modified in such a way as to fit into the total sense of the context concerned. Moreover, since every static unit of meaning enters more than one context, the resistance it opposes to the pressures of the context is generally stronger in dialogue than in monologue. None of the contexts can reduce or absorb the meanings which the unit acquires in the other contexts without its own total sense becoming disrupted. In dialogue, therefore, the unity of each context is ceaselessly attacked by the discordant meanings and shades of meaning carried by its single units.

As a result, the relationship between the several contexts in dialogue is in the nature of a competition. Each one strives to achieve its unity to the detriment of the others, that is, to change the sense of every other one so that they do not disrupt its own sense. The choice of the units of meaning and the shaping of the utterances reflect not only the reality referred to and the sense the speaker attaches to it but also the sense he attaches to the competing contexts or his attitude to them—the speaker tries to make sure that what he says will be understood by his interlocutors in a specific manner and will affect the sense of the contexts they bear. In dialogue, each utterance, and even each word is to some extent an action. The acts by which the other participants transform or modify each unit of meaning chosen by a speaker are reactions to that action; at the same time, they are themselves actions because they also aim to influence the sense of the context from which the unit of meaning in question sprang.

Dialogue has sometimes been described as a chain of actions and reactions. That, however, may be a misleading image because the actions and reactions do not proceed in one dimension. The reaction to the utterance of one speaker consists not only in the reply of another but also in the shifts that occur in each unit as soon as it enters the other contexts, that is, is perceived by the addressees. Coincidences between the play of actions and reactions and the division of dialogue into speeches do exist but they are not vital. The play of actions and reaction is uninterrupted and proceeds not only in time but also, at each point of the time flow, in space. If we need an image, it would be more accurate to say that dialogue is a network, rather than a chain, of actions and reactions.

In the formation of an utterance, the concern with the competing contexts may prevail over the concern with the reality referred to. The commitment of the speech to reality is then weakened and in extreme cases the speech becomes fictitious. In Molière's *Fourberies de Scapin* (II/7), for example, Scapin tries to get from Géronte five hundred écus for his son Léandre, who wants to buy the freedom of his mistress from the gypsies. The entire context associated with Géronte is dominated by his principal characteristic, avarice. Scapin's objective, to disrupt the unity of that context, is extremely difficult to achieve. Therefore, in all his speeches, concern with the facts related is very much subordinated to this objective. He does say he needs the five hundred écus for Léandre, but, rather than trying to present the real reason in such a light as to induce Géronte to give the amount, he resorts to a fictitious reason and says that Léandre will be sold as a slave in Algiers unless he gets that amount within two hours. Only the amount, the fact that it is needed to buy somebody's freedom and the deadline correspond to reality. The rest is invented. Such a treatment of the reality referred to is required by the nature of the context associated with Géronte; even so, Géronte keeps trying to avoid the expenditure.

The extent to which the utterance in dialogue is fashioned with respect to each of the competing contexts is brought out by the semantic reversals that often occur within the same speech when the speaker turns to another addressee. Sometimes, such reversals are as striking as those that appear when one speaker is relayed by another. In dramatic dialogue this can be used in a highly sophisticated manner:

Dorante: Monsieur Jourdain, en voilà assez; Madame n'aime pas les grands compliments, et elle sait que vous êtes homme d'esprit. [Bas, à Dorimène] C'est un bon bourgeois assez ridicule, comme vous voyez, dans toutes ses manières.
Dorimène [bas, à Dorante] : Il n'est pas malaisé de s'en apercevoir.
Dorante: Madame, voilà le meilleur de mes amis.
Monsieur Jourdain: C'est trop d'honneur que vous me faites.
Dorante: Galant homme tout à fait.
Dorimène: J'ai beacoup d'estime pour lui.
Monsieur Jourdain: Je n'ai rien fait encore, Madame, pour mériter cette grâce.
Dorante [bas, à Monsieur Jourdain] : Prenez bien garde, au moins, à ne lui point parler du diamant que vous lui avez donné.

Monsieur Jourdain [bas, à Dorante] : Ne pourrais-je pas seulement lui demander comment elle le trouve?
Dorante [bas, à Monsieur Jourdain] : Comment? gardez-vous-en bien. Cela serait vilain à vous; et pour agir en galant homme, il faut que vous fassiez comme si ce n'était pas vous qui lui eussiez fait ce présent. [Haute.] Monsieur Jourdain, Madame, dit qu'il est ravi de vous voir chez lui.
Dorimène: Il m'honore beaucoup.

(Molière, *Le bourgeois gentilhomme,* III/16)

The same kind of semantic reversal as between the speeches of alternating speakers can also arise within the same speech when part of it is addressed to an interlocutor and part to nobody—the so-called aside. The reversal is due to the fact that the addressed part of the speech takes account both of the reality referred to and of the addressee's context, while the aside, which is more or less addressed directly to the reader, disregards the context of the interlocutor. Where this device is fully developed, a dialogue within the dialogue may take place—within the dialgue among interlocutors, another dialogue may oppose the addressed speeches and the asides of one of them.

Fairly similar in its semantic effect is the exploitation of ambiguity by one of the participants, especially when his speeches are ambiguous only for himself and the reader, while his interlocutor does not grasp their hidden meaning because he does not know some of the circumstances. So when Viola is disguised as a man, Orsino fails to realize that her words secretly express her love for him:

Orsino: Thou dost speak masterly.
My life upon't, young though thou art, thine eye
Hath stayed upon some favour that it loves.
Hath it not, boy?
Viola: A little, by your favour.
Orsino: What kind of woman is't?
Viola: Of your complexion.
Orsino: She is not worth thee, then. What years, i'faith?
Viola: About your years, my lord.
Orsino:
Too old, by heaven. Let still the woman take
An elder than herself; so wears she to him;
So sways she level in her husband's heart.

For, boy, however we do praise ourselves,
Our fancies are more giddy and unfirm,
More longing, wavering, sooner lost and worn,
Than women's are.
Voila: I think it well, my lord.

(William Shakespeare, *Twelfth Night,* II/4)

The concern with the addressee's context can so affect an utterance that the sense put into it by the speaker is entirely beyond the grasp of the reader.

This constant concern with the contexts carried by the other participants is still another of the factors in dialogue which tend to disintegrate the interacting contexts. Weak semantic unity and cohesion is a universal feature of these contexts.

All this does not mean, however, that there is an intrinsic tendency in dramatic dialogue to make the unit of meaning prevail over the context, the semantic statics over the semantic dynamics. No conclusion concerning this general principle of semantic construction can be drawn from the analysis of the competing contexts. They are merely partical contexts. The relationship between semantic statics and dynamics cannot be adequately studied on the level of the unity or lack of unity of these partial contexts but only on the level of that single, integral context that is the dramatic dialogue as a whole; it is a matter of the unification of the dialogue itself.

Notes

1. See Jan Mukařovský, "O jazyce básnickém," *Kapitely z české poetiky,* I (Prague: 1948), p. 124.

2. Edmung Husserl, "Zur Phänomenologie des inneren Zeitbewusstseins," ed. Martin Heidegger, *Jahrbuch für Philosophie und phänomenologische Forschung,* vol. IX (1928).

3. See ibid., pp. 285 f.

4. Ibid., p. 388.

5. See V. N. Vološinov, *Marxism and the Philosophy of Language,* tr. L. Matejka and I. R. Titunik (New York-London: 1973), p. 101.

6. See ibid., pp. 79 f.

7. See Mukařovský, "O jazyce básnickém," pp. 124 f.

8. See ibid., pp. 128 f.

9. See Roman Ingarden, *Das literarische Kunstwerk* (Halle: 1930), paragraph 18.

10. Mukařovský, "O jazyce básnickém," p. 25.

11. See Ingarden, *Das literarische Kunstwerk,* paragraph 19.

12. The existing terminology is very vague in this area. For some dramatists, a scene is what for others is a sequence of scenes. Historians and theoreticians use the term as vaguely as the dramatists. Furthermore, there is no established terminological distinction between the scene that differs from the preceding one only by the set of participants and the scene that also has a different location.

12. Is the Cinema in Decline?

Roman Jakobson

"We are lazy and uninquisitive." The poet's pronouncement still holds.[1] We are witnessing the rise of a new art. It is growing by leaps and bounds, detaching itself from the influence of the older arts and even beginning to influence them itself. It creates its own norms, its own laws, and then confidently rejects them. It is becoming a powerful instrument of propaganda and education, a daily and omnipresent social fact; in this respect it is leaving all the other arts behind.

Art studies, however, seem to remain completely unaware of the emergence of this new art. The collector of paintings and other rare objects is interested only in the old masters. Why preoccupy oneself with the rise and self-determination of the cinema, when one can simply remain content with dreamy hypotheses about the origin of the theater or about the syncretic nature of prehistoric art? The fewer the traces preserved, the more thrilling the reconstruction of the development of aesthetic forms. The scholar finds the history of the cinema too banal; it is virtually vivisection, whereas his hobby is hunting for antiques. Still, it is clear that the search among the early heritage of film will soon be a task worthy of the archaeologist. The first decades of the cinema have already become an "age of fragments." For example, of French films prior to 1907, there remains almost nothing except the Lumière Brothers' first productions, as the specialists report.

However, is the cinema an autonomous art? Where is its specific hero to be found? What kind of material does this art transform? The creator of the Soviet film, Lev Kulešov correctly states that it is real things that serve as cinematographic material.[2] And the creator of the French film, Louis Delluc, has perfectly grasped that in film even man is "a mere detail, a mere bit *de la matière du monde*."[3] But on the other hand, signs are the material of every art. The semiotic essence of cinematic elements is clear to filmmakers. "The shot must operate as a sign, a kind of letter," emphasizes Kulešov. For this reason essays on cinema always speak in a metaphorical

"Úpadek filmu?" *Listy pro umění a kritiku*, 1 (1933), pp. 45-49 = *Studies in Verbal Art* (Ann Arbor, 1971), pp. 150-156. English translation by Elena Sokol, revised by the author.

way about the language of the film and even introduce the notion of film sentences, with subject and predicate, and of film subordinate clauses (Boris Èjxenbaum[4]), or look for verbal and nominal elements in film (André Beucler). Is there a conflict between these two theses? According to one of them, film operates with things; according to the other, with signs. There are observers who answer this question affirmatively: rejecting the second thesis and bearing in mind the semiotic nature of art, they refuse to recognize the cinema as art. However, the incompatability of the two above-mentioned theses was actually eliminated already by St. Augustine. This great thinker of the fifth century, who aptly distinguished between the object meant (*res*) and the sign (*signum*), taught that besides signs whose essential task is to signify something, there exist objects that may be used in the function of signs. It is precisely things (visual and auditory), transformed into signs, that are the specific material of cinematic art.

We can say about the same person: "hunchback," "big-nose," or "big-nosed hunchback." In all three cases the object of our talk is identical, whereas the signs are different. Likewise, in a film we can shoot such a person from behind—his hump will be seen, then *en face*—his nose will be shown, or in profile, so that both will be seen. In these three shots we have three things functioning as signs of the same object. Now let us demonstrate the synecdochic nature of language by referring to our ugly fellow simply as "the hump," or "the nose." The analogous method in cinema: the camera sees only the hump, or only the nose. *Pars pro toto* is a fundamental method of filmic conversion of things into signs. Scenario terminology with its "mid-long shots," "close-ups," and "mid-close-ups" is sufficiently instructive in this respect. Film works with manifold fragments of objects which differ in magnitude, and also with fragments of time and space likewise varied. It changes their proportions and juxtaposes them in terms of contiguity, or similarity and contrast; that is, it takes the path of *metonymy* or *metaphor* (two fundamental kinds of cinematic structure). The treatment of the functions of light in Delluc's *Photogénie* and the analysis of filmic time and motion in Jurij Tynjanov's penetrating study[5] clearly show that each phenomenon of the exterior world changes into a *sign* on the screen.

A dog does not recognize a painted dog, since a painting is wholly a sign —the painter's perspective is a conventional device. A dog barks at dogs on film because the material of the cinema is a real thing, but he remains blind to the montage, to the semiotic interrelation of things he sees on the screen. The theoretician who disclaims cinema as art perceives the film as a mere moving photograph; he does not notice the montage, nor does he want to acknowledge the fact that here a specific sign system is involved— this is the attitude of a reader of poetry for whom the words of the poem make no sense.

The number of those who absolutely reject the cinema is steadily declining. They are being replaced by the critics of sound film. Current slogans state: "Sound film marks the decline of cinema," "it considerably limits the artistic potentialities of cinema," "the style of the film is in inherent contradiction to speech," and so on.

Criticism of sound film is particularly rich in premature generalizations. It does not take into consideration the temporarily limited history and narrow character of certain phenomena in the cinema. Theoreticians have hastily assumed that silence is one of the cinema's structural properties, and now they are offended that its venture into sound makes it deviate from their biased formulae. If the facts do not correspond to their theory, they accuse the facts instead of recognizing the fallacy of the theory.

They have hurriedly assumed that the features of today's films are the only ones that cinema will devise. They forget that the first of the sound films cannot be compared with the last of the silent ones. The sound film is absorbed today with new technical achievements (it's good enough if one can hear well . . . , etc.) and preoccupied with the search for new forms to utilize them. We are in a period analogous to that of the prewar silent film, whereas the most recent silent films have already achieved a standard, have created classical works, and perhaps just this realization of a classical canon contained its own demise and the necessity of a fundamental reform.

It has been stated that sound film has brought cinema dangerously close to the theater. Certainly it has again brought the two closer together, as they were at the dawn of the century, during the years of the "electric theaters"; and it was this new bringing together that prepared the way for a new liberation. For, in principle, speech on the screen and speech on stage are two profoundly different phenomena. As long as the film was silent, its only material was the visual object; today it is both visual and the auditory objects. Human behavior is the material of the theater. Speech in film is a special kind of auditory object, along with the buzzing of a fly or the babbling of a brook, the clamor of machines, and so forth. Speech on the stage is simply one of the manifestations of human behavior. Talking about theater and cinema, Jean Epstein once said that the very essence of their respective expressive methods is different.[6] This thesis remains valid for the sound film as well. Why are "asides" and soliloquies possible on the stage, yet not on the screen? Precisely because inner speech is an instance of human behavior and not an auditory object. On the same grounds that film speech is an auditory object, the "stage whisper" in the theater, which is heard by the audience but by none of the dramatis personae, is impossible in film.

A characteristic peculiarity of speech on screen, as opposed to speech on stage, is also its optional nature. The critic Emile Vuillermoz condemns this freedom of selection: "The convulsive and irregular way in which speech is sometimes imposed upon and sometimes eliminated from an art consistently silent in the past has destroyed the laws of the spectacle and assigned an arbitrariness to the silent segments."[7] This rebuke is erroneous.

If on the screen we *see* people speaking, we simultaneously *hear* either their words or music. Music, but not silence. Silence in the cinema is valued as an actual absence of sounds; consequently, it becomes an auditory object, just like speech, like a cough, or street noises. In a sound film we perceive silence as a sign of real silence. It is sufficient to recall how the classroom grows quiet in a scene of L. Vančura's film *Before Graduation* (1932). In cinema it is not silence but music that announces the exclusion of the auditory object. Music in cinema serves this end because musical art operates with signs which do not relate to any objects. Auditorily a silent film is entirely "nonrepresentational" and for that very reason demands continual musical accompaniment. Observers unwittingly struck upon this neutralizing function of music in the cinema when they remarked that "we instantly notice the absence of music, but we pay no attention to its presence, so that any music whatever is appropriate for

virtually any scene" (Bela Balázs[8]), "music in the cinema is destined not to
be listened to" (Paul Ramain), "its only aim is that one's ears be occupied
while complete attention is concentrated on seeing" (Frank Martin).
The frequent alternation of speech with music in the sound film must
not be seen as an unartistic chaos. Just as the innovation of Edwin Porter,
and later D. W. Griffith, involved rejection of the use of an immobile
camera in relation to the object and brought a variety of shots into film
(the alternation of long shots, mid-shots, close-ups, and so on), similarly
the sound film with its new diversity replaces the inertness of the previous
approach, which consistently discarded sound from the realm of film objects. In a sound film visual and auditory reality can be given either jointly
or, on the contrary, separately from one another: the visual object is
shown without the particular sound to which it is normally connected, or
else the sound is severed from the visual object (we still hear a man speak
ing, but instead of his mouth we see other details of the given scene, or perhaps an entirely different scene). Thus there arise new possibilities of
filmic synecdoches. At the same time the number of methods of joining
shots increases (a purely auditory or verbal transition, a clash between
sound and image, and so forth).

Titles in silent films were an important means of montage, frequently
functioning as a link between shots. In his *Attempt at an Introduction to
the Theory and Aesthetics of the Cinema* (1926), Semen Timošenko even
sees this as their primary function.[9] Thus the film maintained elements of
purely literary composition. For this reason some silent film directors
made attempts to rid film of titles, but these attempts either necessitated
the simplication of the plot or considerably retarded the film's tempo. Only
in the sound film has the elimination of titles actually been accomplished.
Between today's uninterrupted film and yesterday's film interlaced with
titles, there is essentially the same difference as between opera and musical
vaudeville. Laws of purely cinematic shot linkage at present are obtaining
a monopoly.

If someone in a film shows up in one place and then we see him in
another place noncontiguous to the first, a time segment must have lapsed
between the two situations during which the person is absent from the
screen. In the process we are shown either the one place after the person
has already departed, or the other place before his arrival, or, finally, a

"crosscut": some other scene appears in which the person doesn't take part. This principle occurred already in silent films, but there, of course, it was enough to connect such scenes with titles in the vein of: "And when he came home. . . ." Only now is the above-mentioned law consistently realized. It can be dispensed with only when two scenes are not joined by contiguity but by similarity or contrast (the person occupies the same position in both scenes), as well as when the intent is especially to stress the rapidity of the jump from one situation to another, or the interruption, the break between the two scenes. Similarly unacceptable within a scene are unmotivated jumps of the camera from one object to another, noncontiguous one. If such a jump nevertheless occurs, it cannot but emphasize and semantically overload the second object and its sudden interference in the action.

After an event, only a succeeding, not a preceding or simultaneous event, can be shown in today's film. A return to the past can be performed only as a reminiscence or a story narrated by one of the participants. This principle has an exact analogy in Homeric poetics (in the same way as Homeric *horror vacui* corresponds to filmic crosscuts). Simultaneous actions are presented in Homer, as Tadeusz Zieliński points out, either as if they were consecutive events or by the omission of one of the two parallel events, and a palpable gap results if an event is not delineated in advance so that we may easily anticipate its course.[10] Surprisingly enough, the montage of sound film coincides exactly with these principles of ancient epic poetics. An obvious tendency toward the "linear" character of cinematic time already appeared in silent film, but titles allowed for exceptions. On the one hand, announcements such as "And meanwhile . . ." introduced simultaneous actions, and, on the other hand, titles like "NN spent his youth in the village" made possible jumps into the past.

Just as the above-mentioned "law of chronological incompatibility" belongs to the Homeric age, not to narrative poetry in general, so in turn we do not want to generalize hastily upon the laws of contemporary cinema. The theoretician of art who attempts to include the future development of art in his formulae too often resembles Baron Munchausen lifting himself by his own hair. But perhaps one can pick out certain points of departure from which more definite tendencies might develop.

As soon as an inventory of poetic devices takes root and a model canon is established so thoroughly that the literacy of epigones can be taken for granted, then, as a rule, a striving toward prosification usually develops. The *pictorial* aspect of film is minutely elaborated today. And just for this reason filmmakers are suddenly calling for sober, epically oriented reportage and there is an increasing aversion to filmic metaphor, to self-contained play with details. In a parallel way, interest in plot construction, which until recently was almost ostentatiously neglected, is increasing. Let us recollect, for instance, Eisenstein's famous, almost plotless films; or Chaplin's *City Lights,* which in fact echoes the scenario of *A Doctor's Love,* a primitive film by Gaumont from the beginning of the century: a blind woman is treated by an ugly hunchbacked doctor, who falls in love with her but does not dare tell her; he says that she can remove the bandage from her eyes the next day because the treatment Is over and she will see. He leaves, suffers, convinced that she will despise him for his ugliness; however she throws herself upon his neck: "I love you, for you cured me." A kiss. The end.

As a reaction against an overdone sophistication, against a technique reeking of ornamentation, there arises a purposeful looseness, an intentional rawness, a sketchiness as a device (*L'Âge d'or* of the cinematic genius Buñuel). Dilettantism is beginning to delight. In the current vocabulary the words "dilettantism" and "illiteracy" sound despairingly pejorative. Yet there are periods not only in the history of art but even in the history of culture when these factors undoubtedly have a positive, dynamic role. Examples? Rousseau—Henri or Jean Jacques.

After an abundant harvest a field needs to lie fallow. The center of film culture has already changed several times. Where the tradition of silent film is strong, sound film has particular difficulties in breaking a new path. Only now is Czech film going through a period similar to the modest Czech debuts at the threshold of the eighteenth and nineteenth centuries for a new national literature. In the Czech silent film little of significant interest was done. Now, since speech has penetrated the cinema, Czech films worth seeing have appeared. It is highly probable that precisely the lack of a burdensome tradition facilitates experimentation. Real virtue arises from necessity. The ability of Czech artists to profit from the weakness of their native tradition is almost traditional in the history of Czech culture. The fresh, provincial originality of Mácha's romanticism would hardly have been possible if Czech poetry had been burdened with a mature classical norm. And is there a more difficult task for contemporary literature than the discovery of new forms of humor? Soviet humorists imitate Gogol', Čexov, and so on; Kästner's poems echoes the sarcasm of Heine; present-day French and English humoresques largely recall centos (poems composed from quotations). *The Good Soldier Švejk* could emerge only because the Czech nineteenth century did not generate a canonical humor.

Notes

1. Puškin, *Journey to Erzerum.*

2. See Lev Kulešov, *Repeticionnyj metod v kino* (Moscow: 1922).

3. See Louis Delluc, *Photogénie* (Paris: 1920).

4. See Boris Éjxenbaum, "Problemy kinostilistiky," in the collection *Poètika kino* (Moscow: 1927).

5. Jurij Tynjanov, "Ob osnovax kino," in the collection *Poètika kino* (Moscow: 1927). [French translation: "Fondements du cinéma," *Cahiers du cinéma,* 1970.]

6. See Jean Epstein, *Bonjour cinéma* (Paris: 1921).

7. Emile Vuillermoz, "La musique des images," in *L'art cinématographique,* vol. III (Paris: 1927).

8. *Der sichtbare Mensche oder die Kultur des Films* (Vienna-Leipzig: 1924), p. 143.

9. *Iskusstvo kino i montaž fil'ma. Opyt vvedenija v teoriju i èstetiku kino* (Leningrad: 1926), p. 71.

10. "Die Behandlung gleichzeitiger Ereignisse im Antiken Epos," *Philologus,* 1901, Supplementband VIII: 3, p. 422.

Part IV

13. Poetic Reference

Jan Mukařovský

I

The aim of this paper is to differentiate poetic reference from other types of reference. By this term we mean every reference appearing in a text which has a dominant aesthetic function. Thus, we do not mean only figurative references, for figurative reference not infrequently goes beyond the limits of poetry, appearing in informational language as well, and not only in the form of petrified images, but also as any newly created image (for example, an emotional image). On the other hand, not every poetic reference is figurative: there have existed poetic schools that deliberately set out to keep the use of images to a minimum.

What then is the characteristic quality of poetic reference, if not its figurative character? It has been pointed out many times that the specific quality of poetic language does not reside in its "plasticity": a poetic utterance does not necessarily need to aim at evoking a vivid image. It would be equally incorrect to propose "novelty" as the essential quality of poetic reference, since there are frequent instances of poets and whole schools of poetry fond of using traditional references—which are sometimes "poetic" ones but often also of a kind belonging to the vocabulary of ordinary language.

We must, therefore, continue to seek the specific quality of poetic reference. As our point of departure we will take any locution, preferably one which, owing to the neutrality of its semantic coloration, can be understood both as a part of an informational utterance and as an extract from some poetic text. Such, for example, is the sentence, "It's turning dark," which we spontaneously perceive as a piece of information, but which, with a change in semantic direction, we can quite easily interpret as a poetic citation from a hypothetical text. Each of the two cases brings to bear a different semantic aspect. If the sentence is taken as information, the attention of the perceiver is focused on the relationship between the reference and the

"Dénomination poétique et la fonction esthétique de la langue," *Actes du quatrième Congrès international de linguistes* [1936]. (Copenhagen: 1938), pp. 98-104, translated by Susan Janecek.

reality indicated. Perhaps some doubt as to its documentary value would arise; we might ask ourselves: Is it really getting dark? Could this asser- tion be mistaken or false? Or is it an example of grammatical usage with no relationship to any actual concrete situation? and so forth. The answer to these questions—questions which also allow of other, different formula- tions, and which may well remain unarticulated—will determine the import of the communication for appropriate action. Our attitude toward the statement in question changes completely, however, the moment we take it as a poetic citation. At once its relationship to the surrounding context, even though hypothetical, becomes the center of attention. Not knowing the context, we will be puzzled: Is this sentence the beginning, the conclu- sion or a refrain in the poetic text? In accordance with the solution we de- cide on, the semantic aspect of the hypothetical quote will change distinctly. If in place of the imaginary example, we had taken a complete poetic text, for example, a lyric poem, we would be able to establish a whole series of relationships mutually tying together its elements (words, sentences, and so forth) and defining the significance of each in terms of the place it holds in the chain.

Poetic reference is primarily determined, then, not by its relationship to the reality indicated, but by the way it is set into the verbal context. This explains the well-known fact that a word, or a group of words, character- istic of a certain prominent poetic work, if transferred from its own con- text to another one, a discursive context, for instance, carries with it the semantic atmosphere of the work in which it participated and with which it is associated in the linguistic consciousness of the community.

The typical—but not essential—propensity of poetic language for figura- tive references, and especially for new, nonautomatized images, must also be seen as explaining the intimate association of poetic reference with the context. Such images owe their very possibility to the semantic cohesion of the context which allows for introducing a new and original relationship between a word used in a figurative sense and a reality which that word does not ordinarily signify; it is the context that suggests to the reader the signification which has been attributed to the word by the poet's own indi- vidual and unique intention (Tomaševskij). One might even go so far as to assert that all the stylistic devices of poetry, so, for instance, various kinds of sound instrumentation that elicit mutual semantic reactions among the words they bring together, render service to the essential tendency of poetry, namely, to determine reference above all by linkage in context (Tynjanov). Thus, in poetry, as against informational language, there is a reversal in the hierarchy of relations: in the latter attention is focussed above all on the relation, important from the practical point of view, between reference and reality, whereas for the former it is the relationship between the reference and the context incorporating it that stands to the fore. This is not to say that informational reference is absolutely exempt from any effect of the context or that, on the other hand, poetic reference is excluded from any contact with reality. All that is involved is a shift, so to speak, in the center of gravity. As for poetic reference, the weakening of its immediate relationship with reality makes of it an artistic device. That means that the poetic reference is not evaluated in terms of an extralinguistic mission but with relation to the role imposed upon it in the organization of the work's semantic unity.

II

Now is the time—before moving on to further analysis of poetic reference—to recall Karl Bühler's well-known model of the basic functions of the linguistic sign, of which he has presented several elaborations, most recently in his *Sprachtheorie.* According to Bühler, there are three functions inherent in the very nature of language, which are: representation (*Darstellung*), expression (*Ausdruck*), and appeal (*Appell*). Each of these functions consists in an active relation between the linguistic sign and one of three extralinguistic factors necessarily present in any act of discourse. These factors are: the reality indicated by the sign, the person who sends the message, and the person who receives it. As long as we have informational language in mind, Bühler's model is perfectly applicable. Thanks to it, we are easily able to distinguish traces of the three basic functions in any informational discourse, often with one of these functions predominating over the other two. Once we turn to poetic language, the situation becomes quite different. It is not that traces of the three functions enumerated above cannot also be detected here, but rather that here the foreground is occupied by a fourth function unaccounted for by the model in question.   This function stands in opposition to all the others: whereas the latter are oriented toward factors external to language and toward aims reaching beyond the linguistic sign, this new, fourth, function puts the linguistic sign itself at the center of attention.   The first three functions thus make language enter into connections of a practical order; the fourth detaches language from such connections.   Or to put it another way: the first three functions belong to the set of practical functions; the fourth is the aesthetic function.   The focus of the aesthetic function on the sign itself thus comes about as a direct consequence of the autonomy belonging to aesthetic phenomena.   This aesthetic function is something we have already encountered along the way of our analysis of the relationship of reference to reality.   If, in a poetic text, the relation of the reference with the context surrounding it occupies the foreground to the detriment of the relation with thing signified, then this displacement of semantic values is something the language of poetry owes to aesthetic function.

An objection might be raised to the effect that this phenomenon concerns only poetry and that the abuse done to language by playing with it and deflecting it from its practical purposes, justifiable within the confines of that art, makes the conduct of language in poetry incommensurable with language in normal usage; what holds for poetry does not hold for language in general.   To this objection we would respond: (1) Abuse is a necessary, often times even salutary, opposition to normal usage with respect to anything; indeed, it is thanks only to abuse that the world of functions is able to evolve—abuse is often only a means of trying out, whether consciously or unconsciously, a new, previously unknown way of using something. (2) The boundary separating the aesthetic function from practical functions is not always apparent, and, in particular, it does not coincide with the dividing line between art and other human activities.   Even in a fully autonomous artistic expression, practical functions—in our case the three previously mentioned linguistic functions—are not entirely suppressed, so that every poetic work is at least potentially also a representation, an expression, and an appeal.   Indeed, these practical functions often assert themselves rather extensively in work of art—for example, the representative function in a novel, the expressive in a lyric poem.   And vice versa, no practical activity is doomed never to have any aesthetic function; one might well claim that that function is at least potentially involved in every human act.   Thus, even in the most ordinary speech, aesthetic function can be awakened by any procedure giving prominence to semantic relationships that organize context. Any heightened concurrence or opposition of sense, any striking phonetic similarity, any unexpected inversion of word order, or the like, is capable of causing vibrations of aesthetic pleasure. The *potential* aesthetic function is so powerful that it is often necessary, when preparing an intellectual text of purely informational character to revise it so as to remove the slightest suggestions of deformation in semantic relationships lest it attract the attention of the reader. The aesthetic function, thus, is omnipresent. Therefore, even linguistics cannot deny it a place among the basic functions of language.

However, there is still another objection that linguists might raise against our thesis by declaring that, even if one does recognize its import, still the aesthetic function cannot be included among linguistic functions on a par with the other three because it is a function not limited to language. To this we need only respond that aesthetic function, by virtue of its being the dialectical negation of any practical function, always and everywhere takes on the character of the function to which it is opposed in any given case; as the negation of linguistic functions, it becomes linguistic itself. Moreover, the role the aesthetic function plays in the evolution of language and of language culture is a very considerable one, even if we do not follow the example of the Vossler school in exaggerating it; so, for example, lexical innovations, in order to enter into common use, quite often assume an aesthetic aspect.

One final possible misunderstanding remains to be dispelled: theories demonstrating the predominantly emotional character of poetic language (Ch. Bally) seemingly argue against us. It is of course true that there is considerable external similarity between poetic language and emotional language. Both of them, in contrast to intellectual language (where the representative function predominates), have a pronounced tendency to emphasize the person of the author, the sender of the message. In intellectual language, the stronger the intellectual factor, the more the influence of the author's person on the choice of reference is supposed. The ideal goal would be the absolute elimination of that influence and the creation of a definitive bond between the reference and the reality denoted which would be independent alike of the person making the reference and of the context. That is the reason why in science the signification of terms is fixed by definition once and for all. Emotional reference and poetic reference, on the contrary, make the factor of choice stand out and thereby render palpable the very act of reference performed by the author-addresser. In both cases there is a tendency to give rise to the feeling that the reference chosen is only one among other possibilities; behind the actual reference one is always made to sense the potential presence of the entire lexical system of the language in question.[1] Such is the case above all with *figurative* references in both these two languages, poetic and emotional. But the resemblances we have drawn between them are counterbalanced by decisive differences. In emotional language, reference is seen in terms of its relation to the addresser's state of mind: one tries to discern whether the feelings expressed are sincere, what the import of implied volitional elements is, and so on. In poetic language, on the contrary, attention remains once again focused on the sign itself; evaluation in terms of a relation to the state of mind of the author-addresser either becomes secondary or does not come into question at all. With the loss of its import in reality, an expression of feelings becomes an artistic device. Poetic reference, which is subjective as against intellectual reference, takes on an objective character in comparison with emotional reference. Here, once again, we have established that, from whatever side you approach poetic reference, you always find yourself back with the sign itself. The aesthetic function, which is the cause of this return of discourse activity back upon itself, has throughout our analysis shown itself to be an omnipresent dialectical negation of the three basic functions of language and, thereby, also a necessary supplement to Bühler's model.

III

At the end of the first part of our paper, we abandoned the analysis of the relationship between poetic reference and reality once we established that this relationship is weakened in favor of attention concentrated on the sign itself. Is a poetic work, *as* a work of art, deprived, then, of any relevance to reality? Were the answer to this question in the affirmative, then art would be reduced to a game whose sole purpose was to stimulate aesthetic pleasure. A conclusion of that sort would, at the very least, be incomplete. It is, therefore, necessary to resume the analysis of poetic reference in order to demonstrate that the weakness of the relationship between the sign and the reality directly denoted does not exclude, and even does support, the existence of a relationship between the work and the world. We have already established above that poetic reference, in a far more definitive way than intellectual reference, makes manifest, throughout the act whereby it comes about, the active intention of the author of the reference. As a result of the intimate semantic coherence of context that characterizes poetry, this intention is not renewed with each particular reference but remains the same throughout the entire work which, thanks to this unity of referential intention, assumes the character of a global reference (Potebnja). And it is this very reference of a higher order, represented by the work as a whole, which enters into a strong relationship with reality. Does this perhaps suggest that a poetic work, as an artistic creation, "means" what it directly communicates through its theme? To deal with this question, let us take as an example Dostoevskij's novel *Crime and Punishment.* It is highly probable that the majority of those who have read or will read this novel have never committed and will never commit a murder; it is also certain that no crime today could be committed in a social, ideological, and so on, situation just like the one which engendered Raskolnikov's crime. And yet those who read this work by Dostoevskij react to the reading with some of their most intimate experiences; each of the readers has the impression that "sua res agitur." It is highly probable that the psychological associations and semantic combinations set in motion by the reading will differ from individual to individual; and that they, in their totality, can have nothing in common with those of the personal experiences of the author's which gave rise to the work. Be that as it may, in all cases, the life experiences with which an individual will react to a poetic work that touches him deeply will only be partial symptoms of his personal reaction to the poet's attitude toward reality. The stronger that reaction is, the larger the set of experiences set into motion will be, and the stronger will be the influence exerted by the work on the reader's conception of the world.

Since, moreover, the individual is a member of a community, and since his conception of reality is modeled in broad outline on the system of values in force for that community, one may claim that, through the mediation of the individual, poetry exerts an influence on the way the whole society conceives of the world. Therefore we see that the relationship of poetry to reality is considerable, and the more so because a poetic work does not have to do only with concrete realities, but with the entire world. Since a poetic reference, as we have seen, always produces a sense of the whole lexical system of a given language behind it, one might also say that poetry, throughout its evolution, is perpetual confrontation of lexicon with the world of things which the lexicon is meant to reproduce and whose changes it constantly adapts to. We need not assume, however, that the global relationship of a work of art to reality, as we have just described it, is limited only to poetry; it exists in every linguistic performance. There is a mutual counterbalancing between it and the immediate relationship of any particular reference to the reality it denotes; the strengthening of the one weakens the other. The informational function in all its aspects tends toward the pole of immediate relationship, the poetic function, contrariwise, toward the pole of global relationship.

In conclusion, we shall summarize the main theses of this paper. Poetic reference differs from informational reference in that its relationship to reality is weakened in favor of its semantic linkage with context. In poetry the practical functions of language, that is, the representative, expressive, and appellative functions, are subordinated to the aesthetic function, which makes the sign itself the center of attention. The predominance of this latter function accounts for the importance of the verbal context to a reference in poetry. The aesthetic function, as one of the four basic functions of language, is potentially present in every verbal performance; for this reason, the specific character of poetic reference simply resides in a more or less radical displacement of tendencies inherent in any referential act. The weakening of the relationship of poetic reference to the reality denoted directly by any particular sign is balanced by the faculty that a poetic work owes to that weakening itself, namely, to enter as a global reference into a relationship with the entire world as reflected in the life experiences of persons, either senders or receivers.

Note

1. Essentially, any act of reference consists in placing the reality denoted into relationship with the lexical system in its entirety. See in this regard, the following excerpts from a study by S. Karcevskij, "The Asymmetric Dualism of the Linguistic Sign" (Du dualisme asymétrique du signe linguistique," *Travaux du Cercle linguistique de Prague,* I, 1929): "If signs were immobile and had only one function each, language would become a simple repertoire of etiquettes. . . . The nature of a linguistic sign is supposed to be stable and mobile both at the same time. . . . Any linguistic sign is potentially homonym and synonym at the same time. . . . We constantly transpose the semantic value of a sign. But we become aware of it only when the gap between the 'adequate' (usual) value of the sign and its value on a particular occasion is sufficiently wide to impress us. . . . It is impossible to foresee where a sign might be led off to by consequence of its semantic displacements." Thus, poetic reference and emotional reference do no more than shift the accent, in the antinomy of stability and mobility, onto the pole of "mobility."

14. What Is Poetry?

Roman Jakobson

" 'Harmony is the result of contrast,' I said. 'The whole world is made up of opposing elements. And . . . ,' 'And poetry,' he interjected, 'true poetry—the more original and alive its world, the more contradictory the contrasts in which the secret kinship occurs.' " *Karel Sabina (1813-1877), biographer and close friend of the Czech romantic poet Karel Hynek Mácha (1810-1836).*

What is poetry? To define the term, we shall have to juxtapose what poetry is to what it is not. But to determine even what poetry is not is no longer simple.

The list of acceptable poetic themes during the neoclassical or romantic period was quite restricted. The traditional requisites—the moon, a lake, a nightingale, a cliff, a rose, a castle, and the like—are well known. Even the dreams of the romantics were not allowed to stray from the beaten path. "Today I dreamt I was standing among ruins that came tumbling down around me," writes Mácha. "And in the lake below I saw bathing nymphs . . . a lover going to the grave to join his mistress. . . . And then piles and piles of bones came flying out the windows of the old Gothic ruin." Gothic windows, preferably with the light of the moon filtering through, were favored above all other windows. Nowadays, the department-store mirror monstrosity and the village inn's tiny fly-bespattered pane of glass are considered to be of equal poetic worth. And nowadays, just about anything can come flying out of them. The Czech surrealist Vítězslav Nezval writes:

I can be dazzled in mid-sentence by a garden
or a latrine it makes no difference
I no longer tell things apart by the charm
or plainness you have given them

For today's poet, as for Karamazov senior, "there is no such thing as an ugly woman." No nook or cranny, no activity, landscape, or thought stands

"Co je poezie?" *Volné směry*, 30 (1933-1934), pp. 229-239. = *Studies in Verbal Art*, (Ann Arbor: 1971), pp. 20-32. Translated by Michael Heim.

outside the pale of poetic subject matter. In other words, the issue of poetic subject matter has no validity today. Is it then possible to limit the range of poetic devices? Not in the least; the history of art attests to their constant mutability. Nor does the *intent* of a device burden art with any strictures. We have only to recall how often the dadaists and surrealists let happenstance write their poetry. We have only to realize what pleasure the great Russian poet Xlebnikov derived from typographical errors; the typographical error, he once said, is often a first-rate artist. During the Middle Ages, *ignorance* was responsible for the dismemberment of classical statues; today the sculptor does his *own* dismembering, but the result (visual synecdoche) is the same. How is the music of a Musorgskij and the painting of a Henri Rousseau to be interpreted? By the genius of their creators or by their creators' artistic illiteracy? What causes Nezval's grammatical errors? A lack of textbook knowledge or a conscious rejection of it? How would the norms of the Russian literary language ever have been relaxed had it not been for the Ukrainian Gogol and his imperfect Russian? What would Lautréamont have written instead of his *Chants de Maldoror* had he been sane? Speculations like these belong to the category of anecdotal themes like the famous composition topic "How would Gretchen have responded to Faust had she been a man?"

But even if we succeed in isolating those devices that typify the poets of a given period, we have still to establish the line of demarcation between poetry and nonpoetry. The same alliterations and other types of euphonic devices are used by the rhetoric of the period; and what is more they even occur in everyday, colloquial language. Streetcar conversations are full of jokes based on the very figures found in the most subtle lyric poetry, and the composition of gossip often corresponds to the laws of composition followed by best sellers, or at least last year's best sellers (depending on the degree of the gossiper's intelligence).

The borderline dividing what is a work of poetry from what is not is less stable than the frontiers of the Chinese empire's territories. Novalis and Mallarmé regarded the alphabet as the greatest work of poetry. Russian poets have admired the poetic qualities of a wine list (Vjazemskij), an inventory of the tsar's clothes (Gogol'), a timetable (Pasternak), and even a laundry bill (Kručenyx). How many poets now claim that reportage is a more artistic genre than the novel or short story? Although *"Pohorská vesnice"* [A Mountain Village] —a story by one of the leading mid-nineteenth-century Czech prosaists, Božena Němcová (1850-1862)—can boast but few enthusiasts today, her intimate correspondence is for us a brilliant work of poetry.

A short anecdote is in order here. Once, when a world wrestling champion lost to an underdog, one of the spectators jumped up, charged that the bout had been fixed, challenged the victor, and defeated him. The next day a newspaper carried an article saying that the second as well as the first bout had been fixed. The spectator who had challenged the victor of the first bout then burst into the newspaper's offices and gave the editor responsible for the story a slap in the face. But both the newspaper article and the spectator's pique later turned out to be prearranged hoaxes.

Do not believe the poet who, in the name of truth, the real world, or anything else, renounces his past in poetry or art. Tolstoj tried in great exasperation to repudiate his works, but instead of ceasing to be a poet, he forged the way to new unhackneyed forms of literature. As has rightly been noted: when an actor tears off his mask, makeup is sure to be forthcoming.

Do not believe the critic who rakes a poet over the coals in the name of the True and the Natural. All he has in fact done is to reject one poetic school, that is, one set of devices deforming material in the name of another poetic school, another set of deformational devices. The artist is playing no less a game when he announces that this time he is dealing with naked *Wahrheit* rather than *Dichtung* as when he assures his audience that a given work is sheer invention, that "poetry as a whole is one big lie, and the poet who fails to lie audaciously from the word go is worthless."

There are literary historians who know more about a poet than the poet himself or the aesthetician who analyzes the structure of his work or the psychologist who investigates the structure of the poet's psyche. With the certitude of a Sunday School teacher these literary historians map out what in the poet's work is mere "human document" and what is "proof of artistic merit," what is "sincere" and "a natural outlook on life" and what is "sham" and "a labored literary outlook," what "comes from the heart" and what is "affected." All the quotations given here come from the study "Hlaváček's Decadent Erotica," a chapter in a work by Fedor Soldan.

Soldan describes the relationship between an erotic poem and a poet's erotic life as if he were dealing with static entries in an encyclopedia rather than a dialectical alliance with constant shifts, as if he regarded a sign and the object designated by it as monogamously and immutably bound to one another, as if he had never heard of the age-old psychological principle of the ambivalence of feelings—no feeling is so pure as to be free from contamination by its opposite feeling.

Numerous studies in the field of literary history still apply the dualistic "psychic reality vs. poetic invention" scheme, seeking out relations of mechanistic causality between the two so that one cannot help recalling the problem that tortured the old French aristocrat, namely, is the tail attached to the dog or the dog to its tail?

As an example of how sterile these equations with two unknowns can be, let us look at Mácha's diary, an extremely instructive document, which to date has appeared only with considerable expurgations. Some literary historians concentrate entirely on the poet's published work, leaving aside all biographical problems; others try to reconstruct the poet's life in as much detail as possible. While conceding the merits of both these approaches, we very definitely reject the approach of those literary historians who replace genuine biography with official, schoolbook interpretation. Mácha's diary has been expurgated so that dreamy-eyed youths admiring his statute in Prague's Petřín Park will not be disillusioned. But as Puškin once said, literature (to say nothing of literary history) cannot take fifteen-year-old girls into account. And fifteen-year-old girls read much more dangeorus things than Mácha's diary anyway.

The diary described the author's physiological acts—both genital and anal—with epic tranquillity. It records, in laborious code and with the inexorable accuracy of a bookkeeper, the manner and frequency of his sexual gratification with his mistress Lori. Karel Sabina has written of Mácha that "the keen regard of darksome eyes, a sublime brow furrowed with deep thoughts, a pensive mien, which is so often marked by a pale complexion—these plus the feminine traits of refinement and fidelity are what endeared the fair sex to him above all else." And this is how feminine beauty appears in Mácha's poems and stories. The detailed diary descriptions of his mistress's appearance, however, are more reminiscent of Josef Šíma's surrealistic paintings of headless female torsos.[1]

Is it possible that the relationship between lyric poetry and the diary parallels the relationship between *Dichtung* and *Wahrheit*? Not at all. Both aspects are equally valid; they are merely different meanings, or, in more scholarly terminology, different semantic levels of the same object, the same experience, or, as a filmmaker would put it, two different takes of a single scene. Mácha's diary is every bit as much a work of poetry as *Máj* (May, the narrative poem for which Mácha is best known) and "Marinka" (Marinka, a short story). It has no trace of utilitarianism; it is pure art for art's sake, poetry for the poet. Were Mácha alive today, he might well have set aside the lyrical poetry ("Little deer, little white deer, listen to my plea. . . .") for his own intimate use, and published the diary. He would consequently have been compared to Joyce and Lawrence, with whom he has many details in common, and a critic would write that these three authors "attempt to give a true picture of the type of man who has rid himself of all rules and regulations and now merely floats, drifts and rears up as pure animal instinct."

Puškin wrote a poem that begins

I recall a wondrous moment:
You appeared before me like a fleeting vision,
Like a spirit of pure beauty. . . .

Tolstoj in his old age waxed indignant over a bantering letter Puškin had written to a friend in which he referred to the woman of this poem in the following terms: "With God's help I had Anna Petrovna today."[2] But medieval farces like the Czech *Mastičkář [Unguentarius]* are far from blasphemy! The ode and the burlesque are equally valid; they are simply two poetic genres, two modes of expression for one theme.

A theme that never ceased to torture Mácha was the suspicion he was not Lori's first lover. In *May* this motif takes the following forms:

Oh no, it is she! My angel!
Why did she fall before I knew her?
Why was my father her seducer?

and

My rival—my father! His murderer—his son!
He, the seducer of my mistress,
Unknown to me.

At one point in the diary Mácha describes how, after having Lori twice,
he talked with her once more "about her having permitted someone else
to take her. She wanted to die. 'O Gott,' she said, 'wie unglücklich bin
ich!' " There follows another violent erotic scene, after which a detailed
description is given how the poet moved his bowels. The passage concludes: "God forgive her if she is deceiving me; I will not. If only she
loves me. She seems to. Why, I would marry a whore if I knew she loved
me."

Whoever claims that the diary version is a photographically perfect re-
production of reality and *May* a sheer fabrication on the part of the poet
is simplifying the matter as much as the schoolbooks do. Perhaps *May* is
even more revealing than the diary as a manifestation of psychic exhibitionism, intensified as it is by its Oedipal overtones ("My rival—my
father").[3] The motif of suicide in the poetry of Majakovskij was once
thought to be a mere literary trick. It might well be thought so today, had
Majakovskij, like Mácha, died of pneumonia at the age of twenty-six.

Sabina writes that "Mácha's notes contain a fragmentary description of
a person of the neoromantic ilk. That appears to be a faithful picture of
the poet himself as well as the principle model he patterned his lovesick
characters after." The hero of the fragment "slew himself at the feet of
the girl whom he loved ardently and who returned his love even more
ardently. Believing her to have been seduced, he tried to force the name
of the seducer from her so that he might avenge her. She denied everything. He seethed with anger. She swore that nothing had happened.
Then an idea struck him like a bolt of lightening: 'To avenge her I would
have to kill him. My punishment would be death. Let him live. I cannot.' "
And so he decides to commit suicide, firm in the conviction that his mistress
"is a long-suffering angel, unwilling to bring sorrow even upon her seducer."
Then, at the last minute, he realizes that "she has deceived him" and that
"her angel face has turned into the face of a devil." Here is how Mácha
describes his own tragic love affair in a letter to a trusted friend: "I once
told you that one thing could drive me insane. It has come; eine Notzucht

ist unterlaufen. The mother of my beloved died. A fearful vow was taken at midnight by her coffin . . . and . . . it was not true—and I—ha ha ha!— Eduard, I did not go mad, but I did rant and rage."

And so we have three versions: murder and punishment, suicide, and ranting followed by resignation. Each of them was experienced by the poet; all are equally valid, regardless of which of the given possibilities were realized in the poet's private life and which in his oeuvre. Who can draw a line between suicide, the duel that led to Puškin's death, and Mácha's classically ludicrous end?[4]

The many-sided interplay between poetry and private life is reflected not only in the characteristically Máchovian heightened ability to communicate but in the intimate manner in which literary motifs intermingle with life. Moreover, the social function of Mácha's moods is as worthy of investigation as their individual psychological genesis. As Mácha's contemporary, the critic and playwright J. K. Tyl, pointed out in his brilliant pamphlet "Rozervanec" [*The Malcontent*] , Mácha's words "My love has been deceived" are not his private concern, they signify a role since the slogan of his literary school proclaims that "only pain can be the mother of true poetry." On the level of literary history (and only on that level) Tyl is correct in stating that it was all to Mácha's good to be able to say he was unhappy in love.

The seducer versus jealous lover theme is a fitting way of filling up an intermission, the period of exhaustion and melancholy following satisfied desire. A languorous feeling of distrust turns into a conventional motif thoroughly developed by poetic tradition. Mácha himself stresses the literary coloring of the motif in a letter to a friend: "Neither Victor Hugo nor Eugène Sue in their most terrifying novels had the ability to describe the sorts of things that have happened to me. And I was the one who experienced them, and—I am a poet." The question of whether Mácha's ruinous distrust had a basis in reality or—as Tyl implies—was born of free poetic invention is of importance to forensic medicine and forensic medicine alone.

Every verbal act in a certain sense stylizes and transforms the event it depicts. How it does so is determined by its slant, its emotional content, the audience it is addressed to, the preliminary "censorship" it undergoes, the supply of ready-made patterns it draws from. Because the poeticity of the verbal act makes it very clear that communication is not of prime importance, "censorship" here can be relaxed, toned down. Janko Král' (1822-1876), a truly gifted Slovak poet, a poet who in his ruggedly beautiful improvisations brilliantly obliterates the borderline between delirium and the folk song, and is even freer in his imagination, more spontaneous in his exquisite provincialism than Mácha—Janko Král' is, along with Mácha, a classic Oedipal case. Here, in a letter to a friend, is Božena Němcová's description of her first impressions of Král'. "He is terribly eccentric, and his wife, though very young and nice, is terribly naive. He only keeps her as a servant girl, really. He said himself there was only one woman he ever loved, above all else, with all his soul—and that woman was his mother. He hated his father with the same passion: his father tormented his mother (just as he torments his wife). Since she died, he claims to have loved no one. As I see it, that man will end his days in an insane asylum!" But even though it frightened even the intrepid Božena Němcová with its overtones of madness, Král''s extraordinary brand of infantilism elicits no alarm whatsoever in his poems. Published in a collection entitled Čítanie studujúcej mládeže [Readings for Students], they seem little more than a mask. In fact, however, they reveal a mother-and-son love tragedy in such brutally straightforward terms as poetry has rarely known.

What are Král''s ballads and songs about? Ardent maternal love that "never could be shared"; the son's inevitable departure, in the firm belief—despite his "mother's counsel"—that "it was all in vain. Who can go against fate? Not I"; the impossibility of returning "home to mother from far-off lands." Mother searches desperately for son: "Throughout this world my mourning is of the grave, but no news have I of my son." Son searches desperately for mother: "Why go home to your brothers and father, why to your village, winged falcon? Your mother has gone out into the broad field." Fear—the physical fear of bizarre Janko sentenced to destruction—together with Janko's dream of his mother's womb recall the themes of present-day surrealist poets such as Nezval.

Here is an excerpt from Nezval's "Historie šesti prázdných domů" [A Story of Six Empty Houses]:

Mother
Can you leave me forever down there

In the empty room where there are never any guests
I enjoy being your subtenant
And it will be terrible when I am finally forced to go
How many moves await me
And the most terrible move of all
The move away to death.

And now an excerpt from Král''s "Zverbovaný" [The Recruit] :

Oh mother, if you really loved me,
Why did you deliver me into the hands of fate?
Don't you see you have put me out into this alien world
Like a young flower discarded from a flower pot,
A flower no one has ever sniffed.
If they plan to pick it, why do they plant it?
It is hard, so hard for a meadow to be without rain,
But it is a hundred times harder for Janko to be tortured.

The inevitable antithesis of poetry's sudden flow into life is every bit as sudden as its ebb. Here again is Nezval, this time in the vein of poetism, a school he was instrumental in creating.

I've never walked along this path
Have I lost the egg who found it?
A white egg of a black hen
He's been in a fever three whole days

The dog's been howling all night long
The priest, the priest is coming
He's blessing all the doors
Like a peacock with his plumage

There's a funeral, a funeral, it's snowing
The egg is running around behind the coffin
What a joke
The devil is in the egg

My bad conscience spoils me
Then live without the egg
Reader madman
The egg was empty

Out and out advocates of a poetry of revolt were either so embarrassed by these poetistic games that they did their best to hush them up, or so annoyed by them that they spoke of Nezval's decline and betrayal of the cause. I am thoroughly convinced, however, that these childlike rhymes are as significant a breakthrough as the carefully thought out, mercilessly logical exhibitionism of his antilyrics. They are an integral part of a united front, a united front to keep the word from being treated like a fetish. The latter half of the nineteenth century was a period of a sudden, violent inflation of linguistic signs. This thesis can be easily justified from the standpoint of sociology. The most typical cultural phenomena of the time exhibit a determination to conceal this inflation at any cost and shore up faith in the paper word with all available means. Positivism and naive realism in philosophy, liberalism in politics, the Junggrammatiker school in linguistics, an assuasive illusionism in literature and on the stage (with illusions of both the naive naturalist and solipsistic decadent varieties), the atomization of method in literary theory (and in scholarship and science as a whole)—such are the names of the various and sundry expedients that served to bolster the credit of the word and strengthen confidence in its value.

And today! Modern phenomenology is exposing one linguistic fiction after another. It has skillfully demonstrated the prime importance of the distinction between sign and designated object, between the meaning of a word and the content at which the meaning is directed. There is an analogous phenomenon in the sociopolitical field: the heated opposition to muddled, empty, harmfully abstract cant and phrasemongering, the ideocratic struggle against "humbug-words," to use the picturesque expression. In art, it was the motion pictures that revealed clearly and emphatically that language was only one of a number of possible sign systems, just as astronomy had revealed that the earth was only one of a number of planets and thus revolutionized man's view of the world. Columbus's voyage had essentially already marked the end of the myth of the Old World's exclusivity, but not until the recent rise of America did it receive its mortal blow. The film, too, was first regarded as no more than an exotic colony of art, and only as it developed, step by step, did it break asunder the ruling ideology that had preceded it. And finally, the poetry of the poetists and poets belonging to related schools gives a sound guarantee of the autonomy of the word. Nezval's playful rhymes have therefore found effective allies. It has been quite fashionable in critical circles lately to profess certain doubts about what is called the formalist study of literature. The school, say its detractors, fails to grasp the relationship of art to real life, it calls for an "art for art's sake" approach, it is following in the footsteps of Kantian aesthetics. Critics with objections in this vein are so completely one-sided in their radicalism that, forgetting the existence of a third dimension, they view everything on a single plane. Neither Tynjanov nor Mukařovský nor Šklovskij nor I—none of us has ever proclaimed the self-sufficiency of art. What we have been trying to show is that art is an integral part of the social structure, a component that interacts with all the others and is itself mutable since both the domain of art and its relationship to the other constituents of the social structure are in constant dialectical flux. What we stand for is not the separatism of art but the autonomy of the aesthetic function.

As I have already pointed out, the content of the concept of *poetry* is unstable and temporally conditioned. But the poetic function, *poeticity*, is, as the "formalists" stressed, an element sui generis, one that cannot be mechanically reduced to other elements. It can be separated out and made independent, like the various devices in, say, a cubist painting. But this is a special case; from the standpoint of the dialectics of art it has its raison d'être, yet it remains a special case. For the most part poeticity is only a part of a complex structure, but it is a part that necessarily transforms the other elements and determines with them the nature of the whole. In the same way, oil is neither a complete dish in and of itself nor a chance addition to the meal, a mechanical component; it changes the taste of food and can sometimes be so penetrating that a fish packed in oil has begun to lose, as in Czech, its original genetic name, *sardinka* 'sardine,' and is being baptized anew as *olejovka* (*olej-* 'oil' + *-ovka,* a derivational suffix). Only when a verbal work acquires poeticity, a poetic function of determinative significance, can we speak of poetry.

But how does poeticity manifest itself? Poeticity is present when the word is felt as a word and not a mere representation of the object being named or an outburst of emotion, when words and their composition, their meaning, their external and internal form acquire a weight and value of their own instead of referring indifferently to reality.

Why is all this necessary? Why is it necessary to make a special point of the fact that sign does not fall together with object? Because besides the direct awareness of the identity between sign and object (A is A_1), there is a necessity for the direct awareness of the inadequacy of that identity (A is not A_1). The reason this antimony is essential is that without contradiction there is no mobility of concepts, no mobility of signs, and the relationship between concept and sign becomes automatized. Activity comes to a halt, and the awareness of reality dies out.

Notes

1. Poems: Your blue eyes. Rasberry lips. Golden hair. The hour that robbed her of everything had inscribed a fascinating sorrow and melancholy on her mouth, eyes, and brow. . . . Prose: "Marinka"; "Black hair fell artlessly in heavy curls around her pale, gaunt face, which bore the tokens of great beauty, and down upon a pure white dress, which, buttoned up to her neck and reaching down to her tiny feet, revealed a tall, slender frame. A black sash contained her frail body, and a black hairpin spanned her beautiful, high, white brow. But nothing could touch the beauty of her fiery, black, deeply set eyes. No pen can describe that expression of melancholy and yearning." "Cikáni" [The Gypsies] : "Her black curls heightened the beautiful pallor of her tender face, and her black eyes, which smiled for the first time today, had not yet lain aside their long enduring melancholy." The diary: "I lifted up her skirt and inspected her from the front, the sides, and the back. . . . What a fabulous ass. . . . She had beautifully white thighs. . . . I played with her foot, and she took off a stocking and sat down on the couch," and so on.

2. The original has a coarser ring to it.

3. See also "The Gypsies": "My father! My father seduced my mother—no, he murdered my mother—he used my mother—he did not use my mother to seduce my beloved—he seduced my father's beloved—my mother—and my father murdered my father!"

4. Here is how Mácha describes his febrile state three days before his death: "When I read that Lori had been out, I flew into a rage that could have been the death of me. I've been looking very bad ever since. I have smashed everything here to pieces. My first thought was that I had to leave and that she could do what she pleased. I knew why I didn't even want her to leave the house." He threatens her in iambs: "bei meinem Leben schwör ich Dir, Du sichst mich niemals wieder."

15. Signum et Signatum

Roman Jakobson

"The history of what is known as the middle period of Czech verse has not yet been thoroughly examined, but the metrical principles established by the previous century, the era of Czech poetry's maturation and full bloom, retain their validity throughout this period. . . . The development of Old Czech spoken verse—epic verse, in particular—was essentially complete by the second half of the fourteenth century." These words form part of the conclusion to a study I wrote summarizing the results of my research in Czech medieval verse.[1] In my view of fourteenth-century poetry I committed the same error for which I myself had reproached previous treatments of Old Czech poetry. Czech literary historians Josef Král and Jan Jakubec interpreted Gothic literature from a vantage point foreign to medieval aesthetics; they judged Gothic poetic forms by modern criteria obviously far removed from the intent of Gothic poetry. I attempted an immanent analysis of Czech fourteenth-century poetry to determine its own specific missions and goals, and then automatically transferred the concerns of fourteenth-century poetry to that of the following century: I saw the poetry of the Hussite Revolution through the eyes of a contemporary of the pre-Hussite verse allegory *Nová rada* [The New Council]. The results could only resemble what Josef Jungmann, one of the early nineteenth-century reformers of the Czech language, called "the bronze age of Czech poetry, a clear case of dilution, with nothing left but the rhyme."

How does an orthodox classical author look at works of the romantic period? What does an avid romantic think of realism? What does a true disciple of impressionism have to say about later trends in art? They all see a restatement of traditional forms, together with a certain loss in their richness, and find nothing substantially new except deterioration and decay. They fail to understand that new schools have fresh objectives, different systems, a new scale of priorities, that even old features take on new functions when their relationship to one another and to the whole has

An abbreviated version of "Úvahy o básnictví doby husitské," *Slovo a slovesnost,* 2 (1936) = *Studies in Verbal Art* (Ann Arbor: 1971), pp. 200-204 and 218-229. Translated by Michael Heim.

changed. If the historian (especially the historian of culture, literature, or language) views the Hussite period from the vantage point of the Gothic order or Gothic concerns, he will no doubt concur with the conclusions reached by the Czech historian Josef Pekař, who speaks of "the apparent modern spirit and actual medieval spirit" of the Hussite revolutionary movement. According to Pekař's thesis, Hus was in fact a super-Catholic, and the Hussite movement never went beyond the bounds of medieval religious ideology. It was therefore alien to modern social programs and cannot be conceived in terms other than Gothic. Though it doubtless was a revolt, concedes Pekař, the Gothic order sanctioned the right to revolt.

This is all very interesting and instructive, but it is only partially valid. The Hussite period is not only the apogee of the Gothic period; it is also an about-face, an espousal of its opposite. Attempts to amend, perfect, and purify Catholicism merge into the Reformation; super-Catholicism naturally becomes anti-Catholicism—a typical example of how quantity turns into quality. According to Pekař's subtle and stimulating observation, revolt for the sake of reform is a structural component of the Gothic order. But a no-holds-barred revolt and the corresponding no-holds-barred reaction could not but modify the original methods and goals: the quarrel with abuse of authority became a quarrel with authority itself. The result was the spawning of modern methods for contesting traditional authorities.

Despite the fact that the principle idea behind both medieval authority and the Hussites' aversion to it was religious in nature, every attempt at describing the Hussite movement in terms of religion and religion only involves a distortion of the Gothic world view. The Gothic order knew none of the moden era's sharply defined delineations between one field of interest and another, whether religious, artistic, scientific, socioeconomic, national, or erotic. Every phenomenon had several planes, and every event belonged of necessity to more than one sphere. Herein lies the basis for Gothic symbolism. It was not until the Renaissance that individual spheres began to act as independent entities. For ideological reasons, therefore, the Gothic battle with authority could not stop at the religious level; it had no choice but to involve itself in social problems. After all, has there ever been a revolution or counter-revolution in which sociopolitical and religious (or antireligious) concerns were not closely linked? Religion is the controlling, the dominant force in Gothic ideology and makes itself felt in all aspects of Gothic life. Isolating religious problems from social and cultural concerns would be just as unnatural and entail the same atomistic reasoning as cutting off social and cultural considerations from the issue of religion. If the scholar should not seek the all-inclusive key to Hussite turmoil in the quarrel over whether "to eat God's body with gravy or without," as nineteenth-century satirist Havlíček Borovský puts it, he is by no means at leave to treat religious concerns as nothing more than gravy for the Hussite revolution. In fact, as the historian Rudolf Urbánek correctly stresses, all the issues of the time had more of a religious hue than usual. But here, too, quantity shades into quality: the clergy loses its monopoly over ecclesiastical lands and religion undergoes secularization—a basic step in the direction of the secularization of culture as a whole.

It cannot be denied that the social animus of the Hussite period is also an essential component of Gothic ideology. It is based on the demand that the feudal system—in an optimal model—be maintained. For a clear formulation of this position we have only to consult the mid-fourteenth-century author of the *Hradec Manuscript,* in whose moralizing verses scholars have detected progressive, pre-Hussite elements. The poet preaches in the name of an ideal Gothic order founded on religion; every estate has its rights and obligations, and must know its place. "Take note, o ye lords/And leave your poor folk be!/Why do you demand more of them/Than has been established?/You are acting against the will of God,/And thus bringing guilt upon your souls." In other words, do not take more than what has been prescribed. The following passage, however, introduces a drone, and the moral deduced from the drone metaphor is of a completely different order. "The drone consumes the labors of others/Whether in large amounts or small." No longer is there concern over whether a prescribed limit has been exceeded; the concern now is over something having been taken in the first place. "And when summer is over,/The drone grows angry/Because the bees throw him out/And do not let him live with them." All at once a moralizing ditty has turned into a revolutionary slogan. Of course in the *Hradec Manuscript* piece it is still no more than a poetic metaphor. But metaphors generate myths: "*item* they preached and taught that all lords, squires, and knights . . . should be rooted out and have their throats cut." And a myth, even when not fully realized, can become a moving force of history. On the social plane the Hussite uprisings had the class character of a civil war.

How does the Hussite period judge itself? Its most distinguished poet, a representative of the radical wing of the Prague Hussites and author of three extensive works (composed circa 1420 and preserved in the *Bautzen Manuscript*), characterizes Hussite intentions as follows: "These are not new peculiarities;/They are ancient ways of justice/Which people later distorted/And totally transformed."[2] The state of affairs the Hussites opposed is set forth here as a debasement, a violation, a negation of the ancient Christian tradition. Translated into the language of the Hegelian dialectic, this quatrain represents the negation of a negation. But negating a negation never leads to a true return to the positive original, even if the intention to return to a positive past is touted as an official slogan, and people proclaim, "These are not new peculiarities;/These are ancient ways of justice." Pekař's thesis might therefore be reversed to read "apparent medieval spirit and actual modern spirit." Nevertheless, in studying Hussite ideology we must never lose sight of the fact that the general trend was, as the poet says, one of restituting a state of affairs that had been "distorted" and violated, not of inventing "new peculiarities." We must not underestimate the problem of tradition in Hussite innovations. When the Marxist historian and musicologist Zdeněk Nejedlý states that "on religious, national, and social issues the Hussites looked straight ahead, never brooding over what had been" because "they sought what was right, whether it had existed in the past or not," he denies the Hussite movement all historical purpose and divorces Hussite ideology from its motivating forces. He deduces the objectives of the Hussite movement from its ideological consequences. Negative criticism of the Hussites, on the other hand, places paramount emphasis on their historical objectives, even though the consequences (especially the ideological content, which was born of Hussite turmoil and eventually gained wide currency) are qualitatively quite different from their original intent. And yet linguistics, for example, tells us that *energeia* and *ergon*—in other words, language (or any other social value) as creation and as oeuvre—may be inextricably bound to one another, but that they are by no means identical; nor can one aspect be mechanically derived from the other.

With its entire system of cultural values set in motion, Czech poetry of the period, the first half of the fifteenth century, was forced to undergo basic changes.

There can be no doubt that poetry is a self-contained entity set apart by its own signs and determined as an entity by its own dominant feature: poeticity. But it is also a part of higher entities, a component part of culture and of the overall system of social values. Each of these autonomous yet integral parts is regulated by immanent laws of self-propulsion, while at the same time depending upon the other parts of the system to which it belongs; if one component changes, its relationship to the other component changes, thereby changing the components themselves. With the invention of photography, the goals and structure of painting changed; with the invention of moving pictures, the goals and structure of the theater changed. All we mean to do is state the interrelationship between two facts; we are not particularly concerned with ascertaining which came first or finding an unequivocal causal relationship between them. We have said that with the invention of photography came a revision of the goals and therefore the structure of painting. But we might just as well have said that painting, in the course of its internal development, had reached a point at which its goals were so sharply delineated and restricted that photography simply had to be invented and put into practice, if only to assume the burden painting had relinquished. Both formulations are equally legitimate and equally one-sided.

To grasp fully the newness of Hussite poetry, we must place it in a broader context. The development and differentiation of Czech poetic forms is contingent upon the proliferation of the function of the Czech poetic language; the history of poetry and the history of the language are closely intertwined. Semantics, a basic component of poetic form, presents a noetic problem as well. We must therefore confront poetic structure with a comprehensive conception of the sign, which at just this time underwent substantial modification. Via the sign we proceed from the word to a broader concentric circle, that of social context, where a given system of signs, language, and especially poetry comes to fruition.

The language controversy in the Hussite period can also be interpreted on a noetic level. The demand for divine worship in the vernacular is a demand for comprehensibility. It is because Latin was foreign and little understood by the large majority of worshipers that the Hussites equated Latin church music with the howling and barking of dogs. This stand is consistent with the comprehensive concept of the sign. Semiological concerns are a fundamental component and often nothing less than the point of departure for the ideological controversy of the Hussite period (Stanislav Znojemský, Jakoubek ze Stříbra, Gerson), to which both camps made profound and forceful contributions. And yet *philosophia sermocinalis,* the philosophy of discourse, has never become the subject of historical analysis.

In Hussite thought a dialectical reversal turns extreme mysticism into its opposite, strict rationalism. More specifically, the mystery of the sign leads to its condemnation on rationalist grounds. Utraquism, also called calixtinism, the emblematic issue of the Hussite conflict, is especially indicative in this respect. The thought of the Gothic Middle Ages is consistently symbolic, and conceives of the interpenetration of various levels and various spheres of existence as miraculous, mystical cognition. The Gothic metaphor is more than a figure of speech; it is the manifestation of a symbol, and as such has a cognitive value. But the symbol is a mystery, and mystery is binding, mystery is not to be taken lightly. Toward the close of the Gothic period there is an inflation of symbols. The Hussite view of the eucharist reflected a typical inflationary phenomenon: a precious mystery, communion in both kinds, became a common, everyday ritual, and, as is usual with inflation, the value of the ritual declined. Transsubstantiation, the possibility of bread and wine becoming the true body and blood of Christ, was repudiated, disavowed. In the formulation of historian Jan Slavík, during mass the bread remains bread, the wine— wine. Realism, with its proclamation of the immutable, unambiguous quality of the ideal substance of things, could only mean the end of the dialectics of symbols. The Reformation had begun.

As a rule the Gothic was extremely parsimonious of metaphors. Not until the late Gothic did orgies of metaphors like the Hussite ecclesiastical song "Mistr Lepič" [Master Potter] become possible. The overproduction of metaphors (a quantitative phenomenon) suddenly brings about their debasement; the metaphor loses the self-sufficiency of the symbol. Like the poetic symbol as a whole, it becomes a mere token or parable (a qualitative change), to use the terms favored by Hussite writers themselves. The dialectical unity of form and content, of image and thing, of sign and object signified—the dialectical unity that forms the basis of medieval art and philosophy—is completely lost in the Hussite world view. Hus himself said, "It seems to me that I adore the image of Christ not because it is a sign, not because it is an image of Christ; I adore Christ in the presence of the image of Christ because it is an image of Christ and makes me want to adore Christ."[3] The problem of art, a problem that for the Middle Ages was clearly indissoluble, has here been mechanically broken up into the problems of form and content, with form demoted to a mere content container. Gothic nominalism placed a high value on signs (*universalia sunt nomina* [names are universals]); Hussite thought reduced their role to that of a mere ancilla. Hus naturally demanded as transparent a "verbal curtain" as possible, and Hus's friend Jakoubek ze Stříbra, as Nejedlý tells us, finds the artistic image of an object to be of a lower order than its mirror image. To a greater or a lesser extent the Reformation is necessarily iconoclastic— in the literal sense of the word; it tolerates images only insofar as they provide the most practical means of getting at an object. Otherwise, they are gratuitous, contemptible, even pernicious. The author of the *Bautzen Manuscript* puns on the words *obraz* 'image' and *obraza* 'outrage, affront.'

Of course the problem of poetic form is also stated in terms fundamentally different from those of a typical ideologue of the previous period— Tomáš Štítný za Štítného, for example. Štítný writes that "a painted egg tends to be more valuable because of the craft of the person who paints it, but it will be no more useful than an unpainted egg." During the Hussite period, style must not be the crucial or dominant feature of a poem; it must not detract from the message. Any appeal the style may engender on its own is severely condemned for causing the reader "to direct his attention more toward the signs than toward what is being signaled."[4] The role of sound instrumentation is restricted to highlighting and enlivening the content, to enhancing its expressivity.

"Man's Conversation with Death" is a typical Hussite work. Although closely related to fourteenth-century poems about death in theme and, here and there, in actual wording, it differs strikingly in its plainly pro-rational, antimythological intentions and its obvious and brutal naturalism. The poet eschews the circle of metaphors commonly associated with death, and when he does make use of the traditional personification, he takes pains to avoid a graphic confrontation ("Do *not* show me your face"), stresses in a pun that the personification is merely a figure of speech (". . . if I were to catch a glimpse of your face,/I might be frightened *to death"*), and reveal the figure's metonymical nature by answering the question *"What is death?"* in such a way that the actor stands for the act (*"And so death is nothing other/Than the soul separated from the body"*). Likewise, in response to a repeated query about death's "person, form, and appearance," the poet introduces a chain of metonymic images: *umrlčina—umrlce—úmrtí* 'the smell of a rotting corpse—corpses—an instance of death.' In contrast to analogous passages in older poetry, these bluntly physiological images lack even a hint of lyricism or symbolic correspondence and consequently stand out all the more: "Thou shalt watch over my person/ When thou beholdest the corpse's hue:/Terrible, putrid, ghastly,/Ugly, yellow, blackened;/Nothing could be more loathsome/In all earthly creation." The final two lines are a provocative parody of the clichés of the love lyric: "I have met a fair creature/Who hath no equal on earth" or "Though there is a creature on earth.../Than whom no one is dearer to me." Even more indicative of the times than these images of old age and dying are the work's trenchant political observations; death's soliloquies, for example, are forceful attacks on the upper classes. And the most vigorous formulations are underlain by the striking repetition of words with similar sound patterns and by rhymes based on puns; grotesque rhymes and harmonies point up the ironic position of both Death and the author vis-à-vis the man who poses the questions, a prosperous feudal lord who wishes Death to follow the "unjust justice" of man and "wander about doing harm and oppressing the poor while sparing the rich."

Steeped in the literary traditions of the fourteenth century, the author of the *Bautzen Manuscript* enjoys poetic etymologizing (*"Praha* [Prague] comes from *práh* [threshhold] "*) and caustic punning ("Because you Czechs call yourselves *páni* [lords] , you have a *peň* [treetrunk] for a king"), an echo of the gnomic confrontation of *páni* and *peň* in the *Alexandreis,* a fourteenth-century epic. In Hussite works, however, the function of the pun is greatly expanded; the pun becomes a poster variety of sound painting, serving carefully reasoned propaganda and delivering impassioned tirades. There is an urgency about the repetition of certain combinations of sounds, especially vowels and liquids, which seems to unite the words into a strong chain and reinforce the guiding ideas of the text. The pattern *prav.a pravá, plóve prav.a, papr.ové, vr.pra.ové, .lv. pavel prav., pr. prav.* emerges from a passage that reads as follows in English: "God is the eternally true truth/From which every truth flows/As rays from the sun/And springs from the highlands./Paul is speaking of this truth when he says,/"We can do nothing to oppose truth."[5]

The demand for a liturgical language the uneducated could understand and the tendency toward a simpler and more widely accessible literary style coincide with the rationalist bent of Hussite thought. Both phenomena are also clearly connected with another feature of this revolutionary period. We must not overlook the many-sided social changes, especially the distinct trend toward democratization, a salient, yet integral element in the period's system of values and aspirations, and one that historians have amply documented.

Pre-Hussite Czech poetry is inseparable from the ruling estates of feudal Bohemia, both rising and falling with the nobility and high-ranking clergy. It first blossomed forth in the turbulent years when "there were no foreign kings" and the role of the nobility began to increase rapidly. This is the period of such explicit poetic manifestations of the nobleman's ideology as the *Alexandreis*—the canonic historiographical work of Old Czech poetry—and the *Dalimil Chronicle,* the most significant political declaration in all Czech medieval literature. Fourteenth-century Czech literature was for the most part geared to members of the upper classes, and it is primarily their ranks that fed it both practitioners and patrons, the "friends of the Czech tongue" glorified in various works. Smil Flaška z Pardubic, for example, the last important representative of fourteenth-century Czech poetry, was a nobleman and—in his position as leader of the Union of the Nobility, whose goal was to force Wenceslas IV to grant its members concessions—a passionate defender of the interests of his class. The hero of secular poems of the period was always a feudal lord ("I have much land and money. . . . I am a powerful lord; what I want, I have. To no man shall I sell myself."), and the saints about whom *vitae* were written were always of noble birth. The feudal lord was never portrayed as a comic character, while the burgher, artisan, and peasant always served as a target for ironic caricature or harsh class-oriented invective.

Hussite poetry differs radically in social tenor from the aristocratic poetry of the fourteenth century. Contemporaries of the Hussites reproach them indignantly for having "made preachers out of cobblers, tailors and drapers, as well as of millers, potters, butchers, wheelwrights, coopers, bakers and farmers, pewterers and bridlemakers, of spurmakers, tanners and gunners, barbers, tinsmiths, and other artisans." Members of the third estate became the consumers, judges, and, in all likelihood, often the producers of Czech literature. To be sure, the leading lights of Hussite literature included representatives from the privileged estates of feudal society (Vavřinec z Březové, for example, a one-time member of the royal court and, according to Urbánek's plausible hypothesis, the author of the *Bautzen Manuscript*), and these disciples of Gothic culture at its peak assured Hussite works a modicum of literary continuity. But forms requiring a highly educated audience with a well-developed sense of tradition gradually died out, while forms accessible to the masses came to the fore. The exquisite aesthetic experimentation of the author of the *Life of St. Catherine* became impossible at this time, since it assumed an audience in perfect command of poetic canon. Even though the literature of the opposing camp was generally more conservative and traditional, it too was forced to adapt to the habits and views of a lower class of reader if it had any hope of counteracting its enemy's revolutionary propaganda. And because during a civil war putting one's point across effectively becomes the main impetus behind literary activity, anti-Hussite literature underwent a substantial transformation as well.

As the social basis of literature changes, so does its ideology. Once the feudal scale of values was shaken, the burghers gained the floor. Poetry reflected the consequences of this development in various ways.

The right wing of the Hussite party tried to form a coalition of well-to-do burghers and the nobility; as a result, one poet of this persuasion celebrates "the lord, the knight, the burgher of Prague" in his verse. The compositions that make up the *Bautzen Manuscript* call for a much more radical revision of the traditional hierarchy. Nowhere in Old Czech literature is there such a deliberate and daring apostrophe of the burgher class. Prague, not the king, "is and is rightly called" head of the kingdom of Bohemia. If the *Alexandreis* considered a country without a king to be decapitated, the Hussite poet considers a king without Prague—even if he is elected by Czech nobles—to be headless and worthless. Without the consent of the city there is no king, for even a donkey "can be annointed/And crowned with [a] crown." As proof of Prague's primacy the author adduces a modern, highly unchivalric criterion. "The groschen, which measures the value of all things/And provides convenient recompense to all,/ Has at all times been and at all times been called Prague's/and not the king's. . . ." He is willing to recognize the common comparison of the relationship between king and subject to that between head and limb, but only insofar as the monarch does not overstep "the bounds of truth" or tyrannize his people. Otherwise, he prescribes revolt against the "insane head" and proclaims regicide to be God's own tribunal. The revolutionary poet opposes obligatory respect for authority. "Who would have a father/ Who, like a pig that eats its young,/Would eat his sons with great gusto?"

While Hussite literature was undermining the foundations of the traditional ideological system—often even turning it inside out and, in its most extreme form (in "Man's Conversation with Death," for example), severely criticizing both spiritual and secular magnates and identifying with the poor—its opponents bitterly reworked contemporary revolutionary events into the patterns of the phraseology they had inherited. The author of the pre-Hussite *Hradec Manuscript* condemns a man who abandons a woman of high degree for a "coarse slut" and thereby exchanges a beautiful fragrant flower for evil-smelling manure. In the same way, an anti-Hussite pamphlet damns Prague for having repudiated the true king and drafted for its cause the most wretched elements, the worst blackguards of society, "and thereby made fetid what once was fragrant" (as cited by Urbánek). The *Alexandreis* and the *Nová rada* cautioned against nonnoble participation in government; anti-Hussite writings lament its advent in much the same words.

When shifts in social and religious ideology rendered the thematics of the best developed genre of fourteenth-century Czech poetry obsolete, the genre itself—the heroic epic in both its varieties: secular (the knightly epic) and religious (saints' lives)—soon lost its sway. Neither knight nor saint, the two leading human figures of feudal mythology, could claim the role of the hero in Hussite poetry.

Notes

1. Roman Jakobson, "Verš staročeský," *Československá vlastivěda* (Prague: 1934), III, pp. 429-459.

2. For the opportunity to study these works I am indebted to Professor Urbánek, who kindly lent me the copy he himself made of the *Bautzen Manuscript.* I wish to thank him for his aid.

3. "Videtur mihi, quod nec adoro imaginem Christi, quia signum, nec quia imago Christi est, sed adoro Christum coram imagine Christi, quia est imago Christi et excitat me ad adorandum Christum."

4. ". . . plus attendit ad signa sensibilia quam signata."

5. The full Czech text runs as follows: "Bóhť jest pravda věčně pravá,/Z niežto plóve pravda každá,/Jakož z slunce paprslkové,/Z vrchoviště pramenové;/O tejt mluví Pavel pravě:/Nic nemóžem proti pravdě."

16. The Contours of *The Safe Conduct*

Roman Jakobson

A mountaineer walks over a plain. He has nothing to hold on to. He stumbles over its flatness. We draw a clear distinction between our mother tongue and a language we have adopted, though our command of this, too, may be perfect. The difference between the prose of a poet and that of a prose writer is just as striking. Not only does a special stamp mark a poet's prose; a fundamental difference also separates the prose of an age of poetry from that of an age or school oriented toward prose. In the first decades of this century, the vanguard of Russian literature was represented by poetry. It was poetry that was regarded as the unmarked, canonical expression of literature, as its pure embodiment. Almost all the spokesmen both of Symbolism and of the ensuing literary ferment, often subsumed under the general heading of "Futurism," are poets. Apart from a few isolated exceptions, the professional literary prose of this period is typically epigonic work, more or less successfully imitating classical patterns and ingeniously forcing new themes into old molds. While the poetry of the period is charged with internal tension, this prose owes whatever greatness it possesses first to the enormous momentum of quality that Gogol', Tolstoj, and their peers imparted to it and second to the vast dimensions of the present-day reality it deals with. The contribution of this hundredth province of Russian classical realism to the history of literary prose is slight, whereas the prose of V. Brjusov, A. Belyj, Xlebnikov, Majakovskij, and Pasternak—that singular colony of modern poetry—opens up tortuous paths toward a new flowering of Russian prose, as in its time did the prose of Puškin and Lermontov. Pasternak's prose is frankly the prose of a poet in a great age of poetry.

The prose of a writer or of a literary movement chiefly committed to verse is profoundly distinctive, both in those points where it reflects the influence of the dominant—the poetic—element and in those where it strenuously and deliberately reacts against it. The general context in which literature operates, that is, the part it plays in the concert of all the arts, is no less important. Symbolism largely took up the Romantics' slogan about art gravitating toward music as the supreme form of artistic expression.

"Kontury *Glejtu*," Postscript to *Glejt,* the Czech translation of Boris Pasternak's *Oxrannaja gramota* (Prague: 1935), pp. 149-162. Translated by Jarmila Veltruský.

The first art to go beyond the principles of symbolism was painting, and in the early years of Futurist art it was painting that held the leading position. But then, as further development revealed the semiotic nature of art more and more clearly, poetry moved to the fore and became something like a model farm for artistic experimentation. All the poets of the futurist generation evince a tendency to equate art with poetry. But the paths by which individual poets arrive at this order of priorities are different and so are their starting points. Pasternak, a firm disciple of symbolist art, came to poetry from music. Majakovskij's springboard to poetry was painting. For Xlebnikov, the word was always the only conceivable material. We might say that Majakovskij embodies the "Sturm und Drang" in the development of Russian post-symbolist poetry and Xlebnikov its most clear-cut and distinctive achievement, while Pasternak's work connects the new art with symbolism. And although Xlebnikov's poetic character took shape before Majakovskij's, which in its turn developed before Pasternak's, we should be right in the sense that a reader brought up on symbolism was ready to accept Pasternak first, then stumbled his way through Majakovskij and once he had mastered him, embarked on the arduous siege of Xlebnikov's strongholds. But any attempt to view the writers of one particular period as individual links in a single chain of literary evolution and to determine the sequence of these links is always conventional because one-sided. A poet carries on a tradition in certain respects, but he reacts all the more violently against it in others. The elements of rejection and the elements of continuity are discernible only in relation to one another. Therefore Pasternak, who sees his literary mission as the continuation of symbolism, is at the same time aware that the attempt to repeat and perpetuate the older art inevitably gives rise to art of a new kind. Majakovskij, on the other hand, consciously tries to invalidate the old poetry, and yet Pasternak, attuned as he is to symbolism, rightly perceives in Majakovskij's "romantic manner" and in the underlying conception of the world the concentrated heritage of the poetic school that the militant Futurist repudiates. The poetic worlds of Majkovskij and Pasternak are like two related languages, which often differ not only in their neologisms but also in the elements they inherit from their common source: much of what one has retained the other has rejected and vice versa.

Lyric poetry always takes the first person of the present tense for its starting point and principal theme, while the epic takes the third person of the past tense. Russian symbolism is lyrical through and through. Its excursions into narrative are typical attempts by lyric poets to put on an epic mask. In postsymbolist poetry, the two genres diverge: while the lyric impulse, which reaches it supreme expression in the work of Majakovskij, clearly persists and predominates, the purely epic element is embodied, almost unalloyed, in the poetry and prose of Xlebnikov. Pasternak is an exclusively lyric writer, and his prose, especially, is the prose of a lyric poet.

His criticism of Xlebnikov's poetry for having lost touch with real life would certainly have surprized Xlebnikov, who considered on the contrary that his work asserted reality in opposition to the literature of preceding generations which had negated it. For Xlebnikov, every sign, every word uttered is charged with a complete and independent reality, and the question of its relation to some external object, indeed even the question of whether such an object actually exists, is quite beside the point. For Xlebnikov, as for the little heroine of Pasternak's story, a name has the complete and reassuring meaning that it has in childhood. When this heroine grows out of childhood, she begins to suspect for the first time that "a phenomenon conceals something." This adolescent conception of phenomena absolutely matches Pasternak's own. Of course, the epic approach to his surroundings is not open to a poet who is convinced that in the world of prosaic fact the elements of everyday existence enter the soul inertly and vainly and "sink to the bottom—real, hardened and cold, like dull leaden spoons"—and that it is only the passion of the elect that transmutes this "embarrassingly binding truth" into poetry. Feeling alone is recognized as absolutely self-evident and trustworthy. Pasternak bases his poetics on a personal, indeed a proprietary, affective experience of reality. Both in its striving after the purely expressive language of music and in its justification of this conception on the grounds that life-giving passion must triumph over the inevitable, Pasternak's poetry carries on the romantic tradition of symbolism; but as his work matures and takes on a more distinctively personal character, so the original, romantically emotional language increasingly changes into language about the emotions, and it is in the poet's prose that this referential character comes out most clearly.

It is far more difficult to draw a dividing line between Pasternak's work and Majakovskij's. Both are lyric poets of the same generation and Majakovskij, more than any other poet, stunned Pasternak in his youth and continually amazed him. It is easy to discover remarkable correspondences in the tissue of metaphors in the work of the two poets, but the important point is that the function the metaphors perform is entirely different in each case. Majakovskij's *metaphor,* which hones the tradition of symbolism to a new sharpness, is the most penetrating and cogent of poetic figures and the one that determines the construction and the development of the lyric theme. The source of the lyrical impulse is the poet's "I." In the metaphorical lyric, the images of the external world are designed to harmonize with this "I," to transpose it onto other planes, to dissolve the lyric hero in the multiplicity of being and to fuse the multifarious planes of being in the lyric hero. Metaphors operate through creative association by similarity and contrast. The hero is pitted against the contrasting image of his bitter enemy, as multifarious as all the components of metaphorical lyric poetry. This poetry, bound together by the grappling chain of metaphor, fuses the poet's mythology and his being into one indissoluble whole; and the poet, as Pasternak clearly realized, pays with his life for turning himself into an all-embracing symbol. Pasternak's lyrical theme is governed not by metaphorical but by *metonymical* relations. So here it is asociation by contiguity that predominates. The first person appears to have been pushed into the background, but in fact the eternal hero of lyric poetry is present here, too. The images of the outside world function in Pasternak's lyric poetry as contiguous reflections, or metonymical expressions, of the poet's "I." The replacement of an object by one adjacent to it is the simplest form of association by contiguity. But other metonymical courses are open to the poet as well—from the whole to the part and vice versa, from cause to effect and vice versa, from spatial to temporal relationships and vice versa, from simple contiguity to a causal link, and so on. But perhaps the most characteristic of Pasternak's figures is the substitution of the act for the agent, or of the state, expression or attribute for the bearer of it. The poet makes these abstractions autonomous and objectifies them. *Sestra moja—žizn'* (My Sister—Life)—the practically untranslatable title and leitmotif of the most pioneering of Pasternak's collections of poems ("life" is a feminine noun in Russian)—strikingly lays bare the linguistic roots of this mythology.

Majakovskij's element is either the lyric monologue or the dramatic dialogue. The narrative approach is profoundly foreign to him. He prefers second-person to third-person themes. Whatever does not fuse with the poet's "I," Majakovskij regards as an antagonistic opposite. He confronts his adversary face to face, defies him, exposes, crushes, mocks, and anathematizes him. It is not surprising that the only writings in literary prose that Majakovskij completed are his marvelous plays. The reasons that led Pasternak to write his prose stories are equally understandable. No doubt, there are poems interwoven all through with metonymies and narrative prose may be full of metaphors, but nevertheless verse unquestionably has a closer internal affinity with metaphor and prose with metonymy. Verse is based on association by similarity, the verses must be rhythmically analogous in order to be perceived as verses and rhythmical parallelism is most strongly felt when it is accompanied by a similarity (or contrast) of images. Prose is not as a rule deliberately cut up into noticeably similar segments. Its mainspring is association by contiguity: the narration moves from one object to another, in some way contiguous with it.

The essence of poetic tropes is not simply to record the multifarious connections between things but also to displace the usual relationships. The greater the stress under which metaphor operates in a given poetic structure, the more violently are traditional classifications disrupted, while things are redistributed on the basis of new generic traits. Creative (or, as its opponents would say, forced) metonymy also changes the usual order of things. Association by contiguity, the tool Pasternak manipulates so skillfully, transforms their spatial distribution and temporal succession; that is especially striking in the poet's prose experiments, where it is thrown into relief against the background of ordinary referential prose. For Pasternak, these displacements are the effect of emotion or—bearing in mind the expressive function of literature—a means of expressing emotion. In a poetic world governed by metonymy the outlines of things are blurred and the various aspects of one single object turn into independent objects in their own right. These two characteristic features—the decomposition and the mutual interpenetration of objects—link Pasternak's work with the endeavors of the Cubist painters. The contiguities and distances between things change and so do their dimensions. And the relationships between stylistic devices change too—stylistically alien elements join and fuse together.

The wider the range of poetic tropes, the more strongly, to use Pasternak's terms, does "the achieved" overshadow "the object of the achievement." The creative process of connecting throws into the shade the things that are connected; the "charm of autonomous meaning" is brought to light, while the referential link is reduced to a faint glimmer. Like Majakovskij's metaphorical connections or the manifold ways in which the density of language, in its internal and external forms, is heightened in the poetry of Xlebnikov, the metonymical connections created by Pasternak evince the same stubborn urge to nonobjectivity that also characterizes other forms of contemporary art. The creative process of connecting becomes an object in itself. Pasternak continually insists that what is connected is a matter of pure chance: "every detail can be replaced by another." The interchangeability of images is, for the poet, the very essence of art. Images chosen at random not only contain hidden similarities, so that they can serve as reciprocal metaphors, but are also, in one way or another, potentially contiguous: "Who does not have in him something of the dust, something of the motherland, something of the calm spring evening?"—that is Pasternak's apologia for the all-embracing network of metonymic affinities. The harder the affinity is to discern and the more unusual the connection established by the poet, the more the images that are confronted disintegrate and lose their elementary clarity. Significantly, Pasternak consistently opposes "the meaning that is put into things" to their sensory quality, for which he likes to seek out pejorative epithets—in Pasternak's world, meaning necessarily etiolates and sensory quality deadens.

In Pasternak's metonymical poetry, the hero is as difficult to find as in a picture puzzle: he is broken down into a series of component parts and contiguous elements. His place is taken by a chain of his own objectivized states and by the objects, both inanimate and animate, around him. But that which makes him a hero, that is, his activity, in fact eludes the poet's grasp—action is replaced by topography. While in Majakovskij the collision of two worlds necessarily culminates in a duel, the suggestive image found in Pasternak's verses—the world is a mirror to the world—proclaims that the collision is illusory. While Majakovskij shapes his lyric theme as a cycle of metamorphoses undergone by the hero, Pasternak's lyrical prose favors the thematic device of the railway journey in which an excited hero, despite himself unable to act, variously experiences shifts of contiguity and distance. The active voice has been erased from Pasternak's poetic grammar. But if the lyric "I" is passive, is it the "third person" that is the real agent? No. The *agens* remains outside Pasternak's poetic mythology: "As a rule, a man neither knows nor hears that which creates, tunes, and tailors him." The third person, as it appears in Pasternak, designates not the agent but the instrument. The auxiliary, subordinate, marginal part that the third person plays in Pasternak's thematic material is sometimes sharply emphasized: "Another human being came into her life, a third person, absolutely indifferent, nameless or with a merely fortuitous name, arousing neither hatred nor love." All that counts is that this being breaks into the life of the lyric "I." Whatever is not related to this single hero is nothing but "vague agglomerations without names."

This rigorous body of semantic laws also determines the simple organization of the plot in Pasternak's lyrical tales. The hero is possessed, to his delight or alarm, by an external impulse; at one moment he bears its stamp, at the next he suddenly loses contact with it. He withdraws into himself in bewilderment, until the next impulse comes along. The hero's activity is beyond the scope of the poet Pasternak. When he does talk about actions, his language becomes tritely commonplace, and he puts in theoretical digressions upholding his right to platitude. Majakovskij also uses banality as his material, but unlike Pasternak he does so only in describing his adversary. The last of the poet's prose works, *The Safe Conduct,* which replaces the novelistic pseudonyms of the lyric "I" by undisguised autobiography, also provides the clearest revelation of the way Pasternak deals with his subject matter.

There is an obvious connection between Majakovskij's and Pasternak's thematic material and the basic structural features of their poetics. The investigator is entitled to try to find out how the different planes of reality are correlated and facts belonging to one plane may legitimately be inferred from cognate facts belonging to another plane, as a method of projecting a multidimensional reality on to a flat surface. But it would be an error to take this projection for the reality and to disregard the specific structure and internal dynamism of the various planes, that is, to see them as no more than mechanically superposed. From the possibilities that are open at any particular stage in formal development, a given milieu or an individual artist can select what best suits his social, ideological, psychological, and other predispositions. Likewise, when various artistic forms are carried by the laws governing their respective development to a point where they are ready to combine into a single cluster, they seek out an appropriate milieu and a suitable artistic personality to bring this cluster into being. But this harmony between planes must not be regarded idyllically as absolute. It must not be forgotten that there may be dialectical tensions between the different planes of reality. These conflicts between planes constitute the essential mainsprings of cultural history. If many individual traits of Pasternak's poetry are in harmony with the characteristic features of his personality and social environment, his work necessarily also contains those qualities which the poetry of the period stringently imposes (as the indispensable mainstays of its total structure) on every one of its poets, regardless of his individual or social propensities, so that any poet who refused to comply would automatically find himself ejected from the mainstream of this poetry. The poet's artistic mission never enters his biography without a struggle, just as his biography is never entirely absorbed in his artistic mission. The hero of *Safe Conduct* is a chronic bungler, because the actual successes of his original model, the historical Boris Leonidovich Pasternak, are of no use to Pasternak the poet. The tendency to make the sign independent of the object, which we have discerned in the poetry of Pasternak and his contemporaries, is the guiding principle of the whole of modern art, which arose as the antithesis of naturalism. It is inseparable from the pioneering endeavor of this art and does not depend on the biographical features of the individual practitioners. The attempts made by certain observers to link this specifically artistic phenomenon with a limited social sector and an ideology corresponding to it are typically mechanistic aberrations: if we infer from the nonobjective character of an art that the artists' conception of the world is nonrealistic, we artificially obliterate an important antinomy. In fact, the nonobjective tendency in art corresponds more closely with an objectivist tendency in philosophy. Although the idea of belonging to a compact group and a well-defined school is deeply repugnant to Pasternak, who passionately assails all firm contiguities, and although the period was splintered into ideological groups divided to the point of mutual hatred and incomprehension, yet Pasternak's poetry provides clear evidence of his affinity with his generation. It is apparent both in his creative abolition of the object and in his reconstruction of the grammar of art. The heart of this grammar had been the past and the present tense, and the present time, contrasted only with the past, had been conceived merely as an indeterminate, unmarked, "nonpast."

It was futurism which, by its name, theory, and practice, sought to bring the future into the poetic system and make it the crucial category. That is what the verses and manifestos of Xlebnikov and Majakovskij incessantly proclaim and Pasternak's work is imbued with the same endeavor, despite his ingrained propensity for the "deep horizon of memories." Within the context of the new antithesis, Pasternak sets the present time on a new footing as an independent category. He sees that "the very perceptibility of the present is already the future," and it is not by chance that in the closing lines of *The Safe Conduct* reflections of the future fall upon the present and the past. Is there any need to add that this grammatical reform radically alters the very function of poetry in the sphere of social values?

17. Response to Verbal Art

Felix Vodička

Within the framework of structural aesthetics, a literary work is understood as an aesthetic sign intended for the public. We must, therefore, always keep in mind not only a work's existence but also its reception; we must take into account that a literary work is aesthetically perceived, interpreted, and evaluated by the community of readers. Only by being read does a work achieve aesthetic realization, and only thereby does it become an aesthetic object in the consciousness of the reader. Aesthetic perception is closely tied in with *evaluation.* Evaluation presupposes evaluative criteria, and such criteria do not remain unchanged. Therefore, the value of a work, from the point of view of historical origins, is not a constant and invariable quantity. Precisely because the criteria for evaluation and the literary values themselves continuously change over the course of history, it is the natural task of literary historical science to record these changes.

Once published or otherwise disseminated, a literary work becomes the property of the public, which approaches it from the standpoint of contemporary artistic taste. To identify the configuration of this artistic taste in the sphere of literature must be the literary historian's foremost task if he is to comprehend response to, and the actual evaluation of, verbal art. In the study of literary evolution, faced with the task of discerning the evolutionary value of a work, we had to take it as a link in the evolutionary series, without regard to how the work in fact functioned aesthetically and how it was evaluated.[1] Now we must shift our attention to aesthetic objects and to works as aesthetic values. With this aim in mind, we must study the evolution of aesthetic awareness insofar as it has suprapersonal dimensions and encompasses in itself epochal attitudes toward verbal art.

Features of subjective evaluation arising momentarily from a reader's particular disposition of mind or from his personal sympathies or antipathies must be separated from an epochal attitude toward literary phenomena, inasmuch as only features marked by historical universality are the real aim of our inquiry. What this amounts to, in substance, is the recreation of literary norms in their historical evolution for the purpose of

"Dějiny ohlasu literárních děl," *Čteni o jazyce a poesii,* ed. B. Havránek and J. Muka-řovský (Prague: 1942), pp. 371-384. Translated by Ralph Koprince.

investigating the relationships between that evolutionary series and the specific evolution of literary structure. Naturally, aspects of literary norms have some bearing on a work at its inception. Mukařovský characterized a literary work from this point of view as "a dynamic equilibrium of diverse norms, applied in part positively and in part negatively."[1]

Elsewhere, we have traced this relationship in dealing with the genesis of a work.[3] Our further considerations must take into account that the very existence of a set of epochal norms determines in what way a work finds its place in literature. The relationship of the aesthetic norm to new works of literature is instituted by a dynamic tension through which a work often has the power to shift the norm in a direction different from that of the original norm. A work must not, therefore, always be positively evaluated when it conforms with the norm, since aesthetic expectation may be directed toward something new and different from the norm. If we now take literary norms and examine them in their evolutionary continuity, we should be able also to trace the interrelationships this normative historical series has with the historical series of existing literary works, and, consequently, with the evolution of the literary structure. There is always a definite parallel correlation between them, since both kinds of creativity— the creation of a norm and the creation of a new literary reality—proceed from a common basis, from the literary tradition which both are surmounting. Still, the two series cannot be merged together, for all the diversity in the life of literary works springs, in fact, from the dynamic tension between a work and the norm. The most common case is where literary evolution outstrips literary taste, so that the literary norm lags behind. However, the opposite may also happen, particularly when critics, who take upon themselves the function of promoting the development of literary norms, advance requirements which are only subsequently materialized in a literary creation. We must, that is to say, keep in mind that aesthetic perception is not determined solely by traditional conventions but also by the desire for new, concrete works answering to indefinite, intuitively felt, rather than expressible, conceptions of the beautiful which had not hitherto been implemented in literature. The particular state of literary structure serves, to be sure, as the basis for evaluating the norms of a specific period, provided, however, we understand the literary structure as something constantly being surmounted, so that only an exceptional

literary norm will end up rigidly stabilized.   It may also sometimes happen
that a literary theory exists as a norm without being infused with literary
reality, either as a historical anomaly (various dogmatic poetics) or as a
programmatic utopia or in cases where the requirements of a theory are not
realized to the full extent.

Literary norms and requirements provide a base for evaluation. We must
not envisage the literature of a given period merely as a set of existing works
but equally as a set of literary values.   The literary public of any particular
nation or of any particular social stratum at any given time maintains within its purview a certain number of works arranged in a certain hierarchy of
values.   Every new work becomes in some fashion incorporated into this
literature and is evaluated by its readers on a wholly intuitive basis.   This
evaluation, however, has significance for the stability of the scale of literary
values only once it has been made public.   Hence, the importance of the
function carried out by critics.

Just as it is the task of literary history to record the entire wealth of relationships stemming from the opposition between a literary work and
reality, so the dynamics established by the opposition between a work and
the reading public must also become the object of historical description.
Only thus can we obtain a picture of literary life, properly so called, where
works become matters of aesthetic perception and also a value, often with
a bearing not only on the aesthetic sphere but on the entire social life of
any given community of readers, as well.

We may now, by way of a summary, enumerate the following principal
tasks of literary history within the range of the given opposition between a
work and the way it is perceived:

Reconstruction of the literary norm and of the set of literary requirements
of a given period.

Reconstruction of the literature of a given period (that is, of the body of
works that are the object of active evaluation) and description of the
hierarchy of literary values of the given period.

Study of the actualizations of literary works (of both past and present),
that is, a study of that shape a work takes when we encounter it in a given
epoch's frame of reference (especially in literary criticism).

Study of the extent of a work's effectiveness in the literary and extraliterary
spheres.

All of these partial tasks, of course, mutually interrelate with, and reciprocally interpenetrate, one another. Naturally, it is not merely a question of registering all the facts having bearing upon the given tasks. What is involved is the effort to establish the fundamental tendencies of the evolutionary process. The very nature of this process, accompanied, as it is, by a constant tendency toward change, precludes our arriving at laws as understood in the natural sciences, especially since we must keep in mind that in a social organism of perceivers of literary products we will find several strata side by side, each always gravitating toward a different norm, whether this diversity be defined by the changing of the generations (the literary norm of the sons, fathers, and grandfathers), or by a vertical division of the literary public (aesthetically sophisticated readers, the ordinary reading public, readers of substandard literary products). That is precisely why a careful literary historical analysis will avoid the sort of generalization that disregards the elaborate stratification of a literary norm. The very cognizance of local, generational, and vertical divisions in the reading public calls for a study of the interrelations among the literary tastes of the various social strata of readers.

There are, however, additional methodological problems that emerge in connection with the tasks mentioned above. Here we can point out only the most important ones.

The Reconstruction of a Literary Norm

What are the sources for the study of a literary norm?

1. The norms are embodied in the literature itself, that is, in those works which are read, favored, and against which other or new literary works are measured and evaluated.

2. Prescriptive poetics or contemporary literary theories enable us to identify the "rules" to which the literature of a given period "ought" to conform.

3. Critical evaluations of literature, the points of view and the methods of evaluation, and critical requirements bearing on literary creation, constitute an especially substantial source. The attention of the historian is concentrated on this critical activity above all, since this is, as it were, the only remnant of the active and evaluative relationship of the reader to

the work. The critic, as a member of the set of persons actually taking part in literary life and associating around a work, has his assigned function. It is his responsibility to express his opinion about the literary work as an aesthetic object, to record the actualizations of a work, that is, the shape it takes from the point of view of the aesthetic and literary taste of the time, and to express his opinion about its status in the system of established literary values, determining, by his critical judgment, to what extent the work complies with the requirements of literary evolution. It is the literary historian's business to observe how the critics of a given period fulfilled this function, just as it is his task to judge how poets performed their function with regard to given literary tasks. There are periods when criticism has a retarding effect on literary evolution, whereas at other times, conversely, it is a stimulus. There are periods when it assists the public in a change of taste, whereas at other times it stands guard over the traditional values of the past. There are, however, also moments when it neglects some of its functions—for example, the evaluation or description of actualization— which naturally has its consequences in the system of contemporary values: the hierarchy of values is shaken and literary taste finds itself at a state of amorphousness.

Critics operate with certain requirements and employ certain methods that the historians have to unveil. We must not identify the methods of literary criticism with the methods of scholarly analysis of a work of verbal art or with the process of literary history. Thus, for example, the strongly marked psychologizing attitude at the turn of the century (for example, Hennequin's *esthopsychologie*) is not merely the consequence of scholarly understanding of the importance of psychological factors in a work; it is connected with the literary norm in that it emphasizes psychological elements as a requirement in literary creation. Critical methods promote the actualizing and the evaluating of a work from the point of view of given requirements, whereas the methods of literary history make it possible to comprehend and interpret a work in connection with other historical phenomena. In the past, of course, it has often happened that the boundaries of the two fields overlapped, and, unawares, the critic became a historian, the historian—a critic. Therefore, works of literary history may also, to a certain extent, become a source for the understanding of a norm, especially as regards those periods of literary history which emphasize evaluative opinion expounded from the point of view of given postulates independently of historical realities. To be sure, it is necessary to proceed cautiously here, assessing each case individually.

When speaking about a norm and requirements, it is necessary to stress that the requirements cannot pertain merely to how the material is organized from a technical point of view (the rules). According to Mukařovský, norms also embrace ethical, social, religious, philosophical, and other requirements, that is, those which pertain to the thematic questions of literature. From this point of view literature is made to confront tasks that it must master in terms of aesthetic functions. Conversely, it may also be observed how the perception of a work keeps within the range of requirements of contemporary life or ideology, which exert an influence on its aesthetic evaluation, as well. In the perception of any work of art a relationship between the reality of social life and the social values, on the one hand, and the reality communicated by artistic devices, on the other always comes into force with the thematic elements. Consequently, evaluation, too, is the result of a complex process conditioned by the entire epochal structure of life and of its values, as Mukařovský set forth in his book, *Aesthetic Function, Norm, and Value as Social Facts.* Each work that becomes the object of evaluation encounters, in those circumstances, as well, the habits and conventional notions of the perceiving social group, so that the actualization of a work at any particular period materializes against the background of such habits and conventions, whether the evaluation be positive or negative. A work with a theme that is unusual and unsupported by literary or social tradition appears as a violation of the norm in the same way as does any new artistic implementation of themes regarded conventional by the norm of the time.

The criticism of works of literature from the viewpoint of certain religious, social, aesthetic, or other ideas can be so strongly emphasized in the literary norm that the aesthetic function of a work is felt vividly only where it is supported by a coinciding ideological trend (let us recall the religious orientation in medieval literature). There is, of course, a definite line separating the aesthetic perception of a work and ideological judgment of it. Once evaluation of a work focuses only on that reality, about which the work communicates something, and ceases to consider the work itself and its structure, once the work is criticized only in terms of the truthfulness of the message conveyed and not also in terms of the mode of poetic expression in the actual text, then the field of inquiry is deprived of precisely that essential element which so expressly separates the aesthetic sign from other sets of signs which have primarily communicative functions. Inquiry focused only on communication no longer appertains to the field of literary historical research proper and instead becomes a matter of cultural history for which the literary work would be a source. From a methodological point of view, however, we must always keep in mind that a literary work, owing to its aesthetic function, can be regarded a historical source only with discretion and on the condition that its function be respected, since this function may dominate the communication in a given work as well, especially seeing that very often literary works tend toward plurisignification which makes multiple interpretation possible.

The Reconstruction of the Hierarchy of Values in the Literature of a Given Period

An essential feature of the human relationship to the phenomena that constitute the reality surrounding us is that those phenomena be evaluated and, in accordance with their given values, be entered into whole systems of current values. Evaluation includes the desire to overcome uncertainty and indefiniteness in the relationship of the individual or of entire human communities to phenomena; and aesthetic perception, too, is accompanied by evaluation. With respect to literature, what is at stake here is a constant regulation of the tension issuing from the existence of literary works, on the one hand, and the general disposition of the readers' perception, on the other—in other words, the structure of a work and the structure of the literary norm meet in evaluation.

The literary historian's attention focuses on that which constitutes the scope and content of literature at a given moment in literary evolution. We have in mind here living literature, literature that is actively a part of readers' awareness; we are not concerned with historical literary values outside the range of intensive reader interest and, therefore, permanently or temporarily without active aesthetic effect. This reconstruction of the living literary repertoire has its importance for an understanding of the literary norm of a given period and for the study of change in the literary viability of individual works and authors. We investigate which of the works of past and contemporary authors were favored, and we investigate what the relationship to contemporary and past literary trends was. We realize that not every work published finds a place within the literary values of its time, although it might well become an unquestionable value later on (there are also, of course, works that do become historical values as soon as they appear). Conversely, the sphere of living literature may incorporate works which had long ago been ejected from "high" literature or which had never been included in it as works of low literary taste (the cult of the folk song, the cult of the huckster's ditty).

Close and careful attention to the social basis underlying the differentiation of literary taste is a methodological prerequisite in the study of the literary consciousness of a given period. Investigation can discover in what kind of relationship the literary repertoire of the broad reading public stood with respect to the repertoire of readers of "high" literature, what the range of readers' preferences was, whether the reading public was compact and homogeneous in its literary preferences or whether it divided into disparate groups, and so on. Here we confront tasks of a sociological character, but any scholar would be committing an error if he explained the origin of the literary norm of particular social groups solely with reference to the living conditions of the given group, ignoring the power of literary convention and traditional literary processes stemming from the nature of the material. There are, undeniably, certain definite relations between literary taste and the living conditions of a particular social stratum, but the objective evidence is insufficient for a causal interpretation of dependency. As in the evolution of literary structure, the main causal evolutionary elements are immanently contained within the preceding state of the literature. The evolution of the literary norm is determined above all by causes that originate from the organization of the structural elements of the literary norm, since the new evolutionary stage brings to the forefront precisely those elements that were neglected in the preceding norm. Therefore, the evolution of the literary norm can also be interpreted in structural terms. Still, heteronomous factors can, to a certain extent, play a role even here, in the creation of norms and contemporary values. The publisher, the book market, advertising—these are factors that can affect evaluation, and, similarly, sudden reversals in political events or political pressure can contribute to a change in the norm. The historian investigates the relationship of these heteronomous elements to the immanent conditions of the literary norm's new organization and observes whether these external interferences accelerate or retard the autonomous evolution or how the new norms and new evaluations find their expounders and interpreters despite external disruptive interferences or how they so strive to avoid pressure that the latter becomes ineffective. The real norm is not always what passes itself off as such. External interferences can also contribute to a divergence in the paths of literary creation and of the norm. But such discord cannot go so far that all points of contact vanish, for the literary norm—even though it itself can influence arising works—does, after all, more or less depend on existing literary creation. The requirements can, no doubt, temporarily depart very markedly from the possibilities of given literary situations, but if a conception of how literature must have appeared is not to remain a matter merely of endless speculation, literary reality must serve as the basis for further efforts.

Response to Literary Works and Their Actualization

If literary history is to arrive at any understanding of the essential features of literary life, it needs not only to ascertain the positive or negative evaluation of a literary work or to come to certain conclusions about public taste, but also, and much more so, it needs to investigate, in the continuum of history, that concrete shape of literary works which comes about in the act of aesthetically oriented reading. Older literary history used to treat individual works as fixed values, observing how such values were understood and disclosed by critic and reader. Differences and discrepancies in evaluation were construed as errors and deficiencies of literary taste on the assumption that there existed a single "correct" aesthetic norm. Literary historians, aestheticians, and critics never, however, agreed on that single "correct" norm. Since, consequently, there is no correct and single aesthetic norm, there also is no single evaluation, and a work can become subject to multiple evaluation, in the process of which the shape of a literary work (its actualization) constantly changes in the mind of the perceiver. The term actualization (concretization) was used for the first time by Roman Ingarden in his book, *Das literarische Kunstwerk.* He also

issued a call for an inquiry into the life of literary works in their actualizations. Ingarden sees the structure of a work in isolated and static terms, irrespective of the evolutionary dynamics of overall literary structure.
Therefore, he supposes that a work may be actualized in such a manner that all of the aesthetic qualities of the work are asserted; the differences of actualization relate only to those parts of a work which are already in their essence incomplete and require completion in the imagination of the reader (for example, a scheme of description). If, however, we bear in mind the implicit historical state of the structure in a work, on the one hand, and the evolutionary sequence of the changing literary norm, on the other, we realize that not only the incomplete components, but the aesthetic effect of the entire work and, thus, also its actualization, as well, are subject to constant changes. As soon as a work under perception is entered into new contexts (an altered state of language, different literary requirements, an altered social structure, a new system of spiritual and practical values, and so forth), precisely those properties of it can be felt as aesthetically effective, which formerly were not felt as such, so that a positive evaluation could be based upon entirely opposite grounds. Therefore, it is precisely the task of literary history to investigate such changes of actualizations in responses to literary works and in the relationships between a work's structure and the evolving literary norm, since in this way we consistently focus our attention on a work as an aesthetic object and can observe the social dimensions of its aesthetic function. Whereas in studying literary evolution[4] we had placed emphasis on an understanding of what a work was in a series of existing works, now in the study of literary life the emphasis falls on what a work, in the process of aesthetic perception, actually becomes in the minds of those who constitute the literary public.
The vitality of a work depends on properties a work potentially embodies in itself with regard to the evolution of the literary norm. If a literary work is evaluated positively even upon a change of norm, it has, consequently, a great life span in comparison with a work whose aesthetic appeal is exhausted with the extinction of the norm of the time. Response to a literary work is accompanied by its actualization, a change of norm necessitates a new actualization of the work. From the methodological point of view, it must be noted that the source material here will be made up primarily of critical actualizations since such actualizations are

concerned with a work from the standpoint of the whole system of values and promote the incorporation of the work into literature. Furthermore, critical judgments also make a point of discussing what in a work pleases or displeases. Unfortunately, we have only written records of these actualizations and our sources do not always have equal value, so that the historical picture of the life of a literary work is necessarily dependent upon the size and number of sources.

Special methodological problems arise when we investigate the response to a work in a foreign literary environment. Even translation is, in a certain sense, an actualization which the translator effects. The response to a work by readers and critics in a foreign environment is very often quite dissimilar to response to the same work in its indigenous environment, because the norm, too, is dissimilar.

The Literary and Extraliterary Effect of Literary Works

Hitherto we have talked about the impact of a literary work on readers and particularly on the typical intercessor between works and readers, the critics, at the time when a work is the object of aesthetic perception. But a work, which effects readers in its specific shape, can have an influence, as well, on their mental life. Above all, it has an influence on the literary taste of readers who are themselves writers, and may therefore influence, perhaps even without their realizing it, their own literary production. Here we confront the problem of influence. Elsewhere, we treated this problem from a genetic point of view,[5] starting with a finished work and tracing the conditions that influenced its inception and formation, and thus were able to consider other literary works as a source or factor contributing to the work's acquisition of its existing form. Now we will employ the opposite procedure: at the center of attention is not the work influenced but the work exerting influence, and our task is to discern all of those literary phenomena whose origin or aesthetic effect depends on the existence of the work studied. In speaking about the literary effect of a work, we should not overlook, in addition to cases of conscious or involuntary direct influence, those cases where new literary works are able to achieve full aesthetic implementation only against the background of an older work, from which they rebound as from their own antithesis. That happens, for example, where there is identical subject matter but the approach used is different, or where the story is retained but the means of expression change, or where it is a question of an artistically new treatment of the older art.

In addition to its literary effect, we can trace the effect of a work in the extraliterary sphere, particularly when the exposition of some problem in verbal art contributes to its solution in real life. It is commonly known that the specifically aesthetic qualities of a poetic work have the potentiality of acting so powerfully on the excitability of readers that the means by which relations to reality are caught or suggested can produce an influence on their behavior. We need only recall well-known cases where literary character types have effected the conventionalization of contemporary social types, where the moral of a work has influenced the morals of society, where society has attributed a function to a work in the struggle for the introduction of specific social, economic, national or other requirements. Tendentious literature—didactic poetry—has a special place in this connection, since a consideration of the extraliterary effect is part of the author's design. A study of this sort leads us, however, to grounds where literary history encounters the concerns of other historical sciences, which from their points of view can often judge the scope of this extraliterary effect better than can the literary historian, whose attention is centered on the sphere of literary phenomena.

Notes

1. "Vývoj literární struktury," [Evolution of Literary Structure], *Čtení o jazyce a poesii,* ed. B. Havránek and J. Mukařovský (Prague: 1942), pp. 344-355.

2. J. Mukařovský, "La norme esthétique," *Travaux du IXe Congrès International de Philosophie* (Paris: 1937), p. 75.

3. "Genese literárních děl a jejich vztah k historické skutečnosti," [Genesis of Literary Works and Their Relationship to the Historical Reality], *Čtení o jazyce a poesii,* ed. B. Havrávek and J. Mukařovský (Prague: 1942), pp. 355-370.

4. See note 1.

5. See note 3.

18. A Scheme of Narrative Time

Lubomír Doležel

Physical time with its qualities of regular metrics, order, and direction[1] is the basic underlying structure of time structures in narrative literature (fiction). Most of the time qualities and patterns of the narrative work can be described as resulting from a series of operations performed on various forms of physical time, when it enters the process of literary structuring. In the course of these operations, all qualities of physical time are substantially changed; the input forms of physical time appear at the output as forms of the *sign time*.[2]

When studying this transformation, we must first define the set of input forms of physical time. We will eliminate those forms of physical time which—in our opinion—do not participate significantly in the process of narrative time structuring. This concerns, primarily *authorial time*—time of the creative performance which leads to the 'production' of the literary manuscript—and *reader's time*—the time of the reader's perceiving the literary text. There are no direct correlatives of these two forms of physical time in the structures of narrative time.[3] It would be, of course, ridiculous to deny the importance of these time forms as *historical* factors. However, this is a quite different problem which is completely beyond the scope of this study.

Our scheme will take into account the following set of input forms of physical time:

1. The *story time* ('erzählte Zeit'), that is, the succession, duration, and direction of the flow of both human and natural events which the narrative work informs about, either explicitly or implicitly. From the viewpoint of the reader or critic, the story time is, of course, 'deformed' by all those operations it is to undergo in the process of literary structuring; therefore, the only way to describe it is by the method of reconstruction.[4]

2. *The time of the story-telling act,* that is, the time determination (dating and duration) of the story-telling performance which is made responsible for the 'production' of a piece of narrative. It has to be emphasized strongly that this form of physical time is theoretically quite different from authorial time. The story-telling act and its temporal determination is

Slavic Poetics. Essays in Honor of Kiril Taranovsky (The Hague: 1973), pp. 92-98.

a part of the fictional world. Any kind of affinity between the time of the story-telling and the authorial time is a special narrative device, arising from the popular 'playing' of fiction with reality.

3. *The time of the text representation,* that is, the physical time of the sequence of signs forming the text of the narrative work. It is obvious that this textual representation makes use of many different verbal means and narrative devices. However, for our purposes, the time of the text representation can be considered a linear, regular and unidirectional flow of representational units.

Our set of input time forms neglects some forms which are obviously relevant for the structuring of narrative time. We did not account for the role of *the time of the addressee,* that is, the time determination of actions ascribed to a fictitious addressee of the narrative.[5]   Of course, the importance of this form—due to its relatively rare occurrence—for the theory of narrative time is marginal. On the contrary, the form of *the psychological (subjective) time* can be said to play a major role in the formation of the narrative time. However, it is not represented at the input of our scheme because at this stage of investigation it is advisable to avoid the delicate and complex problems of the qualities of the psychological time and of its relationship to physical time.

It is assumed that the transformation of the input forms of physical time into the output forms of narrative time requires two steps: (A) a set of operations which are basically *selective;* (B) a set of operations which can be designated as *formative.*

(A) Selective operations apply to all the input forms of physical time. Their task is to seek out those elements which will participate in the formation of the narrative time. These operations can be briefly specified as follows:

1. The story time ('erzählte Zeit') is transformed into *the action time* ('Erzählzeit,' 'vremja fabuly') by selecting from the sequence of the story only those events which will be represented in the narrative work (as its 'action'). From some portions of the story, events may be selected in a high density, so that a detailed representation of the story is given in the action; other portions of the story, however, can be represented in the action only very cursorily, or can be completely omitted.[6]

As a result of this uneven selection, the physical time of the story is transformed into the sign time of the action. Whereas the former is a continuous flow with regular metrics, the latter is discontinuous and irregular. However, it cannot be assumed that the process of selection leads to a change of time order and direction. The events of the action are ordered unidirectionally according to their 'dating'; in popular form of expression, the action has been characterized as being *chronologic.*

Because the action time in our scheme is based on the physical time of the story only, the scheme cannot account for more complex structures of action time, esp. for those with the component of psychological time. Our scheme accounts only for *simple, linear* action time structures.

2. The time of the story-telling act is transformed into *the narrator's time* (a dimension of the narrator's 'situation'). The selective process which accounts for this transformation can be generally characterized as reduction of the physical-temporal circumstances of the story-telling performance. The degree of reduction determines the quantity and quality of temporal circumstances which will form the time dimension of the narrator's situation, and thus will become relevant for the formation of the narrative time. The notion 'degree of reduction' accounts for the variety of narrator's time structures which is well-known from the history of fiction.[7] The degree of reduction can be absolute, so that all temporal circumstances of the story-telling act will be eliminated in the selective process; a narrative without narrator's time (which is practically equivalent to a narrative without the narrator's situation) results from such an absolute elimination (see the 'classic' Er-form narrative with a consistently 'passive' narrator).[8] On the other hand, the degree of reduction can be relatively low, so that the narrator's time can preserve even the quality of direction; this kind of narrator's time can be manifested in the fictional diary.[9] Between these two extremes, any degree of reduction is possible.

Irrespective of the degree of reduction, the selective operation leads to the same result as in the case of the time of the story: Physical time of the story-telling act is transformed into a discontinuous, irregular and, sometimes even nondirectional ('static') time of the narrator or, in the extreme case, is completely eliminated from the structure of the narrative time.

3. Selective operations affecting the time of the text representation can be described here only in very general terms. We assume that they result in a definite set of verbal means and narrative devices which are introduced

into the text in order to regulate the representation of the narrative time. These special means and devices can be called *textual time regulators;* grammatical forms of verbal tense are an elementary example of time regulators. The density and order of time regulators, interspersed in the text, defines the *regulatory time* of the representation; this time displays the typical characteristics of the sign time.

It has to be emphasized, however, that in the component of the text representation, our scheme has to treat input time differently than in the two preceding instances. Physical time of the text representation enters the structuring of narrative time together with the regulatory sign time. In other words, the structure of narrative time is determined by both the physical, and the sign time of the representation.

(B) The output forms of the selective operations (action time, narrator's time and the two categories of the time of representation) define the input of the formative operations. Formative operations have the characters of an 'automatic process,' resulting from interactions of the input forms. The action time becomes the target of formative operations, whereas the other time forms function as operators. These operators bring about *the transformation of the action time into the time of the plot.* In this way, we arrive at a reformulation of the relationship between action and plot which—since the pioneering studies of the Russian Formalist school[10]—became the fundamental problem of the theory of prose in general and of the theory of narrative time in particular.

The chart that describes the transformation of the input forms of physical time into the output form of plot time can be sketched as follows:

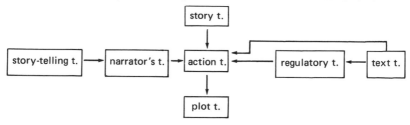

In order to account for the variability of plot time structures, we have to assume that the number of concrete formative operations will be rather high. For this reason, we have to limit ourselves in this study only to an illustrative example of these operations and their results. The basic operations of narrative time structuring in an outstanding novel of the contemporary Czech writer Milan Kundera, *The Joke*,[11] will be outlined. The plot structure of this novel is rather complex; we will limit our description to the story of the main protagonist Ludvík Jahn, even though the other protagonists' stories—as parallels or contrasts to Ludvík's story— have a major role in the overall plot structure of *The Joke*.

The action time. Physical time of Ludvík's story comprises approximately forty years. It is the time of his childhood, his studies in Prague ending with his expulsion, his military service with a special penal company in Ostrava, his imprisonment, rehabilitation and new studies, his work in a scientific institute and, finally, his long prepared 'revenge' executed in his home town in southern Moravia. In the process of selection, this story is transformed into the action of the novel in such a way that the narrated events are concentrated in two time periods—*the Ostrava and the Moravian episodes* (including those directly preceding events which serve as motivations of these episodes). Other events preceding the Ostrava episode (*prehistory*) and those connecting the Ostrava and Moravian episodes (*intermezzo*) are rendered in a minimal selection only. In such a way, the action of *The Joke* is distinctly hierarchical, being concentrated in two primary sections, alternating with two secondary sections:

prehistory   Ostrava episode   intermezzo   Moravian episode
– – – – – – –＝＝＝＝＝＝＝ – – – – – – –＝＝＝＝＝＝＝⟹

The chronological action is transformed into the achronological plot under the impact of two principal operators: (a) the narrator's time, (b) the time regulator of the multiple narrator. The first operator determines the direction of the plot time, the second one its segmentation.

The direction of the plot time. The action of *The Joke* is told by four narrators—protagonists of the story: Ludvík (L), his mistress and 'victim' Helena (H), and his two old friends, Jaroslav (J) and Dr. Kostka (K). One circumstance of the narrator's time has an essential importance for the structure of the plot time: the time of all narrators is simultaneous with the Moravian episode. This circumstance creates a uniform time perspective: the Moravian episode becomes the narrated present and all the other sections of the action are automatically transposed into the narrated past.

The introduction of this perspective into the time structure of the novel determines the direction of the plot time. Whereas the action time—in accordance with the underlying story time—proceeds from the past to the present, *the direction of the plot time is reversed:* it proceeds from the present to the past. In this respect, the plot structure of *The Joke* is analogous to that of the Proustian novel with its "imaginative reconstruction of one's past."[12] At the same time, the reversal of the time direction is a clear argument for a strict theoretical distinction between the action time and the plot time.

Segmentation of the plot time. The specific narrative form of *The Joke* —alternation of four Ich-narrators—operates as a textual time regulator, bringing about a further structuralization of plot time. Various sections of the action are assigned to various narrators, so that instead of a homogeneous plot with a continuous time a segmented plot with a discontinuous time obtains.

Segmented plot can be materialized in various forms. For the plot of *The Joke,* two sets of alternatives are essential:

1. The plot segments can be either equipollent or hierarchical with respect to the rendered action. In the case of *The Joke,* we have to do with a distinctly hierarchical arrangement of the plot; segments of Ludvík's narrative clearly dominate the plot structure, because Ludvík is assigned to render the crucial events of the two primary action sections, the Ostrava and the Moravian episodes. The contributions of the other narrators to the rendering of Ludvík's story are comparatively minor, limited mostly to the events of the prehistory and of the intermezzo.

2. Plot segments can be arranged in either a linear or a cyclic pattern. In the first case, each narrator is assigned to render different sections of the action. This means that each section is narrated only once, with no temporal overlapping. The plot time is *nonrepetitive.* In the cyclic pattern, the action (or at least, some of its sections) is rendered by two or even more narrators; the action is 'viewed' from several perspectives. This means that the plot time is *repetitive.*

Kundera's *The Joke* follows the linear pattern of plot construction. Isolated overlappings of action segments are not sufficiently important to affect our decision about the plot pattern.[13] It can be noted that the linear plot pattern results, in fact, from the supreme dominance of Ludvík as narrator.

The plot segmentation does not affect the general direction of the plot time in *The Joke*. In this respect, most segments repeat in their 'microstructure' the general pattern of the 'macrostructure': They begin in the narrated present (with some events of the Moravian episode); by an event-stimulus in the narrated present, a return to various periods of the narrated past is triggered. Past events are reconstructed by the device of flashback or reminiscence. After having traveled a more or less complicated loop into the past, the segments are brought to a formal conclusion in the present.

In such a way, we arrive at the final structuring of the narrative time in Kundera's *The Joke*. Under the influence of the two operators, the linear and chronological structure of the action time is transformed into a discontinuous and achronologic structure of segmented plot time. The essentials of the plot time structure are outlined in the following chart:[14]

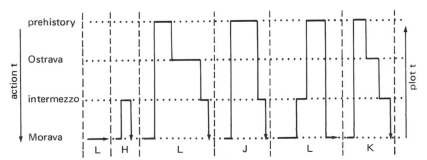

This chart shows clearly how essential are the transformations of the 'raw' physical time in the modern novel. It confirms many previous statements of both fiction writers and critics that the modern novel has become more and more 'liberated' from the norms of physical time, developing its specific time patterns and devices. At the same time, however, it confirms our initial idea that even the most complicated narrative time patterns can be derived from the essential qualities of physical time.

216   Lubomír Doležel

Notes

1. See H. Meyerhoff, *Time in Literature* (Berkeley and Los Angeles: 1955), p. 11.

2. The term *sign time* was used by J. Mukařovský in his essay "Čas ve filmu" *Studie z estetiky* [Praha: 1966], p. 183). In our scheme, it is given a more general meaning: it expresses all temporal qualities of semiotic systems which are different from the qualities of physical time.

3. A. A. Mendilow considers the author's time 'primarily extraneous'; the impact of the reader's time is 'comparatively slight' (*Time and the Novel* [New York: 1965], p. 68, 65).

4. Thus, for example, G. Müller reconstructed the "erzählte Zeit" of Goethe's *Wilhelm Meisters Lehrjahre* (see: "Erzähltzeit und erzählte Zeit," in: *Festschrift Paul Kluckholn und Hermann Schneider* [Tübingen: 1948], p. 196f.).

5. Already D. S. Lixačev distinguished this 'represented' time of the reader from the 'natural' one and described some of its devices in Turgenev's *Sportsman's Sketches* (*Poètika drevnerusskoj literatury* [Leningrad: 1967], p. 215f.)

6. Mendilow points to 'foreshortening' and 'telescoping' as essential devices of the action time (*Time and the Novel*, p. 72).

7. D. S. Lixačev outlines this variety, using, however, the inapposite term 'time of the author.'

8. See my article "The Typology of the Narrator: Point of View in Fiction," *To Honor Roman Jakobson* I (The Hague-Paris: 1967), pp. 541-552 and *Narrative Modes in Czech Literature* (Toronto: 1973).

9. J. Cruickshank described the flowing narrator's time and its convergence with the action time in Gide's fictional diary ("Treatment of Time in La Symphonie Pastorale," *Essays in Criticism* [1957], pp. 134-143).

10. See the best summary formulation of this relationship in B. Tomaševskij's *Teorija literatury, Poètika* (Leningrad: 1925).

11. The first edition of the novel was published in Prague in 1967, the second in 1968. An English translation (with serious omissions) appeared in 1969 (published by Coward-McCann, New York).

12. H. Meyerhoff, *Time in Literature*, p. 52.

13. M. Pohorský suggested that the occasional plot duplications in *The Joke* serve the function of testing the 'reliability' of the particular narrators ("Komika Kunderova Žertu," *Česká literatura* 17 [1969], p. 339).

14. Our description of the plot time structure of *The Joke* (including this chart) is simplified, not taking into account the specific narrative and time structure of the last (seventh) chapter. The chapter consists of narrative segments of three narrators —Ludvik, Helena and Jaroslav—alternating in a relatively rapid tempo. In my opinion, the function of this alternation is primarily rhythmical: the irregular, but generally rapid rhythm of alternating narratives is played off against the slow progress and the monotonous repetition of the leitmotif of the seventh chapter—the ancient folkloristic ritual of the Ride of the Kings.

19. The Translation of Verbal Art

Jiří Levý

We can secure a position of greatest advantage regarding the kind of problems a translator confronts if we first theoretically adumbrate the generative process of the original work of verbal art and then similarly treat the procedure whereby the translation is generated from the original. A literary work of art is created as a representation and a subjective transformation of objective reality. The product of the creative process is a specific ideational-aesthetic content actualized in linguistic material in which both content and material form a dialectical unity.

The individuality of the author is not a wholly independent factor, since it is to a certain extent historically determined. The manner in which the author of a historical novel, for example, selects and reshapes historical events depends decisively upon the particular world view to which he subscribes, upon his political persuasion and upon the current stage in the development of literary art. The milieu in which the author lives, and the distinctive characteristics of his era, which may enter into his work despite their conflict with historical truth, are also components of his creative individuality. For example, many of Shakespeare's plays take place in a non-English setting: the external setting in *The Taming of the Shrew* is Italy, in *Twelfth Night*—Illyria, and in *Julius Caesar*—ancient Rome. The dramatist lived in England, however, and Elizabethan England is therefore reflected in all of his plays as a significant component of his creative personality. The social milieu at the Danish Court of the twelfth century is similar to that of the English Court of the sixteenth century, and the ancient Romans behave exactly like Renaissance Englishmen. Shakespeare departs from historical authenticity, but in so doing his historical perspective acquires a broader validity, for he does not view ancient Rome from some idiosyncratic, capricious viewpoint but rather through the eyes of the Englishman of his age. In the art of the realist even the subjective element in the literary representation is an interpretation of extrapersonal, collective factors, and thus acquires objective validity in a given literary context. However, although the subjective element may not cause overt

"Překladatelský proces," *Umění překladu* (Prague: 1963), pp. 17-24. Translated by Susan Larson.

distortion, it cannot be entirely excluded from consideration, for an artistic representation is never wholly synonymous with reality.

It becomes evident, then, that we must differentiate objective reality from literary reality, the existential fact from the artistic fact—Caesar's Rome is one thing and Shakespeare's Rome another. The substance of an artistic work is not objective reality per se, but the author's interpretation of objective reality, and it is the latter which must be accurately rendered by the translator.

A failure to understand this distinction properly often leads to textual "hypercorrection" or "improvement" upon the original. In the preface to Sládek's unpublished version of a translation of Longfellow's *Song of Hiawatha,* the reader learns that the translator introduced a botanical point of view. The reader is instructed that before the arrival of Europeans in America the pheasant, roebuck, mountain lion, and chicken did not inhabit the area, and, moreover, that Sládek's substitution of the pumpkin for the melon (which did not grow there) is a step in the right direction, though not an ideal solution since the pumpkin originally derived from tropical Asia. The pheasant "should have been replaced by the prairie chicken (*Tympanuchus cupido*) and the Indian term 'bena' should have been deleted altogether." It is suggested that Sládek substituted the closely related bittern for the heron, "since he knew that herons' habitat was further south than the setting of the poem." Furthermore, the translator had to delete the phrase "blue eyes" from the text since it is common knowledge that North American Indians themselves did not have blue eyes and "were astonished when, upon seeing blue-eyed Caucasians for the first time, they noticed that the sky was visible through their eyes." These are the consequences of a failure to understand the fundamental relationship between reality and an artistic work. Since translators, as a rule, tend to have more training in philology than artists do, they indulge in hypercorrections when they discover scientific inaccuracies in the original text. Certainly it is possible to come to terms with a living author about the "correction" of textual details, but to make scientific corrections of botanical and zoological items in a poetic description of nature and in poetic imagery is absurd.

The artistic work, then, is the end result of a process that involves subjective selection and transformation of the elements of objective reality or, to state it more succinctly, a particular ideational-aesthetic content is

actualized in linguistic material. Here it is important to differentiate two
notions which are often erroneously considered identical: (1) the text of
a work, and (2) its semantic value, which, for lack of a better term, we will
denote as "the work in the narrowest sense of the word."

This differentiation is analogous to certain relationships inherent in linguistic material, specifically, the linguistic structure of the minimum free
form—the word. The text of the work is the analogue of the phonological
structure of a word, whereas "the work in its narrowest sense" is the
analogue of the semantic structure of a word. Together the two linguistic
concepts constitute the word, and, similarly, the two literary concepts constitute the literary work. The simplistic opposition between form and content does not suffice here, for "the work in its narrowest sense" is not
content *per se,* but rather "organized" content. Gončarov's *Oblomov* in
Russian and Czech are two different variants of the work, but what is
common to both of them, and what must therefore remain intact, is precisely "the work in its narrowest sense." Modern linguistics utilizes the
term "information" to denote this concept.

The intimate relationship between linguistic expression and thought, between the text of a work and its content, should not lead to the fallacious
identification of one with the other, for in so doing, the distinctive relationship between the content and the linguistic form, which relationship is
fundamental in translation, would be obliterated. The translator must
translate the ideational-aesthetic content with the text serving as the vehicle
of this content. The text is therefore preconditioned by the language in
which the work is written, and, specifically for a Czech translation, this implies that many significant values of the original must inevitably be expressed by different linguistic means than those employed in the original.

This basic theoretical postulate is generally acknowledged with respect
to grammatical form, but has not been heretofore adequately elucidated
with respect to those special national forms of language whose specificity
was more obscure. For example, it is commonly known that in place of
the colon in English, the Czech translator must often use the semicolon,
since the English colon has, in most instances, a terminative function
analogous to the Czech semicolon and does not require further elaboration
as is the case with the Czech colon. A strict adherence to textual configura-
tions would in this case distort the meaning. Or if we were to translate the

German phrase *"Nehmen Sie Platz"* literally with "vezměte *místo*" [take the place], the underlying meaning of the utterance would not be altered, though its stylistic value would be. As opposed to the normal wording *"Posad'te se"* [sit down], the utterance *"vezměte místo"* sounds foreign and awkward, more like a pedantic archaism. This holds true for other special national forms, as well, such as formulae for book titles. In Czech literature the following are common prepositional formulae for book titles: *Z letopisů lásky* [from the Chronicles of Love], *Z českých mlynů* [from the Czech Mills]. Since this formula is not common in English usage, the play *Ze života hmyzu* was translated as *The Insect Play*. Conversely, English titles for a collection of stories for example, usually appear with the title of the first story in the sequence and followed by . . . *and Other Stories;* thus Čapek's *Trapné povídky* [Embarassing Stories] was rendered as *Money and Other Stories*. The same applies to more complex artistic forms such as rhythm. . . .

If our point of departure is not the text of the work but rather its semantic and aesthetic values, then we arrive at the following basis for a proper understanding of the relationship between form and content: It is mandatory to render intact those forms that have a significant semantic function but incorrect to retain intact all linguistic forms indiscriminately. With respect to translation of poetry, this means that the critical point of departure for the translator is not the meter but rather the rhythm of the original. A form may, of course, be of historical value or significant for its local color. For example, the alliterative verse of Old Germanic poetry and the hexameter of ancient poetry are both values that represent the culture and epoch depicted in the original work, and are, therefore, carriers of semantic values, which can, in certain instances, be considered obligatory.

Now we come to the second stage of the generative process in translation: the perception of the work. The translator is first of all a reader. The text of a work functions aesthetically and is socially realized only when it is read. The work comes into the hands of the reader and the translator in the form of a text, and during the process of perception it functions as objective material that is transformed through the individuality of the perceiver-reader. This moment in the process is defined as the reader's actualization (or concretization).

At this juncture it appears necessary to clarify certain concepts in the theory of translation which are sometimes inadequately explained by literary science. We must distinguish between the realization of content and form in linguistic material (that is, the creative work done by the author) and the actualization of the completed work in the mind of the perceiver (that is, the perceptual work done by the reader). Reader actualization is something else again than a scholar's or artist's interpretation. The latter requires active participation and utilizes progressively more sophisticated means of analysis, which allow for a more definitive comprehension of the objective material of the work. We shall operate with a more limited definition of the concept of actualization than Felix Vodička, who conceives of it in much broader terms encompassing such diverse phenomena as theatrical staging ("in dramatic texts staging means actualization"), or critical evaluation, or translation ("the problem of translation is basically the actualization of a work in the context of another language and another literary tradition"). Thus, Vodička's definition embraces phenomena that are fundamentally different. We would define a theatrical performance as the realization of a dramatic text through the medium of the theater, a translation as a realization of a work in a new language, and a critical evaluation as an interpretation.

The subjective understanding of a text is another issue that we must discuss, especially since it not infrequently generates a considerable amount of confusion. What was said earlier with respect to the historical determination of authorial conception also applies to the reader's actualization of a work. The reader grasps the work of art through the prism of his own epoch, and the values emphasized are those ideologically and aesthetically more relevant to him at his point in history. It is the historical determination of the translator's conception that establishes the link between the translation and the translator's cultural milieu.

Lachmann's theory that the *Iliad* and the *Odyssey* were not original epics but derivatives of primeval epic folk songs was a typical product of the romantic predilection for folk poetry. In conformity with this theory, Vinařický translated part of the *Odyssey* using the so-called "folk-verse," that is, (the decasyllabic trochee), and stylistically interpreted the work as a literary derivative of folk ballads. Evidently, even such an extraordinary interpretation of the role of translation as Vinařický's arose out of a specific historical context, and was closely related to the activities of

Čelakovský, Erben, and other revivers of the folklore tradition in Czech Romanticism. The translator, to be sure, is not influenced solely by the external cultural milieu, but also by his own personal biases. The process of perception culminates with the actualization of the text, that is, with the formation of an image of it in the mind of the reader. The difference between the plain reader and the translator lies in the fact that the translator expresses his conception through language. He goes one step further to a linguistic materialization of the semantic values of the work.

Once again we must clarify a fact that is often overlooked: language is not merely the material in which a creative conception is realized—first by the author, then by the translator—but is to a certain extent also an active participant in both creative acts. The linguistic material, which serves as the vehicle for the ideational-aesthetic content, has a distinct effect on this content. The material participates passively in the definitive shaping of the content (by "offering resistance" and molding it only into patterns expressible within that material), and actively (by introducing, through euphonic and similar associations, new meanings that are neither explicitly nor potentially present in the original ideational design.

Only in rare instances is language an active participant. For example, certain semantic associations that emerge in a poem through the use of rhyme pairs, might not emerge in the poetic lexicon of another language. This is most clearly illustrated by cliché rhymes. A conventional rhyme such as *láska-páska* [love-bond] conjures up the motif of love as a "binding" power. The conventional English rhyme "love-dove" conjures up instead, a context of saccarinity, while the cliché rhyme "womb-tomb" promotes the frequency of the birth-death dichotomy as a motif. Often language, due to its structural features, creates conditions that are particularly optimal for a certain repertoire of artistic devices. The English language, which is well endowed with monosyllabic homonyms and synonyms provides a linguistic context that is optimal for the creation of word plays. The abundance of word plays in English literature dating from the time of biblical translations and Shakespeare's plays cannot be explained by pure coincidence alone. Furthermore, the distinctive characteristics of a language system can provide a linguistic context that is particularly optimal not only for the use of individual stylistic devices but also for the development of entire literary trends.

Language participates in the composition of a work primarily in a passive role, that is, it facilitates the expression of those values for which it has adequate expressive resources. The greater syntactic complexity of certain languages (for example, Western) permits a greater semantic flexibility in the associations between thoughts; for example, gerunds in Russian allow an author to embrace several concurrent or successive actions within a single verbal complex, or a German author can use compound substantives to express both an object and its attributive quality. Abstract nouns that are more frequent and stylistically more neutral in French acquire a more concrete and intensified meaning when translated into Czech, for example, "la passion—vášen."

The degree of linguistic determination in a work varies with the author and the genre; the greater the determinacy, however the more difficult the task of translation. It was noted by E. Sapir that the correspondence between language and thought is not uniformly the same for all authors. Certain artists whose spirit moves largely in the nonlinguistic (better, in the generalized linguistic) layer, even find a certain difficulty in getting themselves expressed in the rigidly set terms of their accepted idiom. One feels that they are unconsciously striving for a generalized art language, a literary algebra, that is related to the sum of all known languages as a perfect mathematical symbolism is related to all those roundabout reports of mathematical relations that normal speech is capable of conveying. Their art expression is frequently strained, it sounds at times like a translation from an unknown original—which, indeed, is precisely what it is. These artists, the Whitmans and Brownings impress us rather by the greatness of their spirit than the felicity of their art.

Conversely, there are authors such as Heine, Swinburne, and Shakespeare whose expressiveness derives from the salient features and potentialities of their respective languages. The fact, that there are some literary works stylistically organized more "nationally" than others whose stylistic physiognomy is more "international," was noted already by Belinskij in a critique of the French translation of Gogol':

"Krylov's fables are untranslatable, and for the foreigner to appreciate fully the genius of our great fableist, he would have to learn Russian and live for a time in Russia to become acquainted with the Russian way of life.

Gribojedov's *Woe from Wit* could be translated without extensive loss of quality, but where are we to find a translator who would be equal to such an enormous task? Gogol' is in this respect an illustrious exception to the rule. As a painter predominantly of everyday life, of prosaic reality, the national peculiarity of his literary context would be the very thing that would most fascinate the foreign reader."

The process of translation does not culminate in the translated text, and the text should not be the ultimate goal of the translator's task. The translation, like the original work, acquires a social function only when it is read. Once again—for the third time—we arrive at a subjective transformation of objective material. The reader of the translated work formulates the third conception of the work. First we acknowledged the author's conception of reality, then the translator's conception of the original work, and finally the reader's conception of the translation. The translator's point of departure should not be the text of the original but rather the ideational and aesthetic values contained therein. His goal should not be the translated text but rather the specific content that the text transmits to the reader. This means that the translator must take into account the reader for whom he is translating. For example, in a translation designed for a children's publication, it is necessary to exercise a greater linguistic clarity than in exact translation designed for some fastidious reader in which it is necessary to render intact all the fine points of the original. A dramatic text must also be intelligible upon a first hearing. On the other hand, the theater provides a potential context for elucidating much in dramatic staging that would normally remain obscure in a literary text. When, for instance, in Tolstoj's *Kreutzer Sonata* the lawyer advises a traveler not to disembark from the train until the bell rings once more the reader is probably unaware of the fact that in Russian railway stations a bell rings three times before a train departs. This type of thing was possible to demonstrate in the theatrical staging of Ostrovskij's *Artists and Admirers.* It is equally essential, however, to consider the differences between the social consciousness of the reader and that of the contemporary Czech reader. Many significant values in a work would acquire a different meaning in a literal translation, if a reader with a different social consciousness and a different conceptual framework were to read it.

To summarize, we can say that the seminal problem of the translation process is the relationship among three main components: the objective text of the work and its dual actualization by the reader of the original and the reader of the translation. These three structural components will necessarily be somewhat different; they will vary according to how the following two differentiating factors operate in their formation: (1) the differences between the two languages and (2) the differences in the make-up of the consciousness of the two reading audiences. Defining the boundaries of these two differentiating factors is the critical task of the translator, since fundamental theoretical problems inevitably arise in the attempt to analyze and formulate a normative definition of the relationship between the three aforementioned components.

In classifying the various constituents of the translation process we can also determine the role of various disciplines in our theoretical framework of translation. The following three relationships define the problem of translation:

(1) The relationship between the language of the original and that of the translation (here the findings of comparative linguistics would be utilized).

(2) The relationship between the content and form in the original (here we must discern the aesthetic function of the foreign form) and in the translation (here we must seek indigenous aesthetic equivalents). (To this end we would apply the methods of literary science, comparative stylistics and poetics.)

(3) The relationship between the ultimate value of the original work and that of the translation (here we would apply the methods of literary criticism).

Part V

20. The Essence of the Visual Arts

Jan Mukařovský

The question is: What are the visual arts? At first glance it would seem that its answer should take as its starting point either a definition or an enumeration of these arts—best of all, both a definition and an enumeration. If we attempt to proceed in this way, however, we shall immediately encounter difficulties. In our opinion even the most comprehensive definition, namely the visual arts are those whose material is inorganic matter, those which work with space and disregard time—a definition clearly delimiting the visual arts with respect to poetry and music, theater and dance—can provoke objections. Garden architecture works with organic material. Furthermore, the art of lighting, which claims to be a visual art, is obviously not only a spatial but also a temporal art. Indeed, even a theoretician of the traditional and most intrinsic visual arts could object that the experiencing of time in visual arts occurs wherever a representation of motion is concerned and that even a visual art makes a claim on the viewer's real time itself. This is the case, for example, in architecture when the viewer is compelled by the shape of a structure or that of its surroundings to walk around it in a certain direction before he enters it or to pass through its interior in a certain order. It is by such means that the architect determines the temporal progression and succession in which the viewer is to perceive the separate aspects of a structure or its individual parts. In the same way many objections could arise if we attempted to begin a general characterization of the visual arts by enumerating them. There is very little general agreement not only about what should be considered a visual art (for example, whether photography is an art) but also about how to classify the accepted traditional arts. There are, for example, those who consider ornamental design an independent art alongside of painting and sculpture. As is well known, some movements in architectural theory which are closely linked to practice declare as a principle that architecture is not an art. Were we to proceed from a definition and an enumeration in our characterization of the visual arts, we would encounter these

"Podstata výtvarných umění." [A lecture at the Institute for National Education on January 26, 1944.] = *Studie z estetiky* (Prague: 1966] , pp. 188-195. Translated by John Burbank and Peter Steiner.

and similar difficulties. They are in no way, of course, insurmountable obstacles, but their gradual removal would veil and render unclear our proper task: to penetrate to the *essence* of the visual arts.

Let us therefore choose the opposite course. We should presuppose almost nothing, I think, for we are willing to deduce everything that we shall need through our own reflection.

The first stop on our way will be a comparison of a work of visual art with a natural object. Let us imagine a rock and a statue made from the same stone next to one another. There are undoubtedly many similarities, even more than it appears at first glance. The statue was also once a rock, and there are more than a few instances of a sculptor's finding his inspiration in the shape of a rock. Sometimes the shape of an already finished statue shows the contours of the rock from which it has come . If, on the contrary, a statue is made of a soft material (for example, sandstone) and is exposed to the influence of the weather, it will more and more regain the appearance of a rock in the course of time. Indeed, we can go even further: in its oldest form the most primordial statue—prehistoric, primitive man's statue—was nothing but a mere unshaped, unworked rock. Let us listen to a specialist's words on this point: "The very loosening of a stone from its close contact with the earth's surface represents its first resemblance to man, to human corporeality. If the stone is then erected, the vertical of a human figure together with the point at which this figure is joined to the earth has already been provided."[1] As is therefore obvious, there are really many similarities between a rock and a statue, and the transition between them is completely indistinguishable. In spite of this, however, the difference between a work of art and a natural object is so considerable that their identification, albeit only in certain extreme cases, strikes us as paradoxical. You will say that this is obvious because a work of art is a product of the human hand and human will, whereas a natural object has a shape which is the product of natural forces: erosion, friction, and so on. But be careful; it is not so simple. Even a natural object can strike a viewer as a work of the human hand. We know of rocks resembling statues whose shapes originated through erosion. Hence the difference between a work of art and a natural object does not lie in how the object has originated, whether the human hand and will have participated in its origin, but in the shaping of the object itself. If the shaping of the object strikes us in such a way that we presuppose or rather conjecture some subject behind it, it does not appear to us as a natural object. It appears to us as such only if its organization strikes us as a mechanical consequence of natural forces. Thus we sense *someone,* a subject in general, behind a work of art, but a specific person-originator and his intention are inaccessible and very often even unknown to us. Indeed, as we have already seen, they do not have to exist in the extreme case. Stated clearly: a work of art does not differ from a natural object in the fact that it has an originator who made it but in the fact that it appears as made and in such a way that its organization reveals a specific unified intention. Consequently, we say that a work of art in itself, regardless of whatever is outside it (and thus regardless of anyone's personality) is intentional, reveals intentionality. Let us add to this only a minor but important restriction. If a certain object is conceived by a certain perceiver at a certain moment as intentional or not intentional, what is often decisive is not only its organization but also the way in which the perceiver approaches it. Leonardo da Vinci thus advised young painters: "By looking attentively at old and smeared walls, or stones and veined marble of various colors, you may fancy that you see in them several compositions, landscapes, battles figures in quick motion, strange countenances, and dresses, with an infinity of other subjects. By these confused lines the inventive genius is excited to new exertions."[2] In other words, he advised them to conceive accidentally occurring lines and stains on a wall as preliminary sketches for paintings.

In our foregoing comments we separated the work of art from man-the-originator, and now in making this remark, we are suddenly bringing it closer to man-the-perceiver. We have devoted considerable effort to proving that the organization, the shaping of a work of visual art is not necessarily dependent upon human will, and now it might seem that we are, on the contrary, making it dependent upon human will by introducing the perceiver. Let us not, however, forget that there is a fundamental difference between the originator and the perceiver. The originator is a single, unique individual, whereas the perceiver is anyone. The originator determines the organization of the work, whereas the perceiver confronts a finished work, and he can interpret it in various ways. This conceptual process on the perceiver's part occurs only in a fleeting moment, whereas the work itself endures. Even after our digression concerning the perceiver we can therefore assert the following with confidence: a work of art in itself is organized intentionally, whereas a natural object, in contrast to it, lacks intentionality; its organization is accidental. This difference is fundamentally valid and absolutely definite. The transitions and vacillations to which we have referred several times do not change anything in the fundamental validity of the principle.

In concluding the first part of our discussion, we have thus arrived at a rather important result. The notion of intentionality, which we have just explained as a matter of the organization of the work itself, will accompany us throughout the remainder of our deliberations.

But in defining the work of art as intentional in opposition to a natural object, we are still far from being finished with the essence of the visual arts, even with art in general. For what we have said about intentionality concerns not only artistic creation but all human creativity. Every object that man creates or re-creates for his own purposes bears traces of this intervention forever. Even if its creator has long been forgotten, its organization appears intentional, and this is true even when the purpose it originally served is no longer known. And when an archaeologist, bending over his site, painstakingly searches among fragments of stone for those that bear the slightest traces of intentional organization, he is looking not only for works of art but also for implements of human labor, the objects of everyday life. Hence we now confront the question of whether and how artistic intentionality differs from nonartistic, practical intentionality. We shall start with an illustrative example. We have before us some implement for work or human activity in general, be it a hammer, a plane, or a piece of furniture that has been made with these implements (in the narrow sense of the word). In none of these cases can there be any doubt about intentional organization. Insofar as we view these things as practically designed objects, hence as tools, we judge their properties with respect to the aim which the given thing serves. The shape, the material and every component of the shape and material are evaluated with respect to this goal. Moreover, we pay attention to them only with respect to it: what does not serve this aim simply escapes our attention. Thus, for example, in all probability the color of the handle of the hammer will remain unnoticed. But a moment of decisive reversal can occur when we start to look at a practically designed object in a different way, when we observe the object itself and for itself. At that moment a peculiar change will take place—at least in our eyes. Above all those properties of the object which have no relation to the practical aim and were previously overlooked, which in some cases were not even perceived at all (for example, its color), will come to our attention. But even those properties that have a practical use and were formerly the center of attention now appear to us in a different light. Being deprived of the relation to the aim lying *outside* the object, these properties enter into relations with one another within the object itself, and the object appears to us as if it were constructed from its own properties bound into a unique and integral whole. Whereas in the case of a practically conceived thing a change in any of its properties or parts, undertaken for the purpose of a better adaptation of the object to its aim, would change nothing in its essence, now when we evaluate the object for itself, it appears that the slightest change in any of its properties would touch its very essence, would change the thing into something else. Stated concretely: in the case of a chair conceived as an instrument for sitting, a change in the shape of its back would be only a stage in a gradual adaptation toward the aforementioned aim. In the case of a chair viewed for itself, however, such a modification of its unique set of properties into another equally unique set of properties would be a change in its very essence. In the first case we would conceive the chair as an implement that can be produced in an infinite quality, in the second as a unique work of art that can be imitated but not duplicated. An effort to exclude an object that we have conceived as a work of art from practical usage, even if it is adapted and suitable for a practical use, is connected with its uniqueness and, of course, its isolation.

We have thus succeeded in revealing quite a sharp boundary between a work of art and a practical creation. We have done so on the basis of objects that can be conceived as one or the other without any change in their organization. It is not difficult to find such objects, for almost any practical instrument can be—at least at the moment when we examine it without using it—conceived in itself and for itself regardless of the aim that it usually serves. Certainly every one of us has experienced moments of such artistic involvement with an object of practical use, for example, while standing before a new instrument, a piece of furniture, and so forth, which we have not yet associated with any practical use. Most often, of course, if an instrument of practical use is to attract the perceiver's attention to it-self, to its organization, it will be shaped in a special way. We have in mind products of the so-called craft industry which are sometimes designated in advance not to be used but to be works of art "in the guise" of practically usable objects, for instance engraved glass cups, plastically embellished faience bowls, and so on. If works of art in the proper sense of the word, such as paintings or statues, are concerned, it is quite evident that the atti-tude toward the object is not left to the viewer's whim but that the work itself in its organization directly induces the viewer to focus his attention on itself, on the set of its properties and on the internal organization of this set, and not to look beyond the work for some external aim which it could serve.

We have thus reached the conclusion that products of human activity which in general bear indications of intentionality divide roughly into two large groups. One of them serves some aim, whereas the objects of the sec-ond group are designated, if we may say so, to be an aim in themselves. The objects of the first group can be called implements in the broad sense of the word, the objects of the second, works of art. Each of these two groups is distinguished by a certain manner of intentional organization. An implement suggests that it is designed to serve some purpose; a work of art compels man to adopt the attitude of a mere perceiver. But we have also seen that the organization of an object does not have to function un-equivocally in one of these two directions. There are, on the contrary, many cases in which one and the same object can be evaluated both as an implement and as a work of art. Let us add that one entire important visual art is specifically based upon this ambiguity of organization. This is architecture, the creations of which are simultaneously both an implement (Corbusier even said: a machine) and a work of art.

It would seem that everything is now clear, but it is precisely at this moment that urgent questions begin to arise. Such as: If both a work of art and an implement are intentional, then why is the work of art oriented toward nothing but itself? The idea of being oriented toward a point dif-ferent from that at which we find ourselves follows from the very word "intention." Would it be possible, however, to have an intention that is directed nowhere else but back toward its starting point? Another ques-tion: It is clear that an object which serves a purpose is good for something.

But what is a work of art good for, if we say that it does not serve a purpose? In order to make clear all those things that intimately concern the very essence of art, we must first thoroughly reexamine intentionality as it manifests itself in the work of art. Here is what we see. When consideration for an external aim is suppressed (which is what happens in a work of art), a subject emerges from behind the work, that is, someone who has either intentionally created it or who perceives it intentionally. This is natural. Intentionality deprived of a relation to an aim adheres more closely to its human source. In the case of an instrument of practical activity we do not care either about its originator or its user. What difference does it make who has produced the hammer or who understands what this instrument is for and who uses it? What is important is how well and how reliably it is possible to work with this hammer. In the case of a painting or a statue, on the contrary, the question of use does not arise at all, and attention is necessarily directed toward man. Might the definition of art lie in this fact? There are some theoreticians of this view, and they claim that the work of art is simply an expression of a personality, and therefore that it is necessary for man. We know, however, that the intentionality contained in human creation and hence in a work of art does not at all need to correspond directly to the originator's individual will and personality; the originator can even be lacking in the extreme case (eroded rocks in the shape of statues). Furthermore, if the work of art were exclusively or even only predominantly to be an expression of its originator's personality, what significance would it have for other people, other perceivers? Another view, in its many variations much more widespread than the preceding, sees the definition of the work of art in its effect upon the *perceiver.* The purpose of the work of art is to arouse the perceiver's pleasure, a special kind of pleasure which is not diverted by any external interest—because there is no external aim in art—but which is satisfied only by the observation of the work, by the relation between the perceiver and it. This is so-called aesthetic pleasure. We cannot assume as negative an attitude toward this view as toward the preceding. The work of art no longer appears as a matter of individual but of universal import. An indirect proof of the basic acceptability of this view is the fact that beginning with Kant, who first gave full expression to the idea of the *"interesseloses Wohlgefallen"* [disinterested interest] provided by the work of art, the majority of aesthetic theories have proceeded from this premise. Nevertheless, we do not intend to accept this view passively. We cannot, of course, doubt the existence of aesthetic pleasure: every one of us knows it from personal experience. It is, however, debatable whether aesthetic pleasure is the very kernel of our relation to art or only a mere part of it or a merely external indication of some more profound relation. After all, the mere fact that the powerful effect of a work of art is usually accompanied not only by pure pleasure but also by its very opposite, displeasure, calls for caution. Indeed, nothing is more subjective and changeable than an emotional relation to things. A work of art, and especially a visual work because matter is its material, is something extremely objective, existing independently of changeable emotions. It does not call upon the perceiver primarily to adopt an emotional attitude toward it but rather to understand it. It is not directed toward one side of man but to man in his entirety, to all of his capabilities. Furthermore, it appeals not only to an individual but to everyone. It has been created with a necessary consideration for an audience, hence for a multitude, and a necessary desire on the artist's part was that the work establish an understanding between other people and himself. It has been created with the requisite that all understand it *equally,* that all comprehend it *equally.* Although this requirement is strictly speaking only an ideal, practically unrealizable one, it is an intrinsic property of art and an essential motivation of artistic creation. The work of art is therefore a *sign* that is supposed to mediate some suprapersonal *meaning.* But as soon as we utter the words "sign" and "meaning," the most common and best known signs—the word, language—come to mind. And this is not at all unwarranted. Nevertheless, precisely because of this we must have a very clear awareness of the *difference* between the artistic sign and such signs as linguistic ones. The word—in its normal, nonpoetic usage—serves communication. It has an external aim: to depict some event, to describe some thing, to express some emotion, to stimulate some behavior in the listener, and so on. All of this, however, goes beyond the word itself; all of this is somewhere outside linguistic expression. Language is therefore a sign-*instrument* serving an external aim. A product of visual art, for example a painting, can also, of course, tend to communicate something and hence be a sign-instrument. Thus a picture in an illustrated commercial catalogue serves the purpose of providing information about goods that cannot be depicted in words, and it is a companion and equally important complement of the verbal message. Indeed, even a picture intended as a work of art usually communicates—and often in a very precise way—something: for instance, a portrait of a person or of a landscape (the so-called *veduta*). Nevertheless, the significance of a work of art as a work of art per se does not lie in communication. The work of art, as we have already said, is not oriented toward anything that is outside itself, toward any external aim. But only something that is outside the sign itself can be communicated. The artistic sign in contrast to the communicative sign is nonserving, that is, it is not an instrument. The understanding that the artistic sign establishes among people does not pertain to *things,* even when they are represented in the work, but to a certain *attitude* toward *things,* a certain attitude on the part of man toward the *entire* reality that surrounds him, not only to that reality which is directly represented in the given case. The work does not, however, communicate this attitude—hence the intrinsic artistic "content" of the work is also inexpressible in words—but *evokes* it directly in the perceiver. We call this attitude the "meaning" of the work only because it is rendered in the work objectively by its organization, and it is therefore accessible to everyone and is always repeatable. But by what is this attitude rendered in the work? Reference to a direct analysis of a work gives us the best answer to this question. Let us imagine a painting representing anything: we are not interested in the theme at the moment. First of all, we shall see a plane delimited by a frame and on this plane color patches and lines. How every simple these elements appear to be, but how complex the interplay of meanings in reality! Each of these elements in itself and in its connection with the others is in several respects a vehicle of meaning and a meaning-creating factor regardless of what is represented by it and the others. Here we cannot, nor do we have to, carry out a complete, detailed semantic analysis of the elements of the painting. A brief demonstration will suffice. Let us look at a color patch and for the time being only one of those that are in the painting. This color patch is primarily a vehicle of meaning in itself: the color red affects the perceiver differently from, for example, blue or green. It evokes associated images, stimulates different emotions, different motor reactions, and so forth. This intrinsic meaning of color which is not borrowed from any outside source can sometimes be so strong that it almost becomes concretized: the color blue can evoke a distinct image of sky or water even in such cases when it is used as a pure color quality rather than for the representation of these things. Besides this "intrinsic" meaning, however, color is also a semantic factor in relation to the plane of the picture. For the perceiver the same color patch placed in the middle of this plane will be accompanied by a different semantic nuance than if it were shifted, for example, in a direction diagonal to some corner or perpendicular to some side of the pictorial rectangle—upward, downward, to the right or to the left. It is only with difficulty and imprecision, of course, that we may express in words these different semantic nuances which, on the one hand, influence the meaning of the color itself in the various placements of a color patch on the pictorial plane and which, on the other hand, have an effect upon the "sense" of the pictorial plane. Depending on circumstances a color patch in the middle of the pictorial plane could mean something like calm, balance, or even fixation, immobility, and so on; shifted upwards perpendicularly, it could evoke an image of exaltation, calm hovering; shifted diagonally to a corner, it might mean a sudden movement, an impact, a disturbance of equilibrium, an explosion, and so on. We introduce all of these possibilities, of course, only with the following important reservations. First, words express only awkwardly the meanings that concern us; second, under different circumstances one and the same position of a color patch on the delimited plane can change its meaning even to the extent of becoming an absolute contradiction. Thus a color patch placed perpendicularly above the center of the picture but protruding downward into a point will probably be much more likely to evoke an image of collapsing than of hovering.

But we have not yet exhausted the meanings of which a color patch can be the vehicle in a painting. There is still its relation to the other color patches of the painting and to the color of the surrounding plane in general. If, for example, a red patch is placed on a blue background, it will appear not only optically but also semantically different from the same patch on a green background. The semantic nuances that arise in this way cannot, of course, be expressed in words but can only be felt. We should, however, be aware that a red patch on green, for example, can evoke the image of a flower in a meadow even if its shape has not been elaborated. Of course, this is an extreme case of the concretization of a meaning which originally was completely nonobjective.

Moreover, if a color patch is viewed in relation to what is represented, it can acquire still other semantic nuances. Let me mention only the well-known phenomenon that the qualities of the colors themselves can create a certain foreground and background in a painting. The colors that we call "warm," such as red, manifest a tendency to come to the fore, closer to the spectator, whereas the "cold" colors (for example, blue) retreat to the background. The painter can exploit this property of colors in the semantic structure of a picture in various ways. Finally, there is the relation of a color to the objectivity of the things represented. If the same color, for example, takes up a substantial part of the contour of a thing, it acquires a close connection with the object quality of the thing, it becomes one of its properties, the local color. The *smaller* the part of the contour of the represented thing that it occupies, the more easily it acquires the quality of *light,* of color value. Very complex semantic plays, the investigation of which would lead us too far afield, are also possible. Nor shall we attempt an analysis of the other components of a painting, an enumeration of their semantic variations and nuances. Our concern has been to suggest how complex a semantic structure a painting is if it is viewed as a work of art, as an artistic sign, not as a communicative sign. From mere means of representation devoid of their own meaning all the individual components of a painting become independent meanings codetermining the meaning of the painting as a whole. And this total meaning of the painting, which arises from the complex interplay of these components, is capable of directly evoking in the perceiver a certain attitude applicable to every reality with which he will come in contact. Thus it is not only by means of its theme but precisely by means of its artistic, verbally noncommunicable meaning that a work of art influences the way in which a perceiver who has really experienced it thereafter views reality and behaves toward reality. And this is precisely the most intrinsic designation of art, of *all* the visual arts and not only of these but of all the arts in general. We have demonstrated and justified our claim on the basis of painting alone, but it would not be difficult at all to prove it on the basis of other visual arts as well. Let me mention only in passing a very characteristic circumstance in architecture, an art that oscillates between service to an external aim and artistic semioticity. Buildings in which semantic components (like grandeur, prestige, religious meanings, and so forth) come to the fore—hence palaces, public buildings, churches, and the like—acquire an artistic character more easily and more directly than buildings in which the semantic aspect moves into the background in the face of service to an external aim—purely utilitarian structures like factories, commercial buildings, and so on.

Now let us proceed to a summary of the second section of our paper. Whereas the first section showed us the difference between a work of visual art and a natural object, this second part has concerned the difference between a work of visual art and other products of human activity. We have come to the understanding that a work of visual art differs from other products of human activity essentially in the fact that, whereas intentionality makes the latter serve a particular purpose, the same intentionality renders the work of art a *sign,* not subordinated to any external purpose but self-sufficient and evoking in man a certain attitude toward all of reality.

Our progression from the broadest comparisons to narrower ones, however, has not yet reached an end. The narrowest comparison, namely that of works of visual art with those of other arts, still remains. Only after this comparison with the environment closest to the visual arts has been carried out, will our paper be complete, will the answer to the question "What are the visual arts?" be sufficient. Well, then, how do the visual arts differ from the others? What joins them together? Above all we must be aware of the fact that the interconnection of *all* the arts, not only of that branch which we call visual, is very close. It is not the same as when we compared a work of art with a natural thing and then with a practical product. In those cases the differences between art and what was compared with it lay in the very essence; in this case it is a matter of an intrinsic identity of designations, since every work of art in general is an aesthetic (artistic) sign, a sign, the properties and essence of which we have attempted to ascertain in the course of our paper. And this common designation, already emphasized by the old saying that art is unique and simply has a multitude of kinds (*"ars una, species mille"*—it reads in Latin), this common designation results, on the one hand, in the fact that one and the same artist very often creates simultaneously in several arts, and, on the other hand, in the fact that perceivers specialize in one or another art according to their inclinations and abilities without feeling this limitation as an impoverishing one-sidedness. A further consequence of the common designation of all the arts is the fact that themes migrate freely from art to art as well as that the most varied arts are connected to one another (for example, in the illustration of a poetic work) or combined with one another. There is even an art that in its very nature is a combination of several arts. This is theater. Nevertheless, each art has something that distinctly separates it from the others, and this is its *material*. In this respect the visual arts are separated from the others by a sharp boundary and, again, are very closely connected to one another. Their material, and only theirs, is inorganic, immobile, and relatively unchangeable matter. The tangibility of the material of the visual arts becomes readily apparent in comparison, for example, with music, its inorganic nature in comparison with dance, its unchangeability in comparison with poetry, the material of which, the word, not only changes relatively quickly through development but can also be subject to subtle semantic shifts in passing from perceiver to perceiver. We shall not delay ourselves by enumerating and explaining the minute deviations from the above properties of material that can be found in individual peripheral cases; rather we shall attempt to show how this tangible, inorganic, and unchangeable material affects the arts of which it is the basis. This is an old problem. The most famous treatise on it, Lessing's *Laocoön*, bears the date 1766. Lessing, a rationalist who together with his age understood matters of art from the viewpoint of a norm, albeit not a rigid rule, also conceived this question as something which should be, rather than as a pure assertion of the state of affairs. In his treatise, therefore, he showed that graphic and plastic arts, the visual arts, must adopt a different attitude toward their themes and handle them differently than poetry, an art inspired by the muses. Thus a painting can present the entire appearance of a thing in front of a viewer's eyes at once, whereas poetry must depict the same thing in parts, gradually, in time: for poetry a state changes into events. On the contrary, of course, graphic arts cannot present events otherwise than as a state. For Lessing these are not only assertions but also requirements. He believes that the arts, limited by the nature of their materials, must not attempt to overstep the boundaries thus provided. Although Lessing's treatise contains a great deal of knowledge that has remained a lasting contribution to the study of art up to the present, this basic idea of his has obviously been superseded today. History of art, which in fact developed only after Lessing, instructs us that art, every art, constantly strives to break through the limitation provided by its material, inclining at one time toward this one, at another time toward that one of the other arts. It is, of course, another question whether such a liberation from the preconditions arising from the properties of material can succeed at all. Here it is obvious. In reality even the greatest effort at slipping out of the bonds of material cannot annul the very essence of this material. For this reason everything that a certain art undertakes according to the model of another art necessarily changes its original meaning when expressed by means of a different material. Thus if poetry attempts to depict according to the model of graphic art, it cannot compel words to have an effect upon vision; an attempt at coloration in poetry will therefore have quite a different result than in graphic art. A noticeable shift in vocabulary will occur: adjectives, nouns, and also verbs capable of *signifying,* not directly presenting a color, will increase excessively in the given poet's vocabulary and will provide it with a special character. Still another verbal differentiation of coloration is possible. If primarily adjectives are used for the expression of colors, the colors will appear as fixed properties of things. If nouns signifying individual color shades are used, the color as a nonobjective optical quality (blueness, blackness, and so on) will obtain. Finally, if mainly verbs are used (to redden, to blush, and so forth), the meanings of the colors will gain dynamicity. These individual verbal techniques can, of course, correspond to various manners of painting, but even in that case they will not be their equals but will be only their verbal equivalents. So much for poetry striving for the nature of visual arts. On the contrary, of course, the visual arts can and frequently do strive to overstep the boundaries separating them from the other arts. Thus, just as we have seen poetry attempting to compete directly with painting, painting can exhibit an effort to compete with poetry. This will happen, for example, when painting attempts the narration of anecdotal themes, as it did before the advent of realism in about the middle of the last century. It will also happen if painting is seized with the desire to depict figurative designations (metaphors, metonymies, synecdoches) that are the privilege of the poetic word. Not too many years ago we saw in Prague an exhibition of paintings, characteristically called *Poetry,* that contained pictures of this kind. After all, even today such a sober relative of painting as photography commonly uses synechdoches in showing us a part of an object instead of the whole. Painting can, however, even experience the lure of nonobjective (or rather nonthematic) music and be inspired by its rhythm. We have examples of nonthematic painting which have openly revealed this ambition. Hence the purpose of material in art—and in the visual arts as well—is not to keep a close watch on the boundaries between individual arts but to provoke by means of these limiting and regulating properties the artist's fantasy to fruitful resistance and, of course, agreement. There are countless cases—and very illustrative ones in the visual arts—in which the material meets the artist head on, in which the work grows out of the material. We have already referred to the cases in which the shape of a rock predetermined the shape of the statue that originated from it. However, it is not only the shape of the material that is decisive; so are its other properties. The hardness or softness of stone, the frangibility of stone in comparison with the suppleness of metal, the shining quality of marble, the luster of metal, the pliability of wood—all of these are not only properties of material but also creative possibilities for a sculptor. There are frequent cases in which art historians have been able to say definitely that some old statue is a copy of a lost original executed in a material different from that of the copy. The influence of the material on the original organization of the work was so considerable that the later transference into a different material was not sufficient to conceal it. Hence it is obvious that the material by which particular arts differ from one another and by which, of course, the visual arts as a whole differ from the others is not a merely passive basis of artistic activity but is an almost active factor that directs the activity and constantly intervenes—whether positively or negatively—in it. In entering the sphere of artistic creation, its individual properties are transferred into the elementary artistic meanings about which we spoke above and offer themselves to the artist so that he can knead from them the total complex meaning by which the work affects the perceiver. If we say, therefore, that the visual arts differ from the others in their material, we do not only provide a distinctive feature, as was so in the previous cases, but we get right to the very focal point of artistic creation.

We have come to the end of the road. If something remains, it is the place of the visual arts in man's life, and this requires only a few words. In fact, we have already said or at least suggested the most essential thing about it. The visual arts can and do serve to please the eye and the feelings. In addition, they can be of great value for national self-esteem and prestige. They can and often are—especially in certain periods and in certain places— a very important economic factor whether on the domestic market or in foreign trade or in stimulating tourism. Furthermore, they can serve for the propagation of ideas or principles, and they can perform other tasks as well. In spite of all this, however, their most essential function, without which all the other tasks remain mere shadows or are not even realized, lies in their influence upon man's attitude toward reality. Works of art are primarily nonserving, self-sufficient signs in the sense about which we have spoken in the course of our deliberations. Yet despite their material nature, which at first glance renders them mere things, works of the visual arts are also such signs. Even more: the visual arts are the most effective of all in performing this basic task of art in general. We have to open a book of poetry, we have to enter a theater or concert hall, but we encounter works of visual art on the street, we see them if we look at walls, and even the instruments that we use for the most common daily tasks are for the most part under their influence—either direct or indirect. (Such a great influence, of course, calls for caution in selection and evaluation, but this is the beginning of another chapter.)

Notes

1. K. H. Busse, I, p. 223.
2. Leonardo da Vinci, *The Art of Painting* (New York: 1957), p. 110.

21. Some Aspects of the Pictorial Sign (1973)

Jiří Veltruský

The picture as a sign, and as a specific type of sign, is defined by its material, by the manner in which the *signifié* is connected with the *signifiant* (the signified with the signifier), by the relationship between its referential, expressive, and conative functions and by the construction of its total sense. The present paper deals with the first and the second of these features.

Painting differs in its material from other semiotic systems and most radically from language. It uses material that is by no means exclusive to it. By contrast, the articulated sounds used in language are not used anywhere else and they are part and parcel of language as a semiotic system. The pictorial sign is characterized by the naturalness and materiality of its *signifiant*. This, however, is relative because the same characteristics are even more pronounced in other types of sign. Sculpture, in particular, uses a tridimensional *signifiant* that, moreover, conveys immaterial meanings by such material properties of its own as hardness, fragility, surface texture, and so on. But it is theater, the art which combines signs borrowed from the most varied semiotic systems, that reveals how relative the materiality of the pictorial sign is. When Vsevolod Meyerhold attempted to rid the theater of the materiality of the stage figure created by the actor—in order to bring out the subtle and complex meanings conveyed by symbolist drama—one of the things he did was to make the actors play before a backdrop made of some masterpiece of painting.[1]

Nonetheless, the materiality of its *signifiant* affects considerably the specific way in which the picture conveys meaning. This is most clearly illustrated by certain semiotic effects that different colors produce independently of their referential function—warm and cold colors, advancing and receding colors, and so on, as well as the ability of colors to arouse "affective responses" and the so-called physiognomic perception.[2] Other material components and properties of the picture also produce such immediate semiotic effects. Much has already been said in this respect about the effects of the line and design. Moreover, Schapiro has analyzed the semiotic potential of the properties of the picture field, such as the differences of "expressive quality" between broad and narrow, upper and lower, left and right, central and peripheral, the corners and the rest of the space, and says that: "The qualities of upper and lower are probably connected with our posture and relation to gravity and perhaps reinforced by our visual experience of earth and sky."[3]

The semiotic potential of the material properties of the picture and its components become particularly apparent where the thematic plane of the pictorial sign is weakened. Characteristically, certain modern painters tried to draw from that semiotic potential the whole construction of the sense of the picture; Moholy-Nagy's theoretical formulations are especially outspoken in this respect.[4]

The capacity to convey meanings independently of any referential function, just through the psychophysical effects of the material itself, is a feature that the pictorial sign has in common not only with sculpture, architecture, gestures, theater, and dance but also with music. I am referring neither to tone painting nor to musical quotation but to the semiotic potential of such phenomena as what may broadly be called synesthesia, various qualities of the tone which arouse "affective responses," the impact the rhythm may have on the beating of the heart, the ability of music to bring about "physiognomic perception," and so on. Some students of the semiotics of music are even inclined to conclude, at least tentatively, that meaning conveyed by music derives from "psycho-physiological stimulation."[5] But other musicologists reject this view;[6] it would appear that more investigation is needed.

On the other hand, the material of the pictorial sign differs from that of music by its naturalness: if we leave insignificant exceptions aside, the tones music uses do not occur outside music itself. This opposition is not the same as between the material of painting and that of language. The articulated sounds used in language are an integral part of language as a semiotic system that governs all sorts of usage, both artistic and not artistic. By contrast, the tones are an integral part of an art.

Yet, when all has been said about the difference between the material of painting and of music, both of which convey meaning directly, and the sounds of language, which do not, there is still some residue in the material of language which cannot be dismissed in this way. Jakobson is convinced that even in language the sounds are capable of conveying certain meanings on the basis of their sensory qualities and that sound symbolism is an objective relation due to some sort of synthesia.[7] A similar view is held by

Warren and Wellek.[8] Jakobson considers that research in this area would produce less vague and controversial results if it were more careful as regards the methods of psychological and linguistic inquiry; especially, that such research must operate not with complex phonemic units but with their ultimate components. As an example, he mentions the phonemic opposition between grave and acute and considers that if we ask whether | i | or | u | is darker, some people may say that this question makes no sense to them but hardly one will state that | i | is darker.[9] It may be suggested that research need not even confine itself to meanings relying on what might broadly be called synesthesia, provided the subjects tested are not asked to translate the meanings directly conveyed by the sounds of language into a simple word or phrase. For, like those conveyed by music, these meanings are very faint and vague. They can be described by words but cannot be simply translated into words; they are different from verbal meanings.

Jakobson also points out that "poetry is not the only area where sound symbolism makes itself felt, but it is a province where the internal nexus between sound and meaning changes from latent into patent and manifests itself most palpably and intensely."[10] Though our knowledge is still extremely poor in this matter, it is very likely that when this way of conveying meaning operates outside poetry, it is only in such utterances as are marked by the aesthetic function; while that covers a much broader area than poetry, the effect of the aesthetic function remains the same—it deflects attention from the communication and focuses it on the sign itself, on its properties, and its internal construction.[11] In the pictorial sign, the material properties of the *signifiant* always produce psychophysical effects, and these always have some semiotic implications, no matter whether or not, or to what extent, the sign has an aesthetic function.

This distinction does not concern the opposition between the material of the picture and that of music because music without an aesthetic function does not exist.

The opposition between the material of painting, which does not belong to painting alone, and the material of language, which is an integral part of a semiotic system, has still another important aspect. The components of the picture are incomparably less differentiated than those of language as regards the semiotic potential of each.[12] Consequently, the functions they respectively perform in the construction of the pictorial sense are very variable and to some extent even interchangeable. For example, the function of the basic unit endowed with relatively independent meaning can be performed once by the object or figure, another time by the colored shape, still another time by the color alone, and so on. This is apparently what Benveniste has in mind when he states that painting, drawing, and sculpture are semiotic systems that, unlike language and music, are not founded on units (the difference between language and music consisting in that the units of one are signs and those of the other are not).[13] Nonetheless, it is in my view somewhat rash to conclude that the semiotics of painting should not be founded on the identification and analysis of the simplest components of the picture (and that such an approach would be a mere imitation of the linguistic model).[14] This disregards the very important fact that every component, as soon as it enters a picture, acquires a differential value which it does not have in itself, as a material fact.

The semiotic variability of the material is particularly striking in post-impressionist painting, which chiefly endeavored to bring out and develop the semiotic potential of the individual material, or technical, components— the picture surface and field, its texture, size, form inner articulation, and so on, the line, color, shape, and composition—and to attenuate for this purpose the thematic elements.

This effort has, however, also brought into evidence another aspect of the same problem, namely how limited the semiotic potential of these components is, even when it is developed and exploited to the highest degree possible in the given circumstances. Broadly speaking, the attenuation or suppression of the theme tends to reduce, rather than increase, the wealth of meaning which the picture can have. To illustrate, there is no need to dwell on such extreme experiments as Malevich's *Black Square on a White Background* or *White Square on a White Background*. A great many modern painters have themselves been painfully aware of this effect and searched for means to offset it.

Some of them tried to increase the semiotic potential of the picture through an injection of language. Already Henri Rousseau, though in his painting the weakening of the thematic plane was still fairly moderate, wrote a poem to be attached to *The Dream* in order to explain the picture.

The complex and multifarious interplay between the poem and the picture brings out different meanings of the picture that were not noticed by observers who interpreted it without taking the poem into account.[15] More far-reaching was the cubist experiment between 1911 and 1915 in integrating language elements in the picture itself. This is often interpreted as a formal or compositional matter. Yet the letters, numerals, words, combinations of words, and texts used by the painters assumed a vital role in the construction of the sense of the picture.[16] It goes without saying that when interpreting such devices as symptoms of the painters' awareness of an undesirable impoverishment of the meaning conveyed by the picture, I do not intend to reduce the many aspects of these and similar experiments to this one.[17]

Another symptom of the same awareness is the determination of some modern painters to rely on the psychophysical effects of the material in order to convey meanings independently of the referential function. But the clearest evidence of this painful awareness was the fact that every single current of modern painting in that period, even the most ephemeral among them, set out to create its own interpretative code.

It may be partly because the semiotic functions belonging to the individual components are so slightly differentiated and because their semiotic potential is therefore relatively limited that, as a rule, the structure of meanings tends to be more heavily, even overwhelmingly, dominated by the thematic elements in the picture than in poetry.

The opposition between the respective materials of the pictorial and the linguistic sign is reflected in the manner in which the *signifié* is connected with the *signifiant* in the two types of sign.

In language, specific meanings are conveyed by specific combinations of sounds because they are associated by convention within a given language as a semiotic system. In the linguistic sign, therefore, the *signifié* and the *signifiant* are connected by the contiguity established within the linguistic system: "In referential language the connection between *signans* and *signatum* is overwhelmingly based on their codified contiguity, which is often confusing labeled as 'arbitrariness of the verbal sign.' "[18]

Onomatopoeia and the so-called sound symbolism do not alter this fundamental relation. An attempt to build up a meaningful utterance on this basis, to the exclusion of language units endowed with conventional meaning, is bound to be no more than an experiment—it might be fruitful from the point of view of poetry but as regards the capacity to convey meaning such an utterance would undoubtedly be very, very poor. The "symbolism" of sounds and their patterns and combinations can be used only to modify the meanings due to "codified contiguity."

It is Jakobson again who brought to light another way in which similarity enters into play in the connection between *signifiant* and *signifié* in language. He used the concept of the icon as worked out by Charles Sanders Peirce, and especially of the diagram, defined by Peirce as a variety of icon in which the resemblance between the *signifiant* and the *signifié* pertains only to the relations between the parts. With this tool in hand, he discovered striking instances of "isomorphism" between the two components of the linguistic sign, especially on the morphological and the syntactic plane. The "diagrammatic correspondence" between the *signifiant* and the *signifié* is patent and obligatory, according to Jakobson, in syntax and morphology, whereas on the lexical plane it is merely latent and virtual. This does not seem to challenge the fact that in language the relation between the *signifiant* and the *signifié* consists primordially in contiguity and that this distinguishes the linguistic sign from other kinds of sign.[19] It is indeed decisive that the "diagrammatic correspondence" affects the grammatical, relational level of language rather than its lexical, material level. And, as Jakobson himself points out, the role of this correspondence is subordinate.[20]

The picture is obviously the opposite of the language utterance—so obviously, indeed, that it is tempting to jump to the conclusion that in the pictorial sign the two constituents are related in the opposite manner, namely by similarity. No wonder, then, that a great many scholars take it for granted that the problem of the pictorial sign is essentially how to define resemblance. Yet Schapiro has demonstrated the capital role which nonmimetic elements play in constituting the pictorial sign and the semantic value which they may acquire.[21] The opposition between the two semiotic systems is, indeed, much more complicated than an opposition between A and B.

The part of "codified contiguity" in associating the *signifiant* and the *signifié* in a picture cannot be overestimated. In some instances, social convention is the only basis of this association. Such is the case of the so-called symbolism of colors and of graphic symbols such as the point, the circle, the triangle, the mandorla, the trefoil, and their combinations, all sorts of crosses, stars, and spirals, the opposition between straight line and curve, horizontal and vertical, and so on, but also of the different parts of the picture field. Unfortunately, our understanding of these signs is still very limited—for the good reason that they belong to a semiotic conception of the picture which is radically different from our own, predominantly mimetic conception. As a result, we tend spontaneously either to interpret such contiguity links as traces of some similarity or else to conceive the symbol as a mere label (red means A, blue means B, yellow means C, a circle means P, a square means Q, a swastika means R, location in the upper left-hand corner of the picture field means X, and so on). To interpret the contiguity link by some underlying similarity is rather like, and scientifically about as valid as, substituting the etymology of a word for its semantic analysis. And to read the symbol as a mere label is to disregard the basic fact that—like the word—it may convey different meanings in different situations and in different pictorial contexts, which is a strong indication that the symbol, too, may have a general meaning comprising a set of different particular meanings that will come to the fore in its actual application.

When they deal with the symbolic character of the thematic elements, those art historians and theoreticians who are most interested in the semiotics of the picture are well aware of this problem. Gombrich, for example, points out that such figures and objects "do not have one meaning but a whole range of meanings" and compares this phenomenon to the "multiplicity of meaning" in language.[22] In his study of the symbolism of profile and full-face, Schapiro shows that the respective symbolic meaning of the two positions, and particularly the preference given to one or the other as the vehicle of the higher value, changes from period to period. Moreover, he points out that two senses of the same view may exist in the same style "like the variable senses of a word, a grammatical category, or syntactical form in different contexts."[25] The same approach is needed in the study of nonmimetic symbols, as Schapiro recognizes in his methodological observations concerning color symbolism.[24] It goes without saying that the analogy with language has only an illustrative value.

Another area where contiguity is perhaps the only basis of a *signifié* being associated with a *signifiant* has been eliminated, for the same reason, from the study of the pictorial sign by the division of painting into figurative and ornamental. This dichotomy, which relegates the so-called ornamental painting into a clearly inferior position, has no justification whatever.

There is yet another reason why such types of pictorial sign have been more or less neglected in studies of meaning. Not only is our semiotic sensitivity to the picture conditioned by the tradition of mimetic painting, but our theoretical thinking about the pictorial sign is as a rule still fairly primitive. Contrary to linguistics, which for some time has been increasingly aware of the extremely subtle, varied, and complicated ways in which meaning operates in language and the sense of a message is constructed, there is still a tendency to approach the meaning of the picture as a matter of what the picture "represents" and, on the other hand, to limit the analysis to those pictorial meanings that can be translated into words—broadly speaking, to the thematic meanings. While linguistics studies the meanings of such things as morphemes, grammatical categories, synctactic links, intonation, and so on, most studies in the semiotics of the picture do not go much beyond iconology. Yet iconology is concerned with thematic meanings alone—for Panofsky, "meaning" and "subject-matter" are interchangeable.[25] Partly imputable to some characteristics of the pictorial sign itself, this limitation is nonetheless paralyzing. Perhaps the growing interest in the semiotic approach to music will help to overcome it. The manner in which music and pictures convey meanings—and even some features of the meanings they convey—are likely to be comparable in several respects.[26]

It is not only when there is little or no similarity between the *signifiant* and the *signifié* that contiguity serves to connect them. Even those painters who are convinced that they derived from the model all that they put on the canvas are in fact heavily indebted to convention. Emile Bernard, who accused modern painters of approaching nature with bias and preconceived ideas and claimed that classicism results from unprejudiced observation of nature, nonetheless added that the painters must visit museums and view the great classics of art in order to perceive the "hidden sense" of nature which cannot be discovered by the eye alone.[27]

Matisse, who loathed established conventions as much as any other modern painter, understood surprisingly well that the way to eliminate them was not to abolish convention altogether, as some of his contemporaries believed, but to create new ones:

I have to create an object which resembles a tree. The sign of the tree. And not the sign of the tree such as existed in the work of other artists. . . , for example, of those painters who learned to make leaves by drawing 33, 33, 33, as the doctor makes you say when he listens to your chest. . . . That is only the refuse of other people's expression. . . . Others discovered their own sign. . . . To take it over is to take over a dead thing [. . .]. I have to find signs that are related to the quality of my discovery. They will be new plastic signs which will, in their turn, enter into the common language if what I say by their means becomes important to others. The importance of an artist is measured by the quantity of new signs which he introduces into the plastic language.[28]

Nobody has ever seen a saint's halo except on a picture. Yet, thanks to a convention that generates "codified contiguity," everybody understands "this admirable oriental symbolism which is as profound as it is simple," to use the words of Maurice Denis, who also described the halo as a "circonférence où le chef humain est inscrit, dont la pensée humaine est le centre, et qui en exprime si parfaitement la précieuse splendeur," and as a "rayonnement visible de l'abstrait, de l'immortel, de l'absolu."[29]

Even such a strikingly mimetic principle as perspective cannot work independently of convention. Paul Klee pointed out that the rules of pictorial perspective do not follow from the laws of optics because, by convention, parallel lines are drawn converging if they run into depth but parallel if they run upwards although they recede equally from the eye;[30] Nelson Goodman convincingly refuted the arguments opposed to his demonstration.[31] The role of convention in the operation of perspective can also be seen, in the negative so to speak, in Pontormo's *Joseph in Egypt,* where perspective is used together with several conflicting scales of figures and the two apparently incompatible principles of organizing the picture are perfectly combined.

Shapiro shows how the symbol of the cross is hinted at in mimetic pictures of Abraham's sacrifice, of Moses raising his hands with the help of

Aaron and Hur during the battle with the Amalekites, of Jacob blessing the sons of Joseph, and so on. The cross may be the underlying schematic shape of various figures or objects, such as the ram in the bush, the bush itself, the faggots on Isaac's shoulders, Moses' outstretched hands, Jacob's crossed arms.[32]

In his remarkable analysis of the *Pietà* of Villeneuve-les-Avignon, attributed to Enguerrand Quarton, Michel Butor described the ways in which verbal meanings participate in the semantic construction of this picture.[33] The words written in the *Pietà*—especially the names, "Johannes Evangelista," "Virgo Mater," and "Maria Magdalena," inscribed in the respective halos of the saints—are redundant as far as the identification of the subject matter and its components is concerned—one could also say they have no "metaiconic" function. They rather enter into subtle semantic relationships, both among themselves and with different pictorial symbols, the former founded on the spatial relations between the words and the latter on the circular shape these symbols share with the inscriptions. The meanings resulting from these relationships among words and between words and symbols are linguistic meanings, therefore based on "codified contiguity." Yet they are an integral part of the semantic construction of the predominantly mimetic picture.

Panofsky showed that in the sixteenth and seventeenth centuries Judith could be painted as a handsome young woman with a sword and a charger with the head of a man on it, although according to the Bible the head of Holofernes, whom she had killed, was put into a sack: during the fourteenth and fifteenth centuries a constant link had been established between the image of the charger and that of a man's head, with the result that this configuration came to mean that the man—any man, not just John the Baptist—had been beheaded. Characteristically, several of these sixteenth- and seventeenth-century pictures of Judith were later listed as pictures of Salome by art historians who no longer grasped the conventional contiguity between the charger and the beheaded man and underestimated the importance of the contiguity between the sword and Judith.[34] In fact, what we have here is not only the combination of the charger with a man's head which, by contiguity, conveys the meaning "beheaded man" and of a handsome young woman with a sword which conveys the meaning "Judith," equally by contiguity, but also the combination of the head on the charger with a handsome young woman which may convey, still by contiguity, either Salome or Judith; it is the addition of the sign of the sword that distinguishes Judith from Salome, and the link between the sword and Judith is again based on contiguity.

Still more important is the function of "codified contiguity" in Ottonian painting.[35] Here it may be enough to quote some of the findings of Dagobert Frey:

What is especially striking about the period of romanesque style is the peculiar isolation of the individual figures of which the picture is composed, no matter whether they are juxtaposed without any ornamental bond or whether they receive their particular enclosure and framing through an ornamental articulation of the field. Every single figure, even the individual parts of the body, in so far as they are given prominence as being essential, like for example the head and the hands, every object and every accessory is given in this way an autonomous content and meaning, a *quiditas* of the substance, according to a term of scholastic philosophy, of some well-defined concept, of an "idea" in the platonic sense. In the picture the hieroglyphic signs are fitted together as in some picture writing. [. . .] For instance, rain would be expressed by the conjunction of two symbols: the sky, represented by three stars, and falling drops; dew by the sky, the falling drops and a bush.

In the same manner, individual accessory objects can represent the processes in which they were used. [. . .]

Just as the individual pictorial forms mean conceptual signs, their assemblage in the composition of the picture is purely intellectual, ideal. The elements of the picture are not fitted together according to their concrete spatial or temporal order; their position in relation to one another within the picture is in the first place a symbolic expression of their intellectual relations, of the context of their spiritual meanings, of their position in the religious and cosmic hierarchy. Thus, the circle with lines radiating from the center outwards—already used by the areopagites as a symbol of the radiation of all being from God—the wheel with its radiating spokes, the rosette, become popular basic forms of the visual arrangements of the virtues or vices, of the months or the elements, of the liberal arts or of the vicissitudes of fortune, with all the multifarious related concepts. Even an event of biblical history, such as the descent of the Holy Ghost, is translated into the symbolic form of a flaming wheel with twelve centrifugel torches, around which the apostles are arrayed in a circle. Correspondingly, "higher" and "lower" in the picture must not be understood as meaning a location in space, nor even, as is the case of a later period, as "in

front" and "behind"—it means hierarchical rank. [...] If spiritual rank is
to be expressed, the spatial relation can even be turned upside down, as for
example in the Gospels of Otto III where, on the occasion of Christ's entry
into Jerusalem, the apostles and two of the men who 'spread their garments
in the way' are lined up below the figure of Christ, so that they have to hold
up in the air the garments over which Christ rides. [...]
The linguistic imagery becomes the immediate foundation of pictorial
presentation; the tropes and the similes are crystallized in peculiarly fantastic pictures of objects. In this manner, these mystically symbolic representations often equal obscure puzzles which are difficult to interpret, which
can be solved not on the basis of the unified impression given by the whole
picture but only through the interpretation of the individual symbols and
of their formal relations. [...]
The universal metaphors and purely intellectual symbols of language are
not recast into a new pictorially graphical form of expression but copied
almost word by word in a hieroglyphic pictorial writing. When, in the opposite direction, the pictorial composition is decomposed in the viewer's
imagination into its elements and the picture is read through the individual
pictorial signs, even what is absurd from the point of view of the picture
acquires sense and meaning.[36]

Described in this fashion, Ottonian painting appears to have common
features with postimpressionist painting, not only in its tendency to attenuate the similarity between the sign and what it represents, in its reliance
on "codified contiguity," but also in its striving to match language in its
manner of conveying meaning ("linguistic imagery," "universal metaphor,"
and so forth). This striving is, indeed, one of the characteristic features of
modern painting as well—Henri Matisse's *Blue Nude* is a pictorial translation of the distinction between the adjective and the noun, to mention just
one example.

But the contrast between the two periods is equally striking. The convention on which modern painting had to rely for its ability to conjure up
meanings by contiguity was not a real convention—accepted by society—
because modern painting was by definition experimental, therefore ephemeral in each of its particular varieties (or "isms"). This quasi-convention
consisted in the painters' directly or indirectly informing their particular,
circumscribed public—it has been said, in an extreme formulation, that the
public of modern art is artists themselves—of the code they were using and

this code being accepted as the intellectual key to the pictures.

Moreover, modern painting in general, and even abstract painting, is not really a new mode of associating the *signifié* with the *signifiant* but rather a dialectical negation of the established mode, the resemblance of the latter to the former:

> In abstract painting the system of marks, strokes and spots and certain ways of combining and distributing them on the field have become available for arbitrary use without the requirement of correspondence as signs. The forms that result are not simplified, abstract forms of objects; yet the elements applied in a non-mimetic, uninterpreted whole retain many of the qualities and former relationships of the preceding mimetic art. This important connection is overlooked by those who regard abstract painting as a kind of ornament or as a regression to a primitive state of art.[37]

This explains the phenomenon already mentioned, namely that the endeavor to increase the semiotic potential of the picture resulted in actually reducing this potential. The meaning that dots, lines, colors, shapes, the size, texture, shape, and articulation of the field and such like can convey by themselves, independently of the subject-matter of the picture, are vague unless social convention makes them more definite by means of "codified contiguity."

As strong as it may become in certain communities at certain periods, the codifying power of pictorial convention can hardly ever match that of linguistic convention because language is the basic instrument of communication. So, despite its ability to connect the *signifié* with the *signifiant* by contiguity, the pictorial sign tends more often to connect them mainly by similarity.

If, however, it is to become a reliable tool of semiotic description, the concept of similarity must be carefully defined. Gombrich has probably contributed more than any other scholar to the necessary critique of the loose and naive way in which the concept of resemblance has been used in art history.[38] Yet it has still to be defined. Physical resemblance must be carefully distinguished from diagrammatic correspondence (isomorphism). Furthermore, similarity is inseparable from contrast because there is no similarity without dissimilarity and no resemblance without dissemblance—

otherwise similarity and identity would be one and the same thing. This has far-reaching implications for the operation of the sign that conveys meaning by way of similarity. Every one of the lines, colors, forms on a picture has some similarity with some other visual reality. The picture cannot convey the meaning intended unless all these similarities are classified into those that are relevant as similarities and those that are to be disregarded as dissimilarities because they resemble realities that are alien to the intended meaning.

This visual semiotic classification itself relies on contiguity, which operates to this effect in at least three distinct ways: not only through pictorial convention, but also through subject matter and through the differential value each component acquires within the picture.

As already pointed out, the structure of meanings tends to be overwhelmingly dominated by thematic elements. It is true that this is often overstated, as when Boas and Wrenn claim that Pisanello's *Vision of St. Eustace* "would be meaningless unless one had some idea of the story which lies behind it"[39]—none of the people to whom I showed the picture found it meaningless, and none even tried to find out what story lies behind it. But the fact remains that it is through the subject matter and its components—figures, objects, actions, scenery, and so on—that the viewer is guided in selecting, from among all the similarities which link the components of the picture to the realities outside it, those that are relevant to the picture as such. Yet it is by contiguity, not by similarity, that certain visual qualities, for which the viewer is led to look in the picture, are connected with such thematic meanings.

The manner in which this function is performed by the subject matter may be illustrated by a very simple example borrowed from Georges Seurat's *Le Chahut.* In the lower part of the right side the viewer sees a sequence of four almost identical, and almost identically colored, parallel forms about equally far apart. The sequence reappears in the upper part of the middle two-fifths in a somewhat modified form (the forms point in the opposite direction, their slant is different, they are slightly slimmer, they are gradually decreasing fractions of the shapes composing the first series, and so forth). Because of the trunks, arms, and heads of the four chahut dancers depicted in the space between these two sequences, the

viewer immediately connects the forms in question with the meaning
"legs." And he connects them with that meaning by similarity. Yet the
similarity is remote, so remote that the same degree of similarity could be
found with any number of entirely different things—provided they were
suggested by the thematic meanings. Moreover, this semiotic operation is
hardly affected by the obstacles put into its way: indeed, the forms are
nearly identical although the subject matter leads the viewer to perceive
them as alternately female and male legs; the only visible difference is that
the "female" forms, unlike the "male" ones, are marked by small separate
shapes which accompany them, representing bows on the ladies' shoes. It
is of course by contiguity that the trunks, arms, and heads depicted evoke
the meaning "legs."

The differential value the material elements acquire when they become
pictorial components—that is, when they enter a picture—may best be illustrated by the presentation of darkness. The darkness in a picture can never
be so deep as in reality—characteristically, not even Malevich painted, to
my knowledge, a *Black Square on a Black Background.* To represent the
night, it is sufficient for the painter to reduce the brightness of the colors
and, maybe, to substitute the colder "tones" for warmer ones.[40] In more
general terms, the respective numbers of hues, brightness levels, and degrees of saturation used in any single picture are fairly limited. Moreover,
a high degree of contrast in brightness seems to attenuate the contrast of
hue—that is what Florentin meant when he wrote almost a hundred years
ago: "A mesure que le principe colorant diminue dans un ton, l'élément
valeur y prédomine."[41] The use of a wide range of hues seems to reduce
the saturation effects.

Naturally, this semiotic process is not limited to colors. All the components are endowed, within the picture, with differential values that
they do not have in themselves. Matisse made the point perfectly:

Claude Lorrain, Poussin, have ways of their own of drawing the leaves of a
tree, they discovered their own way of expressing leaves. So skillfully,
that they are said to have drawn their trees leaf by leaf. Simply a manner
of speech: in fact they represented perhaps fifty leaves for two thousand.
But the way the sign "leaf" is placed multiplies the leaves in the mind of
the viewer who sees two thousand of them.[42]

Still another illustration of the way the differential value of the components classifies the similarities can be found in the example drawn from Seurat's *Le Chahut.* As already pointed out, the "female" and the "male" forms are nearly identical except that the "female" ones are accompanied by small separate shapes representing bows on the shoes. A very similar small shape appears at the same spot of what represents the raised leg of the first male dancer from the left. The viewer immediately interprets this shape not as a shoe bow but as the last two fingers of the first female dancer. Yet the shape resembles a bow as much as it resembles two raised fingers and, what is more, the position of the remaining three fingers by no means requires that the two others be visible as well. The viewer is guided in this case by the differential value of a compositional pattern. Since in the two sequences the small distinctive "bow" shapes combine with the odd, not the even, "leg" forms, he automatically rejects the association that would create the only exception to this rule and retains only the similarity with two fingers.

This differential value of the components, which itself depends on no resemblance between the *signifiant* and the *signifié,* is as important in the pictorial as in the linguistic sign. It is a condition without which the sign cannot function: "In a semiological system, the sign necessarily has a differential character, that is to say, it is constituted by an element of particularization within a series of facts founded on a common, identical and consequently general character."[43] The difference between the pictorial and the linguistic sign consists in that the material of language has these differential values irrespective of any specific utterance because it is integrated in the linguistic system, while the material of the picture, due to its naturalness, acquires them only when it is used in a picture.

The system from which these differential values of pictorial components derive may be either preestablished by the rules of a style, a school, a genre, a tradition, and so on, or created by the specific picture itself; moreover, even where there is a preestablished system, it can be freely changed, unlike the linguistic system, by any single picture.

There is no symmetry, then, between the function of similarity in connecting the *signifié* with the *signifiant* in the language utterance and the function of contiguity in connecting the two constituents in the picture.

First, it would be all but impossible to construct a meaningful utterance on the basis of linguistic elements conveying meaning by way of similarity, that is, onomatopoeia and sound "symbolism" with the assistance of morphological and syntactic "diagrammatic" correspondence, whereas pictures relying exclusively upon association by contiguity exist. Second, in the language utterance the similarity-based "symbolism" of the sounds and the "diagrammatic" correspondence can only modify the meanings with which the units of the utterance are endowed by contiguity—whereas in the mimetic picture the connection by similarity itself cannot operate without the connection by contiguity performing its selecting and classifying function.

The question arises whether to connect the *signifiant* and the *signifié* some sort of contiguity is not necessary in any kind of sign. But our present knowledge of the various semiotic systems is still so limited that the question has to remain unanswered. Evidently, the problem has something to do with Benveniste's contention that all other systems of communication are derived from and presuppose language.[44]

Notes

1. Cf. Edward Brown, *Meyerhold on Theater,* London: 1967; Vsevolod Meyerhold, *Écrits sur le théâtre,* vol. I, Lausanne, 1973.

2. See E. H. Gombrich, "On Physiognomic Perception," *Meditations on a Hobby Horse and Other Essays on the Theory of Art,* London: 1963, pp. 45 ff.

3. Meyer Schapiro, "On Some Problems in the Semiotics of Visual Art: Field and Vehicle in Image-Signs," in A. J. Greimas, R. Jakobson, et al., ed., *Sign, Language, Culture,* The Hague: 1970, p. 492.

4. See L. Moholy-Nagy, *Malerei, Photographie, Film,* Munich: 1925, pp. 6 and 9.

5. See Jean-Jacques Nattiez, "Situation de la sémiologie musicale," *Musique en jeu,* 5, and "Analyse musicale et sémiologie: Le structuralisme de Lévi-Strauss," ibid., 12.

6. See Nicolas Ruwet, *Language, musique, poésie,* Paris: 1972, p. 13.

7. See Roman Jakobson, "Linguistics and Poetics," in Thomas A. Sebeok, ed., *Style in Language,* New York-London: 1960, pp. 372 f; see also "A la recherche de l'essence du langage," *Diogène,* 51, and *Child Language, Aphasia and Phonological Universals,* The Hague: 1968, pp. 82 f.

8. See Austin Warren and René Wellek, *Theory of Literature*, London: 1949, p. 164.

9. See Roman Jakobson, "Linguistics and Poetics," in Sebeok, *Style in Language*, pp. 372 f.

10. Ibid., p. 372.

11. See Jan Mukařovský, "Estetika jazyka" [Esthetics of Language"], *Kapitoly z české poetiky*, vol. I, 1948, pp. 45 ff.

12. See Roman Jakobson, "On the Relation between Visual and Auditory Signs," *Selected Writings*, vol. II, The Hague: 1971, p. 341.

13. See Emile Benveniste, "Sémiologie de la langue," *Semiotica* I/1-2.

14. See Hubert Damisch, *Théorie du nuage*, Paris: 1972, pp. 26 f.

15. See Roman Jakobson, "On the Verbal Art of William Blake and Other Poet-Painters," *Linguistic Inquiry*, 1970/1.

16. See Susan Markus, "The Typographic Element in Cubism, 1911-1915," *Visible Language*, Autumn 1972.

17. In fact, in a paper entitled "Zur Soziologie der modernen Malerei" (1948), I dealt in some detail with the general tendency of modern art to transplant the components, devices, and semiotic principles from one art into another or even into all the others.

18. Roman Jakobson, "Linguistics and Poetics," in Sebeok, *Style in Language*, p. 372.

19. See Roman Jakobson, "A la recherche de l'essence du langage," *Diogène*, 51.

20. See Roman Jakobson, "Language in Relation to Other Communication Systems," *Selected Writings*, vol. II, p. 700.

21. See Meyer Schapiro in Greimas, Jakobson, et al., in *Sign, Language, Culture*, pp. 487 ff.

22. See E. H. Gombrich, *Symbolic Images: Studies in the Art of the Renaissance*, London: 1972, pp. 8 and 12.

23. Meyer Schapiro, *Words and Pictures: On the Literal and the Symbolic Meaning in the Illustration of a Text*, The Hague: 1973, p. 44.

24. See ibid., pp. 47 f.

25. See Erwin Panofsky, *Studies in Iconology*, New York-Evanston-San Francisco London: 1972 (paperback), pp. 3 ff.

26. The role of the Prague School in the study of the semiotics of music is largely unknown. Penetrating analyses of the ways in which music conveys meaning were made by one of the Czech predecessors of the Prague school, Otakar Zich—see

especially his "Estetické vnímání hudby" [Esthetic Perception of Music], Česká mysl, XI, 1910, and Estetika dramatického umění, Prague: 1931, pp. 277 ff. In 1932, an important discussion on musicology took place in the Prague Linguistic Circle—see Roman Jakobson, "Musikwissenschaft und Linguistik," Prager Presse, December 7, 1932. From 1945 to 1948, several papers dealing with the semiotics of music were presented and various related problems were examined in the Esthetics Seminar and the Theater Seminar of Prague University, both directed by Jan Mukařovský; prominent among the young musicologists who contributed to this work were Eduard Herzog, Antonín Sychra, and Adolf Scherl. Whatever progress was then made toward the semiotics of music seems to have been destroyed during the subsequent period when structuralism was officially banned. Some echoes of the ideas initiated in the two seminars can be found in Sychra's early writings and in his work during the last years of his life, including his popularizing book, Hudba očima vědy [Music through the Eyes of Scholarship], Prague: 1965.

27. See Claude Chassé, Le mouvement symboliste dans l'art du XIXᵉ siècle, Paris: 1947, p. 104.

28. Henri Matisse, Ecrits et propos sur l'art, Paris: 1972, pp. 1/1 t.

29. Maurice Denis, Théories 1890-1910, Paris: 1912, p. 34.

30. Paul Klee, Pedagogical Sketchbook, London: 1972, p. 41.

31. Nelson Goodman, Languages of Art, London, 1969, pp. 16 ff.

32. See Meyer Schapiro, Words and Pictures, pp. 14 f, 17 ff, and 28.

33. See Michel Butor, Les mots dans la peinture, Geneva: 1969, pp. 52 ff.

34. Erwin Panofsky, Studies in Iconology, pp. 12 ff.

35. I use here the term "Ottonian" not to take sides in, but to stay out of, the conflict between the art historians who consider Ottonian art as romanesque and those for whom it is a precursor of this style.

36. Dagobert Frey, Gotik und Renaissance, Augsburg: 1929, pp. 40 ff.

37. Meyer Schapiro, "On Some Problems in the Semiotics of Visual Art: Field and Vehicle in Image-Sign," in Words and Pictures, p. 501.

38. See especially E. H. Gombrich, Art and Illusion, London: 1972; "Meditations on a Hobby Horse or the Roots of Artistic Form" and "Illusion and Visual Deadlock," Meditations on a Hobby Horse and Other Essays on the Theory of Art; "The Mask and the Face: The Perception of Physiognomic Likeness in Life and Art," in E. H. Gombrich, Julian Hochberg, and Max Black, Art, Perception and Reality, Baltimore-London: 1972; "The Visual Image," Scientific American, September 1972.

39. George Boas and H. H. Wrenn, *What Is a Picture?*, New York: 1966 (paperback), p. 1.

40. The clumsy term "tones" is used here on purpose. Indeed, I am not sure that the opposition between warm and cold colors is a matter of hues (see Rudolf Arnheim, *Art and Visual Perception,* London: 1967, p. 328).

41. Eugène Florentin, *Les maîtres d'autrefois,* 1965 (paperback), p. 237.

42. Henri Matisse, *Ecrits et propos sur l'Art,* pp. 171 f.

43. Serge Karcevskij, *Système du verbe russe,* Prague: 1927, p. 13.

44. Emile Benveniste, "Coup d'oeil sur le développement de la linguistique," *Problèmes de linguistique générale,* vol. I, Paris: 1966, p. 28.

Postscript. Prague School Semiotics

Ladislav Matejka

1.

The semiotics of art, the study of art as creative usage of sign systems, has become one of the major areas of scientific quest in the school of structural linguistics known since the 1920s as the *Prague Linguistic Circle.*
   In Prague, the modern science of sign emerged against the background of an illustrious semiotic tradition. Students of sign structures and of the systematic usage of signs in human communication had a remarkable predecessor in the Prague-born Bernard Bolzano. While professor of philosophy at Prague University (1805-1820), Bolzano introduced his grand design for a theory of science, including within its scope speculations about the "interpretation of signs" and "their relationship to the objects signified," about "the use of signs to produce ideas in others," about natural, contingent and conventional signs and their "metonymic and metaphoric usage," and about "the sign of signs" (such as "written signs signifying spoken language").[1]
   However, the Prague tradition of semiotic thought might be traced even further back to the medieval nominalists and realists who, in the fourteenth century, virtually split Charles University asunder with their dispute over whether universal phenomena subsisted in themselves or were mere names invented to express the qualities of particular things. On this peripatetic journey into the past, one should recognize, of course, the impact of the schoolmen who restated St. Augustine's binary concept of *signum* as *signans* and *signatum* (whereby something stands for something else—*aliquid stat pro aliquo*) and detect the even more distant echo of the Stoic concept concerning the relation between what is expressed and what is meant.
   Yet, the most decisive stimuli for the rise of structural semiotics in the *Prague Linguistic Circle* must be sought in a number of more modern phenomena: the legacy of the Russian school of Formal Method, the *Cours de linguistique générale* of the Geneva professor Ferdinand de Saussure,[2] and Karl Bühler's model of the bond between *Sprechakt* (speech act) and *Sprachgebilde* (language structure).[3] This list must also include the semiotics of the American pragmatists who were closely studied by Thomas G. Masaryk and his school. Indeed, it was one of Masaryk's disciples, Vilém Mathesius, professor of English at Charles University in Prague, who, in

1926, became the first chairman of the *Prague Linguistic Circle,* while Masaryk himself, by then president of Czechoslovakia, acted as an interested and well-informed observer of the movement and the *Circle's* generous benefactor.

Captivated by observations about static and dynamic linguistics in Masaryk's *Concrete Logic,* Mathesius, as early as 1911, launched a powerful attack on the simplifying schemes of the linguistic positivists, especially as manifested in Schleicher's conception of language as a biological organism. Mathesius's study, entitled "On the Potentiality of Language Phenomena," particularly decried the influence of the exact sciences which had led the Neo-grammarian school to an aprioristic belief in the absolute regularity of sound-laws and to the disregard for the co-occurrence of variants as a source of potential change. "Linguistics," Mathesius insisted, "should not merely endeavor to discover general regularities, it must also struggle, even more energetically, against excessive, mechanistic simplifications of language phenomena."[4]

Mathesius believed that the danger of methodological simplifications lay in the fact that the classificatory schemes were confused with the actual make up of language. Therefore, he called for the study of concrete usage in every possible aspect with due attention to vacillation in speech habits, whether on the level of sound, grammar or meaning. It was the study of co-occurrence of variants which Mathesius regarded as directly relevant to an illumination of language not only in its practical (informational) function but also in its creative application in verbal art. In his view, stylistics and rhetoric, the disciplines concerned with the special functions of a language system, differed from linguistics only in terms of aims: in verbal art, the co-occurrence of variants becomes a source of creative usage and should be studied accordingly.

Mathesius's proposal of a static (synchronic) linguistics, as distinguished from dynamic (diachronic) linguistics, was published the same year that Ferdinand de Saussure offered the last part of his course in general linguistics at the University of Geneva and four years before the first publications of Saussure's posthumous *Cours de linguistique générale.* Although Saussure's insistence on the distinction between static and diachronic linguistics obviously had no direct relation to Mathesius's proposal, the striking conceptual coincidence may have resulted from the common need of both authors to respond to the deadlock in the neogrammarian trend and to search for a new, more productive path of linguistic investigation. No doubt, the same common need also constituted the basis for the mutual understanding between Mathesius and the members of the *Moscow Linguistic Circle,* such as Roman Jakobson, Sergej Karcevskij, and Petr Bogatyrev, who had left the Soviet Union in the early twenties to live in Czechoslovakia and, in 1926, helped found the *Prague Linguistic Circle.*[5]

2.

In Russia, Saussure's *Cours* and his inspiring concept of semiotics (*semiologie,* as Saussure himself called it) was enthusiastically promoted by Sergej Karcevskij, who had spent several years in Geneva as Saussure's student and who, upon his return to Russia in 1917, joined the *Moscow Linguistic Circle.* Jakobson recalls the lively discussions among the students in Moscow at that time: "We learned," he writes "to sense the delicate distinction between the *signatum* (the signified) and the *denotatum* (the referred-to), hence to assign an intrinsically linguistic position, first to the *signatum* and then, by inference, to its inalienable counterpart as well—that is, to the *signans.*"[6] Saussure's impact on Russian linguists in the 1920s is well documented by M. N. Peterson's outline of the Sassurian doctrine in the journal *Pečat' i revolucija* (1923), by laudatory remarks of R. Šor in Marr's *Jafetičeskij sbornik* (1927), and particularly by V. N. Vološinov's extensive analysis in his *Marixism and the Philosophy of Language* (1929).[7] "It can be claimed," Vološinov wrote in 1929, "that the majority of Russian thinkers in linguistics are under the determinative influence of Saussure and his disciples."[8] In fact, Vološinov's own semiotic design was heavily influenced by Saussure's observations about signs and their role in human communication, although Vološinov, speaking from the Marxist point of view, rejected as a Cartesian fallacy Saussure's insistence on absolute separation of the concrete linguistic performance (*la parole*) from the abstract language system (*la langue*).

In Prague, Saussure's deliberations over synchronic and diachronic linguistics and his outline of a general science of sign found ready ground. His incentives, whether approved or critically modified, are clearly discernible in the "Theses" of the *Prague Linguistic Circle,* presented at the

First International Congress of Slavists in Prague and published in the first volume of *Travaux du Circle Linguistique de Prague* in 1928. The "Theses" argue that the practical function of language is primarily directed toward what is denoted in the external world while the poetic function takes place "when language is directed toward the sign itself."[9] Thus the poetic function, implying heightened awareness of the semiotic process, appears in juxtaposition to the practical (informational) function. Accordingly, the investigation of the poetic function is expected to take into account the fact that the text of verbal art principally attracts attention to its sign structure and only obliquely or figuratively imparts information relevant to the social context. This early formulation of the poetic function in terms of orientation toward sign, although, of course, subsequently elaborated, stands as one of the Prague School's fundamental concepts of semiotics and as a common denominator of its investigation not only of various verbal phenomena, verbal art included, but also of art in general.

The section on poetic language is one of the most comprehensive components of the entire "Theses," despite the fact that, with the exception of Jan Mukařovský, the majority of the early members of the *Prague Linguistic Circle* were linguists or primarily linguists. In fact, in the first issue of the *Travaux,* where the "Theses" were published, only Mukařovský's discussion of "The Connection between the Prosodic Contour and Word Order in Czech Verse" was directly concerned with problems of verbal art. Two studies by N. S. Trubetzkoy were devoted to phonology and morphology; Mathesius discussed the phonology of Czech lexicon; Bohumil Trnka dealt with the problem of synchrony and diachrony in comparative linguistics; Bohuslav Havránek focused on the question of standardized language, and Sergej Karcevskij speculated upon the asymetric dualism of the sign in the verbal system. Nevertheless, the variety of problems that were represented in the *Travaux,* whether in its first issue or subsequent ones, exercised impact both directly and indirectly on the formation of a semiotic trend in the *Prague Linguistic Circle.* This was particularly true as regards the concept of phonology which Roman Jakobson had introduced into studies of verbal art years before the *Prague Linguistic Circle* was founded.[10]

3.

There cannot be any doubt that the "Theses" of the Prague Linguistic Circle reflect, whether directly or in a further developed or critically modified aspect, certain concepts proposed earlier by the Russian school of the Formal Method. The Russian school was not an entirely homogeneous movement, however, and the Prague group was particularly responsive to the trend represented by Boris Ejxenbaum, Boris Tomaševskij, Jurij Tynjanov, while largely ignoring the taxonomic branch of the scholastic formalists or their eclectic "fellow travelers," who tended towards a merger of the Formal Method with the German tradition of literary morphology and compositional analysis. Thus, to some extent, the "Theses" mirror the methodological split within the movement which, since 1915, has been known as Russian Formalism, often with disregard for the fact that the very interpretation of the concept of *form* caused a growing conceptual disagreement and an early schism.

A year before the "Theses" were issued in *Travaux,* Roman Jakobson, in collaboration with the outstanding Russian literary theoretician Jurij Tynjanov, published a sharp repudiation of those formalists who saw the goal of literary analysis in cataloguing, classifying, and labeling details without adequate study of the literary system and its specific structural laws from a functional point of view:

. . . academic eclecticism, scholastic "formalism"—which replaces analysis by terminology and the classification of phenomena—and the repeated attempts to shift literary and linguistic studies from a systematic science to episodic and anecdotal genres should be rejected.
The history of literature (art), being simultaneous with other historical series, is characterized by an involved complex of specific structural laws. Without an elucidation of these laws, it is impossible to establish in a scientific manner the correlation between the literary series and other historical series.[11]

In virtually the same vein, Boris Ejxenbaum, in 1925, had repudiated the classificatory predilection of "scholastic formalism" in his lucid survey of the Formal method's first decade. Singling out Viktor Žirmunskij, Ejxenbaum accused him of having "found the Formal method of interest only as one of a set of possible scientific rubrics—as a technique for breaking material down into various grouping under various labels."[12] However, in his classificatory attitude toward form, Žirmunskij was not alone. Among the followers of the Formal method, there was an entire group of scholars who became devoted adherents of the taxonomy and descriptive morphology. The most outstanding among them was Viktor Šklovskij.

The attitude of the *Prague Linguistic Circle* toward Šklovskij's brand of formalism and particularly toward his compositional analysis of prose might best be illustrated by Jan Mukařovský's review of Šklovskij's *Theory of Prose,* a book that appeared in 1925 and included almost ten years' worth of Šklovskij's compositional studies. Mukařovský's review was written in 1934, when the Czech translation of the *Theory of Prose* was published.[13] This review clearly reflected the two decades that had elapsed since the origin of the earliest studies in Šklovskij's book. It was precisely during these two decades that many of the crucial concepts of the Russian Formal method had crystallized. Thus, Mukařovský's review represented, to a certain extent, a confrontation between one branch of Russian formalism and Prague structuralism. In fact, Mukařovský intentionally used the opportunity of reviewing Šklovskij's book to reject certain formalistic excesses, which he compared with Herbart's aesthetic of pure form, and to explain the principle of structuralism as a way out of the blind alley of rigorous preoccupation with the taxonomy of the text. He developes his argument by taking up the analytic credo from the introduction to *Theory of Prose,* where Šklovskij proclaims that his sole interest is in the material aspects of verbal art: what material is used and how the work is made. Using the textile industry as an analogy, Šklovskij asserts that he is merely interested in the types of yarn and the techniques of weaving and not in the situation on the international wool market or in the politics of trusts. This analogy provides Mukařovský with a spring-board for his claim that the techniques of weaving, with their figurative implications for art, necessarily reflect the needs and pressures of the market in accordance with its law of supply and demand. In the spirit characteristic of Prague structuralism, Mukařovský concludes that the techniques of art cannot be studied in a vacuum, artificially isolated from the related systems and, implicitly, from time and space. Being a social structure, verbal art ought to be analyzed not only with regard to its autonomous properties but also in its relationship to other social systems, to "structures such as science, politics, economy, social stratification, language, ethics, religion, each having its own immanent development."[14] Accordingly the immanent evolution of the system of art is viewed as an intrinsic force which responds to the impact of related systems but transforms that impact in its own terms. Since the specificity of each social structure, including art, is defined by its gravitation toward autonomy, the interrelationship of structures appears as a dynamic system of interacting forces displayed in a hierarchy of dominating and dominated constituents. It is this complex role played by the interrelationships of systems that becomes the very basis of structuralism for Mukařovský.

4.

The same year that Mukařovský published the review of Šklovskij's *Theory of Prose*, he wrote his "L'art comme fait sémiologique." This was his first attempt to argue the feasibility of the model of sign not only for literary study but for the study of art in general, according to the premise, now made explicit, that the structural approach to the complex interrelationships of art offers best insight if the work of art, whether verbal or nonverbal, is recognized as a special operation of signs mediating between the creator and his reader, listener or viewer. "Unless the semiotic character of art is adequately elucidated," Mukařovský insisted, "the study of its structure will remain necessarily incomplete."[15]

By implication, the semiotics of art became an important aspect of the entire structural concept defined by the Prague School. It helped to safeguard structural analysis from the pitfalls of purely formal considerations of the artifact in its physical implementation. By the same token, the notion of art as a sign structure mediating between the creator and his consumer guarded against viewing the phenomenon of art as a direct reflection of the artist's mind or as a mirror of the external world with its ideological, economic, social, cultural, and other problems.

The model of sign as a vehicle conveying meaning helped to establish an analytic framework for the structural observations about the signifying means and the domain of signification and, at the same time, about the nature of the link between the external and internalized aspects of art. The very notion of communication by means of art turned attention to the preconditions needed to make a communicative contact by art possible. It became clear that the study of the perceptible elements, however rigorous that study might be, would not explain the meaningful usage of the artifact, its understandability, the changeability of its functions, and, in general, the problem of its value. It was the function of the work of art as a sign structure rather than the artifact itself to become the focal point of scrutiny.

In the opening paragraph of "L'art comme fait sémiologique," Mukařovský refers to Saussure's science of sign and makes use of the term "collective consciousness," which Saussure saw as the foundation of every semiotic system. Applying Saussure's concept to the domain of art, Mukařovský explains that "the artifact functions merely as an external signifier (*signifiant* in Saussure's terminology) for which in the collective consciousness there is a corresponding signification."[16] In the domain of art, as Mukařovský sees it "the signification is given by what is common to the subjective state of mind aroused in individuals of any particular community by the artifact."[17] In other words, individual responses to a work of art are governed by an internalized system analogous to the system of verbal language. Thus the concrete construction of an artifact *in praesentia* is juxtaposed to the abstract internalized system in *absentia:* the perceivable properties appear in opposition to the corresponding intelligible aspects, the concrete to the abstract, the individual to the social. Accordingly, the artifact functions as a sign only if the internalized underlying system makes it meaningful.

In his conclusion Mukařovský insists that the structure proper of the work of art lies neither in the perceivable signifier, created by the artist, nor in the reference of the work of art to the social context but rather in the signification registered in the collective consciousness and shared by the members of the art community (artists and consumers of art). Consequently, it became of primary importance to deal with the fact that the artifact or text remains virtually the same in the course of time (or undergoes the changes due to merely the aging of matter), while the special apparatus of norms and rules (grammatical, aesthetic, ethical, and other) may change quite substantially and, at any given stage of evolution, appears as a co-occurrence of older and newer, higher and lower, more stable and less stable norms and rules.

5.

In 1935, the principles of the semiotics of art were restated in the first issue of *Slovo a slovesnost* /Word and Language Culture/, a literary magazine founded by the *Prague Linguistic Circle.* The introductory article, signed by Bohuslav Havránek, Roman Jakobson, Vilém Mathesius, and Bohumil Trnka, proclaimed semiotics to be the most crucial issue in the intellectual and cultural resurgence of modern times. The characteristic properties of the sign and of its usage were singled out as the foundation of human interaction, the very constituent factors of mankind's culture and civilization. "All of reality, from an immediate perception to the most abstract train of thought, appears to modern man as a vast, complexly organized realm of signs."[18] The proclamation, recognizing that inquiry into the realm of signs had just begun, called for attention first and foremost to those areas of human culture where the various internal structures of sign stand out most sharply in all their complexity. From this point of view, the verbal system acquired particular importance, as the proclamation revealed:

Language is the most fundamental set of signs (though by no means the simplest) in view of the fact that a permanent feature of the entire realm of signs is the tendency to express everything in verbal terms. Verbal discourse can be particularly instructive to us because of its referential relationship, that is to say, the relationship between a sign and the reality to which it refers, inasmuch as language, both spoken and written, aims above all at expressing reality, at acting upon reality even if only indirectly.[19]

Thus, verbal communication appeared not only as the analytic focus of attention but also served as a model for other types of sign systems--other "languages." Among them the arts, especially verbal art, were regarded as the most promising domain for semiotic inquiry. A comparison between the normal referential usage of language and the manipulation of sign structures in art served as a fundamental angle of observation:

Verbal art and art in general provide the prime material for studying the internal structure of the sign itself, for disclosing the interrelationship between a sign vehicle (that is, sound, color, etc.) and its meaning, and for investigating the manifold stratification of meaning. This is due to the fact that the referential relationship in art is attenuated: the work of art is not measurable in terms of the veracity of the information conveyed; rather, it is a sign that lives its own life and freely travels between artist and audience.[20]

As can be seen, the principles of art were sought in the operation of the sign system itself. The referential relationship of the sign structure in art to the designatum, the outside world, was viewed as intentionally subordinated, due to the focus on the sign structure itself, to the world of the signs standing in an oblique and even antithetical relationship to the real world.

The emphasis on such an indirect, figurative relationship was not meant, however, as a defense of the notion of self-contained art, completely isolated from the social context and its system of values. On the contrary, the focus on the sign structure added complexity and depth to the ultimate understanding of art by encompassing the system of art conventions, norms, and rules relevant to a value judgment. The concept of art as a sign system, mediating between members of a certain community made it necessary that the study of art, a social phenomenon by its very nature, include adequate consideration of society and its organization:

The entire dynamics of social development, the ongoing regrouping and conflict of each of its strata and its environment, the struggle of classes, nations and ideologies—all that is intensely reflected in the relation between art and society and even in the development of art itself, despite the fact that the changes in the structure of art appear as continuously sequential and ordered.[21]

The change in art was accordingly defined as an essential topic of structural investigation. The immanent, self-propelled force striving toward the autonomy of art was recognized only as one among a set of forces interacting within the system of a culture—each affecting the others and each restricted by others while transforming their impact into its own terms. This position, which is very characteristic of structuralism in its Prague version, did not transform the study of art into the sociology of art—it merely recognized the fact that the autonomy of art is not absolute and that the functions and values of art are by definition social, and, for that reason, must be studied in connection with the overall system of social values.

6.

The nature of the relationship between the world of signs and the real
world denoted by the sign systems gradually emerged as one of the central
topics of the Prague School semiotics. It constituted an essential theme in
Jakobson's study of Hussite poetry (1936) where he explicitly rejected the
restrictive nature of his own approach toward the immanence of evolution
in his earlier investigation of medieval Czech poetry. The relation between
signum and *denotatum* also became an important topic in Mukařovský's
book *Aesthetic Function, Norm and Values as Social Facts.*[22] Subsequently, it underwent new scrutiny in his "Dénomination poètique et la fonction
esthétique de la langue" (1938).[23] In this study Mukařovský refers extensively to Karl Bühler's observations about the speech act (*Sprechakt*) in its
relationship to the language system (*Sprachgebilde*) as well as (1) to the
thing spoken about, (2) to the speaker, and (3) to the listener.[24] Bühler,
one of the contributors to the *Travaux* of the *Prague Linguistic Circle,* although not a regular member, regarded the three essential relations as the
underlying base of the three principal functions of the speech act: (1) the
representational function referring to what is spoken about, (2) the expressive function referring to the speaker, and (3) the 'appellative' (that is,
conative) function referring to the person spoken to. Although Mukařovský in principle considered Bühler's three basic functions perfectly acceptable with regard to a normal informational utterance, he felt that it was
necessary to add a fourth function in order to account for the poetic usage
of language. In Mukařovský's dialectical interpretation, the fourth basic
function, which he calls *aesthetic,* appears in opposition to all other functions. The aesthetic function makes the very structure of the linguistic
sign the center of interest and pushes the three practical functions into the
background. By negating them, the aesthetic function becomes a function
in its own right.

   The prominence of the aesthetic function in verbal art, Mukařovský argues, does not entirely suppress the other three practical functions. They
are present but hierarchically subordinated to the fourth function, which
specifies the work as verbal art. This explains why the text of verbal art
can, at least potentially, exercise the representative function referring to
the extralinguistic context, the expressive function referring to the artist,

and the appellative function affecting the reader. The three practical functions, Mukařovský points out, "often assert themselves rather extensively
in a work of art: the representative function in a novel or the expressive
function in a lyric poem." By the same token, the aesthetic function is
not restricted to the domain of art only: it is potentially involved in every
human activity, even in the most ordinary kind of speech. In art, however,
"it appears in the *foreground.*"[25]

There is no doubt that this view provides for the autonomy of verbal art
without isolating art from those factors which, by extension of the realm of
sign, belong to the extralinguistic context. It represents a truly structural
view, at least in terms of the structuralism conceived by the *Prague Linguistic Circle.* Although the work of art remains at the center of attention as a
semiotic system with certain autonomous properties, there is no intentional disregard for its relationship to the general domain of language and to
other cultural and social systems. At the same time, neither the creator
and the corresponding problems of the genesis of art nor the reader and
his evaluation are removed from consideration.

Subsequently, Bühler's model was taken up and further developed by
Roman Jakobson, who added two additional basic functions and introduced certain conceptual and terminological changes. Bühler's distinction
between *Sprechakt* and *Sprachgebilde,* which, in many respects, could be
compared with Saussure's dichotomy of *la langue* and *la parole,* was redefined as code and message, terminologically and conceptually attuned to
modern information theory. In his closing statement to the Conference on
style in 1958 in Bloomington (Indiana), Jakobson outlined the redefined
model in terms of six principle factors capable of determining the dominant function: (1) the addresser, the emotive function; (2) the addressee,
the conative function; (3) the context, the referential function; (4) the
code, the metalingual function; (5) the contact, the phatic function; and
(6) the message, the poetic function.

Thus Bühler's representative, expressive, and appellative functions were
restated as the referential, emotive, and conative functions, respectively,
whereas Mukařovský's aesthetic function became the poetic function.
While Mukařovský's aesthetic function "makes the very structure of the
linguistic sign the center of interest," Jakobson's poetic function is "the
set (Einstellung) toward the message as such, focus on the message for its

own sake." This assertion, however, was qualified in full accordance with the Prague structural trend: "The poetic function is not the sole function of verbal art but only its dominant, determining function, whereas in all other activities it acts as a subsidiary, accessory constituent."[26] Thus there is a clear continuity in emphasis on the relation of the work of art to all basic factors of the semiotic operation. The concrete message is not isolated from the abstract code shared by both the artist and the consumer of art. Although the corresponding psychological, physiological, and sociological aspects do not become the primary target of observation, their relevance is not ruled out but rather placed in proper perspective. It is clearly recognized that, in contradistinction to formalized, artificial codes such as those found in the domain of mathematics and information theory, the code of verbal art cannot be studied merely in terms of its vocabulary and its operational rules without adequate attention to its social character, to the nature of its acquisition, and to its role in the production of new, previously unknown cultural values.

7.

The hierarchy of functions attributable to the usage of sign became the paramount concern of all Prague semioticians, whether they specialized in verbal art or in other arts such as music, theater, film, architecture, and so on. Petr Bogatyrev even extended the investigation of functional hierarchies into the broad area of folk art and showed that the functional study of sign could open up new vistas for the scientific probing of culture in general.

In his study, "The Folk Song from a Functional Point of View" (1936), Bogatyrev suggested that semiotic inquiry should become an immediate task for musicology in order to lead it out of the dead end of pure formalism.[27] In Bogatyrev's view, the folk song represented a particularly revealing case of semiotic multifunctionality, because here it was possible to study the aesthetic function in hierarchic tension with magic, ritual, religious, erotic functions, as well as with various practical functions.

Bogatyrev's suggestive idea provoked an active response among a whole group of Prague musicologists. One of them, Antonín Sychra, applied Bogatyrev's functional approach to his thorough and methodologically consistent investigation of Moravian and Slovak folk songs, while paying special attention to the effect of functional criteria in forming or deforming musical structure.[28]

According to Sychra's findings those folk songs that tend to involve the activity of a whole group of people, such as dance songs or songs for marching, are, as a rule, strictly dominated by metrical schemes and characterized by the prominent role of dynamic stress (intensity, loudness). In contrast, the folk songs that can be linked to the needs of individual expression are characterized merely by scattered metrical signals and by the heightened role of quantity (duration) rather than by regular metrical schemes and stress. These drawn-out songs restrict the individual performance far less; by the same token, the resulting variants are often unique and unrepeatable: a truly individual expression on the spur of the moment. Sometimes two songs have the same text but different from each other in their musical structure, one being, for example, a dance song with a strict metrical scheme and the other a love song with metrical impulses providing for the freedom of individual expressivity. Thus it is the difference in the musical arrangement which profoundly affects the general meaning of such songs, even though the verbal arrangement (that is, lexical selection, morphology, syntax) remains unchanged. The sound of song is revealed as a sign structure, the meaning of which is capable of overpowering the lexical and grammatical meaning of the text. The text itself becomes secondary and, in fact, is often suppressed, deformed, or even made unintelligible.

The nature of the transformation that accounts for the difference in the musical structure is at the very center of Sychra's scrutiny. In this way, he is able to approach systematically the difficult problems of variability and invariability and study the underlying principles of musical meaning with great subtlety. At the same time, the general meaning of the musical genres, models, and patterns in their relationship to regional, ethnic, national, and multinational characteristics occupies the foreground of his scrutiny.

In many respects, the hierarchical multifunctionality of the folk song shows striking parallels to the functional structure of the folk costume. This parallel is outlined by Bogatyrev in his study "Costume as a Sign" (1936), where he makes a special point concerning the fact that the folk costume, in contrast to the folk song, is used not only as a sign structure but also as a material object in its own nonsemiotic terms.[29] Thus, the folk costume indicates sex, religion, national, ethnic and regional affiliation; professional as well as social categories while, at the same time, it covers the human body and performs many strictly practical functions. On the one hand, the wearer of the costume considers his physical needs and personal taste while, on the other hand, he is forced to conform to the norms pertaining to semiotic functions—to the meaning of the folk costume, its ideology. "In order to comprehend the social functions of costume and uniforms," Bogatyrev asserts, "we must learn to understand these objects as signs in the same way that we learn to understand different words of language."

It became clear that the study of the code relevant to the use of the folk costume as a sign required an approach conceptually different from the study of the folk costume in terms of its material, the technique of weaving and the rules for combining the parts of the garment into the folk costume as a whole. It was fully realized that a classificatory, morphological study of the folk costume merely in terms of its material properties, parts and wholes, and the rules of their composition could perhaps satisfy the needs of a scientific description of the folk costume as an object but not as a sign structure.

Bogatyrev's semiotic comparison of the "languages" of the folk costume with the verbal language is used by Nikolay Trubetzkoy in his *Grundzüge der Phonologie,* one of the most important contributions of the Prague School to the functional (phonological) study of verbal systems.[30] Within this framework, Trubetzkoy points out that among the various forms of folk costume only those which engage a system of norms can function as signs. Moreover, Trubetzkoy calls attention to the striking fact that the isoglosses which distinguish areas or strata of costume types often correspond to the dialectal isoglosses of expressive phonology. In this way, the semiotics of folk costume represents to a certain extent a dialect or a dialectal league overcoming narrow regional, ethnic, and even national boundaries.

It was through Trubetzkoy's *Grundzüge* that Bogatyrev's comparison reached Rolland Barthes, who devoted to the language of clothing a substantial portion of his witty, although somewhat abstruse and controversial, essay *Eléments de Sémiologie* (1964) later expanded into an entire book *Système de la Mode* (1967).[31]   In this way, the Prague semiotics indirectly contributed to the prodigious fermentation of French structuralism, or at least to the branch represented by Barthes, who more than anyone else (perhaps with the exception of Claude Lévi-Strauss) led Paris literary criticism in the 1960s toward a rediscovery of the doctrine of sign.

8.

The most thorough elaboration of the Prague semiotics of art took place in the domain of dramatic art, where several semiotic systems appear in mutual interrelationship and interaction.   Perhaps more than in any other area of semiotics, Prague studies of theater show a distinct link to the local scholarly tradition represented most notably by Otokar Zich, an outstanding theorist of dramatic art.   His book *Estetika dramatického umění [Aesthetics of Dramatic Art]* (1931), which was dedicated to his teacher, the Herbartian aesthetician Hostinský, represented an impressive attempt to grasp the complexity of dramatic art in terms of a single system of systems.[32]   Naturally, Zich's concept of mutual interrelationship and interaction of heterogeneous systems within a single unifying structure appealed to the structuralists.   They enthusiastically acknowledged Zich's claim that all components of dramatic art, whether verbal language or pantomime, music, lighting, architecture, or dance, must be studied in their mutual interaction rather than in isolation.   Moreover, Zich's detailed discussion of "things representing other things" in the realm of theater lent itself to reinterpretation within the framework of a doctrine of sign.   Thus, for the young generation of Prague theorists, Zich was both potentially a structuralist and a semiotician although, of course, they recognized that in many respects Zich represented the traditional Czech aesthetics firmly rooted in its central European origins.   Admiration for Zich's *Aesthetic of Dramatic Art* certainly did not preclude disagreements of a conceptual nature.   For one thing, his model was found too narrow and his rules, deducible from the model, were recognized as too general and often incapable of covering the known empirical facts.   Although the final paragraph of Zich's book claimed that dramatic art in its continual revival on the stage was the most atemporal of all the arts, and thus truly immortal, many of Zich's own observations were tinted by his obviously time-bound predilection for realistic theater. Moreover, Zich's model of the autonomous existence of dramatic art among other arts did not properly provide for specific problems of folk, primitive, medieval, and avant-garde theater and for distinct dramatic traditions in both the temporal and the spatial sense. In this respect, Karel Brušák's concise study of Chinese classical theater figured as an important supplement that not only turned attention toward the neglected non-European cultural domain but, at the same time, contributed to the epistemology of semiotics by its conceptually consistent approach.[33] It clearly showed that the primary requirement for grasping dramatic art should be sought in the nature of the underlying code comprising schemes, norms, and rules relevant to the corresponding cultural values. The acquiring of such a code, like learning a language, was revealed as a necessary precondition for understanding and adequate evaluation.

Bogatyrev's specialization in folklore contributed both directly and implicitly to a better grasping of the difference between dramatic art in the proper sense and folk drama where the norms of ritual might dominate the aesthetic function and the magic function might prevail.[34] It was only natural that Bogatyrev, as a folklorist, found the most distinctive feature of the theater to be its capacity for transformation, a concept which began to fascinate the structuralists at that time.

In contrast to Bogatyrev's emphasis on the role of transformation, Jindřich Honzl, a stage director by profession, concurred with Zich's emphasis on action and proclaimed action the dominant feature of dramatic art, connecting all other components and creating a unifying structure.[35] Jiří Veltruský in turn accepted the importance of action but recognized it only as one pole in the dialectal opposition, all other components being the second pole.[36] He made it particularly clear that each system participating in the unifying superstructure of a work of dramatic art should be analyzed not only in terms of its own signifying means and the corresponding system of signification but above all in their total interaction leading to a new semantic potentials. Or, as he put it:

Words cannot be fully translated into gestures, pictures, music, the meaning of a picture cannot be fully conveyed by language, music, the play of facial muscles, etc. Each of these types of sign is entirely different, each has its own unique ability to refer to certain kinds and certain aspects of reality and each is deficient in some other respects. Language for instance is inferior to painting in indicating colors, the location of objects or people within a certain situation, the distance between them, etc. Painting is at a disadvantage in comparison with sculpture and architecture in referring to time sequence, the time flow, etc. Music is superior to any other semiotic system in the articulation of the passage of time while it is inferior to all of them, except maybe architecture, in calling up a concrete reality. If not all, at least several semiotic systems combine, complement, and conflict with one another in dramatic art. The same reality is referred to, either simultaneously or successively, by signs as different as, for instance, speech, picture and music. None of them can denote that reality in its entirety; each has a different meaning even though they all refer to the same thing. In this sense theater offers an opportunity to study in optimal conditions— almost as in a laboratory—both the common and the distinctive features of different sign systems or, to put it differently, contrastive semiotics.[37]

9.

Through the years one of the outstanding features of the Prague School of linguistics has been its unwavering insistence on the inseparability of the two conjoined poles of every sign system, whether called *la langue- la parole, Sprachgebilde- Sprechakt* or *code-message.* Essentially the same conceptual position has characterized all the Prague semioticians of art: they have been reluctant to dissolve the dichotomic structure in favor of one of the two poles and to study in isolation either the concrete signifier (artifact) or the abstract system of schemes, patterns, and rules. Since the very relationship within the dichotomic structure has been of paramount interest, the Prague School has kept its methodological distance from those followers of Saussure who regarded only the abstract system worthy of scientific scrutiny and who, like Hjelmslev, insisted that language as a system was fundamentally the same whether spoken, telegraphed by Morse code or signaled by flags. Thus in contrast to the Copenhagen structuralists, the Prague semioticians have considered the relation between sound and meaning and, in general, between the signifier and the system of signification as an indissoluble opposition. Therefore, they have resisted all temptation to change linguistics into "an algebra of language, operating with unnamed entities, i.e., arbitrarily named entities without natural designation."[38] By the same token, the Prague theorists have not embraced the empiricists or Marxist-mechanists who have been chiefly concerned with the concrete implementations of works of art in the hope that a rigorous segmentation and classification of the material properties in terms of economy or logic will uncover the apparatus which produced their data. By recognizing the indissoluble bond between the internalized system and its concrete products, the Prague School has implicitly accepted the fact that the social system of norms and rules which makes human communication possible and meaningful cannot be reached merely by rigorous abstraction of concrete utterances. In this respect, the Prague structuralists have profoundly differed from the American structuralists of the post-Bloomfieldian era. This is clearly indicated by the critical remarks of Zellig Harris, the leading American structuralist, made in his review of Trubetzkoy's *Grundzüge:*

> The Prague Circle terminology gives the impression that there are two objects of possible investigation, the *Sprechakt* (speech) and the *Sprachgcbilde* (language structure), whereas the latter is merely the scientific arrangement of the former.[39]

This comment makes it clear that "language structure" (*Sprachgebilde*) is something else for Harris than for Trubetzkoy and other members of the *Prague Linguistic Circle.* Harris's "language structure" is nothing more than one among several possible scientific observations about a certain number of recorded speech acts. By definition, such a "language structure" cannot account for the fact that a language system is capable of producing an *infinite* number of speech acts characterized by an *uncountable* number of combinations and creative potentials. Clearly, Harris's "language structure" is profoundly different from Saussure's *la langue* as well as from Jakobson's *code.* In contradistinction to the American structuralists such as Harris, the Prague structuralists have indeed recognized the necessity of dealing with two objects of investigation, although the primary focus of their scrutiny has been the very interaction of the "two objects." In outlining the "organon" of verbal discourse, Roman Jakobson even speaks of two distinct vehicles of communication:

> Both the message (M) and the underlying code (C) are vehicles of linguistic communication, but both of them function in a duplex manner: they may at once be utilized and referred to (pointed at).[40]

Moreover, in his investigation of encoding and decoding impairments in aphasia, Jakobson was naturally forced to distinguish between language competence and its products manifested in concrete messages. And his statement that "without a confrontation of the code with the message no insight into creative power of language can be achieved"[41] clearly recalls the classical tradition of the Prague School.

Observations about speech acts in opposition to language systems have been particularly productive in those Prague studies that dealt with the difference between verbal languages and nonverbal semiotic systems or, as in the case of theater, with a semiotic suprasystem involving both verbal and nonverbal subsystems. In this connection, certain comments made by Bogatyrev as especially revealing:

We can carry over the concept of *la langue* and *la parole* from the field of language phenomena to art. Thus, just as the hearer, in order to comprehend the individual utterance of the speaker, must have command of the language, that is, language as social fact, so also in art the observer must be prepared to receive the individual performance of the actor or of any other artist—his special speech acts, as it were—in terms of his (the observer's) command of the language of that art, its social norms. This is the point of congruence between the fields of language and the field of art.[42]

Thus, it is the "language" of the particular art which comes to the fore as an essential component of art communication: the artifact (text, musical composition) can properly function as a sign structure relevant to the values of the given cultural community only if the corresponding "language" system is engaged. It follows that the art consumer must be attuned to the "language" of the artist if the sign structure of art is to function as a mediator between them. Accordingly, the "language" of the classical Chinese theater or Chinese music becomes the primary prerequisite for adequate appreciation of corresponding performances, or (to use the example, cited by Jakobson) the degree of mastering the system, which underlies the Gregorian chant, determines the recognition of its qualities as distinct from contemporary music and other types of music, viewed spatially and temporally.[43]

10.

The ominous preludes to the Second World War virtually dismembered the very core of the Prague Linguistic Circle: Trubetzkoy died under tragic circumstances, Bogatyrev returned to the USSR after twenty years in emigration, while René Wellek and Roman Jakobson chose to live in the West. In the United States, Wellek soon attuned his epistemological scrutiny of literary criticism to the Anglo-American tradition. In cooperation with Austin Warren, he synthesized his views in the *Theory of Literature,* a book that subsequently became a best-seller around the world. Here Wellek's guarded sympathies for the Prague School and the Russian Formalists are critically presented within the general framework of many other literary theories. Wellek's own contribution clearly reveals his high esteem for the phenomenology of literature as outlined in Roman Ingarden's stratificational model linking the stratum of language with other, higher strata.[44]

Meanwhile Roman Jakobson became increasingly interested in the problems of invariants and universals in their opposition to variables whether in verbal language or in semiotic systems in general. The dichotomy between *la langue* and *la parole,* which had never been elaborated by Saussure in all its essential components, remained the most crucial conceptual challenge for Jakobson. He clearly recognized the dangers of the radical dualism manifested by Saussure's attempt to isolate the poles of dichotomies rather than to see them in dialectical terms as an indissoluble opposition. Thus, in contrast to Saussure and his Cartesian orientation, Jakobson became interested above all in the features binding the antithetic properties together.

An awareness of the crucial importance of the internalized system naturally guided Jakobson's analytic inquiries toward the problems of language acquisition in its mirror relation to aphasic regression of language usage. While his *Kindersprache, Aphasie und allgemeine Lautgesetze,* written in Sweden, was primarily concerned with the sound system, several studies, written after his arrival in the United States, were devoted to those aspects of language acquisition and pathology which he found essential for the grammatical system and the operation of language in its entirety—whether in daily communication or in the domain of art. Pursuing this analytic strategy, Jakobson succeeded in showing the direct relevance of aphasic disorder of contiguity for encoding procedures and, in general, for the metonymic usage of language, while the disorder of similarity was defined in its essential relation to the decoding procedure and to the metaphoric usage. "While each of these two types of aphasia tends toward unipolarity," Jakobson observes, "the normal verbal behavior is bipolar." He points out, however, that "any individual use of language, any verbal style, any trend in verbal art displays a clear predilection either for the metonymical or for the metaphorical device."[45] Thus the observable symptoms of language pathology in contrast to normal verbal communication were used by Jakobson as a concrete base for his conclusions about the system underlying the use of language in all its aspects—including verbal art. The course of Jakobson's exploration naturally brought into focus the fact that verbal art, like language itself, has been attested in every known human community. Thus along with his search for the distinctive features common to all human languages, Jakobson has become increasingly interested in those universal aspects of auditory and visual signs which would characterize the semiotic communication of all mankind.

11.

Today the theorists of art descending from the conceptual platform of the Prague School are clearly polarized. The polarization is not restricted to the old guard of the Prague Linguistic Circle. It is also detectable among those who, since the 1960s, have tried to revive the tradition of the Prague School in Czechoslovakia or who pursued their own traditions of semiotic research in France, Poland, Canada, the Soviet Union, Holland, East and West Germany, Italy, and so on.[46] Those scholars, who have been primarily concerned with the functions of concrete work of art in a given time and space position may feel that the exploration of schemes, patterns, and general laws imposes a system on the material while disregarding true evaluation of art in its integrity. On the other hand, the search for the underlying systems of art, viewed as special types of semiotic communication, may find the evaluative interpretations of concrete works of art too eclectic, unsystematic, and likely to lapse into unchecked subjectivism. The crisis, moreover, is complicated by various efforts to include into the framework of the semiotics of the art the psychoanalytic criteria of Freud or Jung, the Marxist point of views, phenomenology, sociolinguistics, anthropology, information theory, modern logic, algebra, or advanced statistics—or to regard semiotics as a philosophy of life. In some areas the diversification within the realm of semiotics may appear as a virtual chaos or "hodgepodge of methods," to use Wellek's characterization of the contemporary French scene.[47] Nevertheless, the chaos seems to display amazing vitality and, perhaps, it just represents a process of crystallization: a necessary step toward a more profound insight into the complexity of art—and of human intercourse in general.

Notes

1. Rolf George, *Bernard Bolzano: Theory of Science* (Berkeley: 1972), pp. 308 ff.

2. Ferdinand de Saussure, *Cours de linguistique générale* (Geneva: 1916); see *Course in General Linguistics*, tr. W. Baskin (New York: 1959).

3. Karl Bühler, "Die Axiomatik der Sprachwissenschaften," *Kant-Studien*, 38 (1933), pp. 19-90.

4. Vilém Mathesius, "On the Potentiality of the Phenomena of Language," *Prague School Reader in Linguistics*, ed. J. Vachek (Bloomington: 1964), pp. 1-32 = the English translation of "O potenciálnosti jevů jazykových," *Věstník královské české společnosti nauk: třída filosoficko-historickojazykozpytná* (Prague: 1911).

5. Victor Erlich, *Russian Formalism: History—Doctrine* (The Hague: 1955), pp. 129 ff.

6. Roman Jakobson, "Retrospect," *Selected Writings*, vol. 1 (The Hague: 1971), p. 631.

7. Valentin N. Vološinov, *Marxism and the Philosophy of Language*, tr. L. Matejka and I. R. Titunik (New York: 1973) = the English translation of *Marksizm i filosofija jazyka: osnovnye problemy sociologičeskogo metoda v nauke o jazyke* (Leningrad: 1929/1930).

8. Ibid., p. 58-59.

9. "Thèses," *Travaux du Cerle Linguistique de Prague: Mélanges linguistiques dédiés au Premier Congrès des philologues slaves* (Prague: 1929), p. 14. (The English translation in manuscript by H. Diament and E. C. Berksdale.)

10. See Roman Jakobson, O češskom stixe preimuščestvenno v sopostavlenii s russkim (Berlin: 1923). Reprinted in *Brown University Slavic Reprint VI* (Providence: 1969).

288   Ladislav Matejka

11. Jurij Tynjanov and Roman Jakobson, "Problems in the Study of Literature and Language," *Readings in Russian Poetics: Formalist and Structuralist Views,* ed. L. Matejka and K. Pomorska (Cambridge: 1971), p. 79 = the English translation of "Problemy izučenija literatury i jazyka," *Novyj Lef,* 12 (1928).

12. Boris M. Éjxenbaum, "The Theory of the Formal Method," *Readings in Russian Poetics: Formalist and Structuralist Views* (Cambridge: 1971), p. 23 = the English translation of "Teorija 'formal'nogo metoda,' " *Literatura: teorija, kritika, polemika* (Leningrad: 1927).

13. Jan Mukařovský, "K českému překladu Šklovského *Teorie prózy,*" *Čin,* 6 (1934); reprinted in *Kapitoly z české poetiky,* 1 (Prague: 1948), pp. 344-350.

14. Ibid., p. 349.

15. Jan Mukařovský, "L'art comme fait sémiologique," *Actes du huitième Congrès international de philosophie à Prague, 2-7 septembre 1934* (Prague: 1936), pp. 1065-1073. = "Art as Semiotic Fact," in this anthology.

16. Ibid.

17. Ibid.

18. "Úvodem" [Foreword], *Slovo a Slovesnost,* 1 (1935), p. 5. (The English translation in manuscript by A. Levitsky.)

19. Ibid.

20. Ibid.

21. Ibid.

22. Jan Mukařovský, *Aesthetic Function, Norm and Value as Social Facts [Estetická funkce, norma a hodnota jako sociální fakty],* tr. M. E. Suino (Ann Arbor: 1970) = Michigan Slavic Contributions, no. 3.

23. Jan Mukařovský, "Dénomination poétique et la fonction esthétique de la langue," *Actes du quatrième Congrès international des linguistes* (Copenhagen: 1938), pp. 98-104 = "Poetic Reference," in this anthology.

24. See Karl Bühler, "Die Axiomatik der Sprachwissenschaften," *Kant-Studien,* 38 (1933), pp. 19-90; also see *Sprachtheorie: die Darstellungfunktion der Sprache* (Jena: 1934).

25. See A *Prague School Reader on Esthetics, Literary Structure, and Style,* ed. Paul L. Garvin (Washington, D.C.: 1964).

26. Roman Jakobson, "Closing Statement: Linguistics and Poetics," in *Style in Language,* ed. Thomas A. Sebeok (Cambridge: 1960).

289 Postscript: Prague School Semiotics

27. Petr Bogatyrev, "La chanson populaire du point de vue fonctionnel," *Travaux du Cercle linguistique de Prague,* 6 (1936) = "Folk Song from a Functional Point of View," in this anthology.

28. Antonín Sychra, "Lidová píseň s hlediska semiologického," *Slovo a slovesnost,* 9 (1948-1949), pp. 7-23.

29. Petr Bogatyrev, "Kroj jako znak," *Slovo a slovesnost,* 2, 1936, pp. 43-47 = "Costume as a Sign," in this anthology.

30. N. S. Trubetzkoy, *Grundzüge der Phonologie* = *Travaux du Cercle Linguistique de Prague,* 7 (1939), p. 19.

31. Roland Barthes, *Eléments de Sémiologie* (Paris: 1964); *Système de de la Mode* (Paris: 1967).

32. Otakar Zich, *Estetika dramatického umění* (Prague: 1931). See Oleg Sus, "Poetry and Music in the Psychological Semantics of Otakar Zich," *Sborník prací filosofické fakulty,* 44 (Brno: 1969), pp. 77-93.

33. Karel Drušák, "Znaky na čínském divadle," *Slovo a slovesnost,* 5 (1939) = "Signs in the Chinese Theater," in this anthology.

34. See Petr Bogatyrev, *Lidové divadlo české a slovenské* [Czech and Slovak Folk Theater] (Prague: 1940).

35. Jindřich Honzl, "Pohyb divadelního znaku," *Slovo a slovesnost,* 6 (1940), pp. 177-188 = "Dynamics of the Sign in the Theater," in this anthology.

36. Jiří Veltruský, "Dramatický text jako součást divadla," *Slovo a slovesnost,* 7 (1941), pp. 132-144 = "Dramatic Text as a Component of Theater," in this anthology; see his "Drama jako básnické dílo," *Čtení o jazyce a poesii* (Prague: 1942), pp. 403-502.

37. Jiří Veltruský, "Notes Regarding Bogatyrev's Book on Folk Theater" (written in 1942; unpublished).

38. Louis Hjelmslev, *Prolegomena to a Theory of Language* (Bloomington: 1935), p. 60.

39. Z. S. Harris, review of N. S. Trubetzkoy's *Grundzüge der Phonologie* in *Language,* 17 (1941), p. 345.

40. Roman Jakobson, "Shifters, Verbal Categories, and the Russian Verb," *Selected Writings,* vol. 2 (The Hague: 1971), p. 130.

41. Roman Jakobson, "Retrospect," *Selected Writings,* vo. 2 (The Hague: 1971), p. 718.

42. Petr Bogatyrev, "Znaky divadelní," *Slovo a slovesnost,* 4 (1938), pp. 138-149 = "Semiotics in the Folk Theater," in this anthology.

43. Roman Jakobson, "Musikwissenschaft und Linguistik," *Selected Writings,* vol. 2 (The Hague: 1971), pp. 551 ff.

44. René Wellek and Austin Warren, *Theory of Literature* (New York: 1942), p. 154.

45. Roman Jakobson, "Aphasia as a Linguistic Topic," *Selected Writings,* 2, p. 238.

46. See René Wellek, *The Literary Theory and Aesthetics of the Prague School* (Ann Arbor: 1969) = *Michigan Slavic Contributions,* 2; Josef Vachek, *The Linguistic School of Prague* (Bloomington: 1966); *Poetics,* 4 (1972) = *To Honour Jan Muka-řovský;* L. Doležel and J. Kraus, "Prague School Stylistics," in *Current Trends in Stylistics,* ed. B. B. Kachru and H. F. Stahlke (Edmonton: 1972), pp. 37-48; T. G. Winner, "The Aesthetics and Poetics of the Prague Linguistic Circle," *Poetics,* 8 (1973), pp. 77-96.

47. René Wellek, *Discriminations* (New Haven: 1970), p. 334. See René Wellek, "Stylistics, Poetics, and Criticism," in *Literary Style,* ed. S. Chatman (New York: 1971), pp. 65-75; Edward Stankiewicz, "Structural Poetics and Linguistics," in *Current Trends in Linguistics,* 12:2, ed. T. A. Sebeok (The Hague: 1974), pp. 629-659.

Index

KING ALFRED'S COLLEGE
LIBRARY